ACCOUNTING 101: EASY ACCOUNTING AND BOOKKEEPING FOR BEGINNERS

Denver G. Pettigrew, Ph.D., CPA, MBA

"I READ TO LEARN; I READ MORE TO LEARN MORE"—DR. DENVER G. PETTIGREW

Denver Pettigrew, Ph.D., C.P.A., M.B.A.

ACCOUNTING 101: EASY ACCOUNTING AND BOOKKEEPING FOR BEGINNERS

Denver G. Pettigrew, Ph.D., CPA, MBA

A life-long learner of business and economics-related topics, Dr. Pettigrew is a Certified Public Accountant (CPA); Doctor of Philosophy (Ph.D.) in Business Administration with a specialty in Advanced Accounting; Master's in Business Administration (MBA); and Bachelor of Science (BS) in Accounting. With over 30 years of working experience in accounting and many years as a successful professor of accounting and business at online and on-campus universities and colleges in the USA, Dr. Pettigrew hopes to motivate more students to consider careers in accounting and finance. Previous publications include: *The Zen of Bookkeeping and Accounting: Basic Accounting for Pre-College and New Learners*, published on Amazon.com; and *Investigating Differences in Annual Profitability Rates in Developed and Emerging Markets: A Multiple Case Study*.

Accountants and bookkeepers use a systematic step-by-step set of activities to *record*, update, and report on the financial activities of an organization, maintained and reported in three main sets of financial records: (1) *Journals,* to *record* financial/economic transactions; (2) *General Ledger accounts,* to *post* the journal entries to the appropriate accounts; and (3) *Financial statements* including the balance sheet, income statement, statement of retained earnings, statement of changes in owners' equity account, and statement of cash flows to summarize and report on the activities in the general ledger.

Accounting 101: Easy Accounting and Bookkeeping for Beginners

Copyright © 2018 Denver G. Pettigrew, Ph.D., CPA, MBA

ISBN-13: 978-1727370171

ISBN-10: 1727370171

All rights reserved. Parts of this book may not be reproduced in any form without the written permission from the author with the exceptions of the following quotations: "If you can read, write, use a simple calculator to add, subtract, multiply, and divide, you too, can learn basic accounting and bookkeeping," and "I read to learn; I read more to learn more."

Sections of information in this book were previously written and published in *The Zen of Bookkeeping and Accounting: Basic Accounting for Pre-College and New Learners* by the author.

Written requests and inquiries may be sent to Denver G. Pettigrew, Ph.D., CPA, MBA Denver Business Academy LLC., P.O. Box 8305, Sebring Florida 33872, U.S.A.

Cover Design by Denver G. Pettigrew, Ph.D., CPA, MBA

Important Disclaimer: Accountants use specialized language to describe accounting activities and often use similar terminology to express accounting and economics concepts, principles, and activities. The author, a professor of accounting, has taken great steps to avoid any appearance of plagiarism or similarity with other accounting books; any similarities found in this book are purely coincidental.

Accounting 101: Easy Accounting and Bookkeeping for Beginners

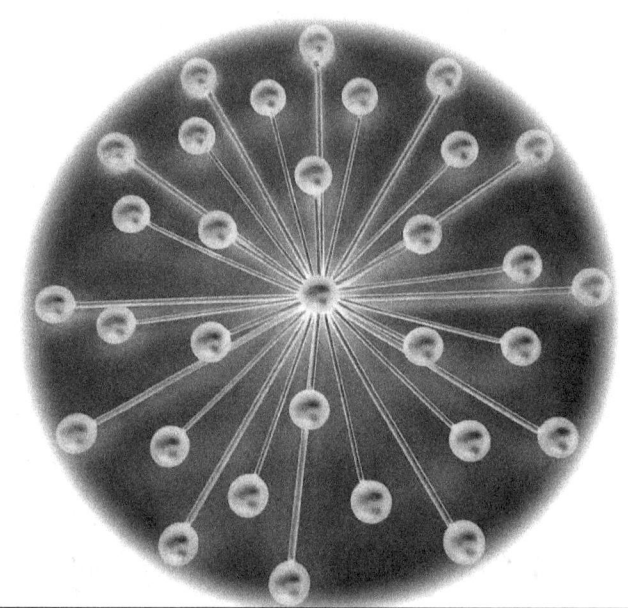

Collaborative learning. "Superior learners seek at least two to six additional sources of information." Dr. Denver Pettigrew

Denver Pettigrew, Ph.D., C.P.A., M.B.A.

Contents of Accounting 101: Easy Accounting and Bookkeeping for Beginners

Introduction to Accounting 101: Easy Accounting and Bookkeeping 1

Chapter 1: Must Read Overview of Accounting and Bookkeeping 3
- OK, Where Do I Start? A simple Example 3
- Cash Transactions 6
- Non-Cash Transactions—On Terms (Payments Delayed) 7
- The Double-entry Concept of Accounting 9
- The Accounting Equation 10
- Summary Overview of Accounting Activities 11
- Summary questions of financial activities chapter 1 12
- Answers to Summary questions of financial activities chapter 1 13
- Cumulative Comprehensive Hands-on Example 1 15
- Solutions to Cumulative Hands-On Example 1 15

Chapter 2: Business Transactions, Chart of Accounts, and General Journal 17
- Business Transactions 17
- The Chart of Accounts (COA) 18
- The General Journal (GJ) 19
- Special Journals 20
- Summary questions of financial activities chapter 2 23
- Answers to Summary questions of financial activities chapter 2 24
- Cumulative Comprehensive Hands-On Example 2 26
- Solutions to Cumulative Hands-On Example 2 27

Chapter 3: The General Ledger and the Trial Balance 29
- The General Ledger (GL) 29
- The Trial Balance (TB) 32
- Summary questions of financial activities chapter 3 34
- Answers to Summary questions of financial activities chapter 3 35
- Cumulative Comprehensive Hands-on Example 3 37
- Solutions to Cumulative Hands-On Example 3 37
- 38

Chapter 4: Elements of The Balance Sheet 39
- The Balance Sheet (BS) 39
- Assets 39
- Liabilities 44
- Equity 46
- Expenditure and Expense 47
- Summary questions of financial activities chapter 4 48
- Answers to Summary questions of financial activities chapter 4 49
- Cumulative Comprehensive Hands-on Example 4 51
- Solutions to Cumulative Hands-On Example 4 52

Chapter 5: Elements of the Income Statement 57
- The Income Statement AKA the Profit and Loss Statement 57
- Revenue 58

Denver Pettigrew, Ph.D., C.P.A., M.B.A.

  Expenses 59
  Summary questions of financial activities chapter 5 66
  Answers to Summary questions of financial activities chapter 5 67

Chapter 6: Adjusting Entries, Post-Adj. TB, Closing Entries, and Net Income 69
  Adjusting Entries 69
  New General Ledger Account: Income Summary Account 72
  End of Period Closing Entries 74
  Summary questions of financial activities chapter 6 80
  Answers to Summary questions of financial activities chapter 1 81

Chapter 7: Income Statement, Balance Sheet, Changes in Owner's Equity 83
  The Income Statement 83
  The Statement of Retained Earnings 84
  The Balance Sheet 86
  The Statement of Changes in Owner's Equity/Stockholder's Equity 86

Chapter 8: Simple Payroll and Payroll Expenses 89
  Wages and Salaries 89
  Additional Employer's Payroll Expenses 94

Chapter 9: The Cash Flows and Bank Reconciliation Statements 109
  The Cash Flows Statement 109
  The Bank Reconciliation Statement 116

Chapter 10: Basic Introduction to Financial Ratios and Trend Analysis 123
  Trend Analysis 123
  Financial Ratios 127

Chapter 11: Final Thoughts and Encouragement 129

Appendix A: Combined Chart of Accounts and Trial Balance 131

Appendix B: Typical Check Register 132

Appendix C: General Journal 133

Appendix D: General Ledger 134

Appendix E: Combined Income Statement & Retained Earnings 135

Appendix F: Balance Sheet 136

Appendix G: IRS Percentage Method Tables for Income Tax Withholding 137

Appendix H: IRS Wage Bracket Tables for Income Tax Withholding 2018 139

Denver Pettigrew, Ph.D., C.P.A., M.B.A.

Introduction to Accounting 101: Easy Accounting and Bookkeeping

The material in the book is based on a simple framework for teaching and learning accounting and bookkeeping using activities related to the elements of a *Simple Combined Chart of Accounting and Trial Balance* shown on the following page and throughout the book. Beginners tend to get overwhelmed at the number of concepts and theories contained in the chapters in accounting textbooks, that they lose sight of the *main reasons* for studying each chapter. I hope that by including "What is the purpose of this chapter?" in the first few lines of each chapter, the reader will see its purpose.

Accountants and bookkeepers use a systematic step-by-step set of activities to *record*, update, and report on the financial activities of an organization, maintained in three main sets of financial records: (1) *Journals* (JEs), to initially *record* financial or economic business transactions; (2) *General Ledger accounts* (GL), to *post* the journal entries to the appropriate accounts; and (3) *Financial statements* including the balance sheet, income statement, statement of retained earnings, statement of changes in the owners' equity account, and statement of cash flows, to summarize the GL accounts and report on the operations and financial health of the organization. The terms *firm, company,* and *organization* will be used interchangeably throughout the book.

As the famous far-eastern saying goes "a picture is worth ten thousand words," I have used many examples, diagrams, and figures to demonstrate simple accounting and bookkeeping concepts and practices used in the accounting and bookkeeping profession in the real world (Barnard, 1927). I hope you enjoy reading the book and realize that you too can learn accounting and bookkeeping.

Best wishes for a successful career in accounting.

Dr. Pettigrew

A Simple Combined Chart of Accounts and Trial Balance

CHART OF ACCOUNTS	TRIAL BALANCE	
Account #, Classification, and General Ledger Descriptions	Debit $$	Credit $$

Balance Sheet

Assets: 1000

- 1010 Cash — XXXX.XX
- 1020 Accounts Receivable — XXXX.XX
- 1021 Allowance for Bad Debts — XXXX.XX (Credit)
- 1030 Merchandise Inventory — XXXX.XX
- 1040 Prepaid Accounts — XXXX.XX
- 1050 Fixed Assets — XXXX.XX
- 1051 Accumulated Depreciation — XXXX.XX (Credit)

Liabilities: 2000

- 2010 Accounts Payable — XXXX.XX (Credit)
- 2020 Salaries & Wages Payable — XXXX.XX (Credit)
- 2030 Long-term Payable — XXXX.XX (Credit)
- 2040 Unearned Revenue — XXXX.XX (Credit)

Equity: 3000

- 3010 Owner's Capital/Equity — XXXX.XX (Credit)
- 3020 Drawing — XXXX.XX (Debit)
- 3030 Retained Earnings — XXXX.XX (Credit)

Income Statement

Revenue: 4000

- 4010 Sales Revenue — XXXX.XX (Credit)
- 4020 Other Revenue — XXXX.XX (Credit)
- 4030 Cost of Goods Sold (COGS) — XXXX.XX (Debit)

Expenses: 5000

- 5010 Rent Expense — XXXX.XX
- 5020 Salaries & Wages — XXXX.XX
- 5030 Office Expenses & Supplies — XXXX.XX
- 5040 Utilities Expense — XXXX.XX
- 5050 Insurance Expense — XXXX.XX
- 5060 Advertising & Promotion Expense — XXXX.XX
- 5070 Depreciation Expense — XXXX.XX
- 5080 Vehicle, Travelling & Entertainment Expense — XXXX.XX
- 5090 Bad Debt Expense — XXXX.XX

Totals: XXXX.XX | XXXX.XX

Chapter 1: Must Read Overview of Accounting and Bookkeeping

OK, Where Do I Start? A simple Example

Question: What is the purpose of this chapter?

Answer: To introduce you to the objectives of an accounting and bookkeeping system and important fundamental concepts and tools.

Before we can start recording the financial activities of the firm, we must define what accounting and bookkeeping is about. Because accounting and bookkeeping activities are inter-related and sometimes used synonymously, for simplification of explanations we will use the terms interchangeably although technically they are different. Accountants must know bookkeeping and attain a much higher level, and variety, of education and certification, to provide operating and strategic expertise to different levels of managers in firms.

The public uses the generic term *accounting* in business and non-business formats such as when we have to (a) *account* for our whereabouts last Wednesday, (b) *account* for how we did in the test on a particular date or particular subject, (c) *account* for what we did with the book we borrowed from the library last month, (d) *account* for how we spent the money that was in our bank account at the beginning of the month, (e) *account* for where we got the money to put into our bank accounts (sources) how we spent (uses) the money and how much is the remaining amount (balance) at the end of the month, etc. You get the idea that accounting for something is explaining the results of specific activities or money. In this book, we focus only on financial accounting: Accounting for the sources and uses of valuable monetary resources (values shown in dollars) in a business.

There are three fundamental concepts new learners *must* understand in learning accounting and bookkeeping: (1) business transactions, (2) the *double entry* concept of *debits* and *credits*, and (3) the *accounting equation.*

1. **Business Transactions** Bookkeepers record only transactions completed on behalf of a business firm—business transactions; not the personal transactions of the business owner.

2. **Double-entry System of Accounting** Business transactions consist of debits and equal amounts of credits. In other words, every transaction has an equal movement of value *to* (debit or DR) a receiving general ledger (GL) account *from* (credit or CR) a source GL account, to properly record the transaction in journal entries (JE); if we subtract all the credit entries from all the debit entries in a journal, the result must be

Accounting 101: Easy Accounting and Bookkeeping for Beginners

zero if recorded correctly. The journal entries are posted periodically to the corresponding general ledger accounts (GL) indicated in the journal.

DEBIT DR   **CREDIT CR**

3. **The Accounting Equation** The accounting equation is based on the same double-entry system of accounting used for recording transactions in the journal and provides a summary of all amounts posted in GL accounts in a simple formula: Total Assets (A) equal the Total of Liabilities (L) plus Owners' Equity (E), or A = L + E.

> **Important**: You *must* fully understand how to make a simple journal using the double-entry concept of debit and credit.

The following is a simple demonstration of steps taken to record a few ordinary business transactions in a general journal. I will use a fictitious firm, MZ LLC., owned and operated by a fictitious person, Master Zen. New firms generally begin operations using cash for all transactions until the business is operating successfully. We will discuss this further in a later chapter, but for now, MZ LLC operates on a cash basis.

- On January 1, 20xx, Master Zen invests $20,000.00 of his savings into starting a firm, registered as MZ LLC., in Florida, to buy and sell books. He opens a bank account in the name of the firm and deposits the $20,000.00. He receives a checkbook and check register to keep track of receipts and payments for the firm. All receipts are promptly deposited to the account and all purchases and payments are done using the business checks

- On Jan. 2, 20xx MZ LLC buys 200 books for $2,000.00 using business check number 1. Note that whenever a business operates by buying and selling finished products, such as books, they are often referred to as merchandize and the firm is called a retailer of merchandize, or retailer, for short.

- On Jan. 5 MZ LLC sells 100 books for $3,000.00 cash and deposits the amount in the bank.

Chapter 1: Must Read Overview of Accounting and Bookkeeping

- On Jan. 7, the end of week 1, MZ LLC pays Mr. J. Bookkeeper $800.00 for services using business check number 2.

Let us first look at how these transactions are recorded in the check register supplied by the bank when the firm's account was opened. The transactions would be recorded as indicated in the *Check Register* shown below. We will create a simple general journal from information recorded in the check register using the chart of accounts shown on page 2 and Appendix A. Hint: Three key questions to consider when recording journals using the chart of accounts are (1) Which account is receiving cash or value? This account is *debited*. (2) Which account provided (source) the cash or value in (1)? This account is *credited*; and (3) What is the purpose of the transaction? This is explained on a separate line below the transactions.

A Typical Check Register

PLEASE MAKE SURE TO DEDUCT CHARGES THAT AFFECT YOUR ACCOUNT								
ITEM NO. OR TRANS. CODE (a)	DATE (b)	TRANSACTION DESCRIPTION (c)	ADDITIONS: AMT OF DEPOSITS OR INTEREST (+) (d)		✓ T	FEE IF ANY (-) (e)	SUBTRACTIONS: AMT OF PAYMENTS OR WITHDRAWALS (-) (f)		BALANCE (g)	
	Jan. 1, 20XX	Investment from Master Zen	20,000	00					20,000	00
Check # 1	Jan. 2	Books Unlimited- 200 books					2,000	00	18,000	00
	Jan. 5	Cash Sales 100 books	3,000	00					21,000	00
Check # 2	Jan. 7	Mr. J. Bookkeeper					800	00	20,200	00

The transactions in the check register would be recorded in a typical general journal using the GL account numbers shown in the chart of accounts (COA). Notice that *each* transaction involves the *cash* account either receiving cash or spending (paying) cash. Remember that each transaction must be recorded on a separate line and contains a debit *and* a credit. It is customary to record the debit entry first, followed by the corresponding credit entry and then the explanation for the entries. Carefully compare the check register with the following general journal.

General Journal

General Journal			Page No. 1		
Date 2017		Description	GL Ref.	Debit	Credit
Jan	1	Cash	1010	20,000.00	
		Owner's Capital	3010		20,000.00
		Cash Invested by Master Zen			

Accounting 101: Easy Accounting and Bookkeeping for Beginners

Jan	2	Merchandize Inventory	1030	2,000.00	
		Cash	1010		2,000.00
		Purchase books 200 from Books Unlimited			
Jan	5	Cash	1010	3,000.00	
		Sales Revenue	4010		3,000.00
		Cash sales of 100 books to customers			
Jan	7	Salaries & Wages Expense	5020	800.00	
		Cash	1010		800.00
		Salary paid to J. Bookkeeper			

Hint: Whenever a transaction narrative contains the words *cash* or *check*, or phrase such as *paid* to or *received money* from; one of the GL accounts in the transaction is the *cash account*! look at the following cash transaction examples to identify the accounts affected and position (DR or CR) when recording the related journal entries using the chart of accounts. We will use transaction numbers instead of dates for this practice exercise:

Cash Transactions
1. Paid check for $1,000.00 to landlord for a month's rent of office space.
2. Paid $75.00 for business telephone service to phone service provider.
3. Bought for cash $1,000.00 books to sell to customers.
4. Received $1,500.00 for sale of books to cash customers.
5. Paid $400.00 to local newspaper to advertise business to the public.
6. Paid electric bill for $200.00 to electric utility company.
7. Purchased a used van for cash, $3,000.00

Solutions using the chart of accounts
1. GL account *5010* is DR and GL account *1010* is CR for $1,000.00
2. GL account *5040* is DR and GL account *1010* is CR for $75.00
3. GL account *1030* is DR and GL account *1010* is CR for $1,000.00
4. GL account *1010* is DR and GL account *4010* is CR for $1,500.00
5. GL account *5060* is DR and GL account *1010* is CR for $400.00
6. GL account *5040* is DR and GL account *1010* is CR for $200.00
7. GL account *1050* is DR and GL account *1010* is CR for $3,000.00

Chapter 1: Must Read Overview of Accounting and Bookkeeping

Each transaction would be recorded on three separate lines: (a) debit entry, followed by (b) credit entry, then (c) explanation for the transaction.

You might be wondering, "What if the transactions were not paid for immediately in cash by the firm or by its customers?" Great question!

In that case, we would replace the cash account with a *non-cash* account from the balance sheet section of the chart of account as follows:

Non-Cash Transactions—On Terms (Payments Delayed)

1. ~~Paid check~~ Received bill for $1,000.00 to landlord for a month's rent of office space.
2. ~~Paid~~ Received bill for $75.00 for business telephone service to phone service provider.
3. Bought ~~for cash~~ on terms $1,000.00 books to sell to customers, firm will pay suppliers at a later date.
4. ~~Received~~ Sold $1,500.00 ~~for sale~~ of books on terms, amount ~~cash~~ to be received from customers at a future date.
5. ~~Paid~~ Received bill for $400.00 ~~to~~ from local newspaper to advertise business to the public.
6. ~~Paid~~ Received electric bill for $200.00 to electric utility company.
7. Purchased a used van for ~~cash~~ $3,000.00, firm to pay seller at a future date.

Solutions using the chart of accounts

1. GL account <u>5010</u> is DR and GL account ~~1010~~ <u>2010</u> is CR for $1,000.00
2. GL account <u>5040</u> is DR and GL account ~~1010~~ <u>2010</u> is CR for $75.00
3. GL account <u>1030</u> is DR and GL account ~~1010~~ <u>2010</u> is CR for $1,000.00
4. GL account ~~1010~~ <u>1020</u> is DR and GL account <u>4010</u> is CR for $1,500.00
5. GL account <u>5060</u> is DR and GL account ~~1010~~ <u>2010</u> is CR for $400.00
6. GL account <u>5040</u> is DR and GL account ~~1010~~ <u>2010</u> is CR for $200.00
7. GL account <u>1050</u> is DR and GL account ~~1010~~ <u>2010</u> is CR for $3,000.00

Each transaction would be recorded on three separate lines: (a) Debit entry, followed by (b) Credit entry, then (c) Explanation for the transaction.

Notice that for non-cash transactions, the *Cash* account *1010* is replaced by the *Accounts Receivable* GL account *1020* for the delayed *receipt* of cash from customer, and the GL *Accounts Payable* account *2010* replaces the Cash account *1010* for the delayed *payments*. We will describe Accounts Receivable and Accounts Payable in more detail in Chapter 4.

3 Key Questions when Recording Journals

> Three key questions to consider when recording journals using the chart of accounts are (1) Which account is receiving cash or value? This account is debited. (2) Which account (source) provided the cash or value in (1)? This account is credited; and (3) What is the purpose of the transaction? This is explained in a separate line below the transactions.

> Accountants and bookkeepers use a systematic step-by-step set of activities to *record*, update, and report on the financial activities of an organization, maintained in three main sets of financial records: (1) *Journals,* to *record* financial/economic transactions; (2) *General Ledger accounts,* to *post* the journal entries to the appropriate accounts; and (3) *Financial statements* comprising the balance sheet, income statement, statement of retained earnings, and statement of cash flows to summarize and report on the balances in the general ledger.

The definition used for this simplified book is in terms of the activities involved in the accounting *process*: Accounting is both a process and a means of summarizing and reporting of financial transactions and activities of a business for a specific period. The process involves identifying and recording financial transactions in *journals* and posting them to related accounting *ledgers*; the accounting ledgers are then summarized, classified, and reported in financial statements such as the *balance sheet, income statement, statement of changes in owner's equity,* and *cash flows statement* to be used by users for decision-making purposes. In other words, accounting is a systematic step-by-step set of activities by the accountant to (1) identify, analyze, and record financial transactions, (2) record the transactions in the journal using a chart of accounts, (3) post the journal entries to the general ledger, (4) prepare a trial balance of the general ledger accounts, (5) make adjustments at the end of accounting periods, and (6) summarize and report on the activities of the firm using financial statements.

Notice that the process begins with identifying and recording financial transactions of the business.

Steps in the accounting process can be illustrated as follows:

Steps in The Accounting Process					
STEP 1	STEP 2	STEP 3	STEP 4	STEP 5	STEP 6
Analyze Transactions	Record Journal Entries	Post to General Ledger	Prepare Trial Balance	End-of Period Adj. Entries	Compile Financial Statements

Chapter 1: Must Read Overview of Accounting and Bookkeeping

The general ledger accounts shown in the combined chart of accounts and trial balance are sometimes referred to as *elements* in the balance sheet and income statement. The Cash account, Accounts Receivable, Merchandise Inventory, Accounts Payable, Long-term Payable etc. are referred to as *elements* in the balance sheet. Likewise, Sales Revenue, Cost of Goods Sold, Rent Expense, Salaries and Wages etc. are referred to as *elements* in the income statement.

To correctly analyze, record, and post transactions of a firm, new learners must know and fully understand what I believe to be are the two most important concepts in accounting: (1) the *double-entry system of accounting,* and (2) the *accounting equation*. These two concepts are fundamental and directly related and must be fully understood and memorized to successfully learn accounting.

The Double-entry Concept of Accounting

The double-entry concept states that every business transaction involves an *equal* exchange of value between the two sides of every transaction: a receiver and a giver. Business transactions are therefore referred to as give-get activities because when value is given, the same value must be received by someone on the other side of the transaction. In accounting, the give-get transactions are recorded in the journal and posted in representing general ledger accounts. The account *receiving* the value is *debited* and the account *giving* the value is *credited* for an equal amount. Accountants look at the *chart of accounts* to identify the general ledger accounts in which to record *transactions*—debiting one or more accounts receiving value and simultaneously crediting one or more accounts giving up the value.

THE DOUBLE-ENTRY SYSTEM OF ACCOUNTING: DEBITS MUST EQUAL CREDITS		
DEBIT DR	⬅	***CREDIT CR***
DEBITS (LEFT)	MUST EQUAL (BALANCE)	**CREDITS (RIGHT)**
GET	MUST EQUAL (BALANCE)	GIVE
RECEIVE	MUST EQUAL (BALANCE)	SOURCE
IN	MUST EQUAL (BALANCE)	OUT
TO	MUST EQUAL (BALANCE)	FROM

A "T" account structure (because it looks like a giant T) is generally used to provide a visual representation of the general ledger accounts to assist students in understanding the recording process using debits (DR) and credits (CR). In the T format it is easier for the student to see the Debits on the left side of the ledger account and the Credits on the right side;

sometimes, the sides might be labeled DR and CR. To remember which side is debited or credited, the words *credit* and *right* both contain the letter "R".

Two popular styles of the conceptual "T" general ledger accounts are: the horizontal and vertical or perpetual "T" (in **bold**) styles are shown in the following diagrams.

Example of The Horizontal or Balancing "T" Style of General Ledger Account							
Account Name: Fixed Assets				**Account No.: 1050**			
Date 2017		Trans. Description	JL Ref.	*Debit*	Date 2017	Trans. Description	JL Ref.	*Credit*
Jan.	1	General Journal	J1	2,000.00	Jan.	1		

Example of The Vertical or Perpetual General Ledger Account "T" Style						
Account Name: Fixed Assets					**Account No.: 1050**	
Date 2017		Trans. Description	JL Ref.	Post JL here		Updated Balance	
^		^	^	*Debit*	*Credit*	*Debit*	*Credit*
Jan.	1	General Journal	J1	2,000.00		2,000.00	

Notice with the vertical or perpetual style of general ledger accounts, also referred to as *four* columns style because it has two sets of debit and credit columns, the updated balance columns on the right side of the account contains the *updated* or *running* (also called *perpetual*) balance in the account *after* the posting of the journal transaction to the general ledger account.

The Accounting Equation

The accounting equation concept, *Assets = Liabilities (debts) + Owners' Equity*, demonstrates the relationship between groups of items and their values owned by the firm for use in the business—assets, and the sources of financing for the assets—liabilities plus owners' equity. Ledger accounts for assets usually have debit balances, and the ledger accounts for liabilities (debts) and owners' equity (capital) normally have credit balances. It is called an *equation* because, if you recall the double-entry system of accounting concept discussed in the previous section, the total of the accounts with debit balances must equal the total of the accounts with credit balances.

The Accounting Equation				
ASSETS	=	**LIABILITIES**	+	**EQUITY**
LIABILITIES	=	**ASSETS**	-	**EQUITY**
EQUITY	=	**ASSETS**	-	**LIABILITIES**

Chapter 1: Must Read Overview of Accounting and Bookkeeping

The accounting equation can be viewed as a summary of a firm's balance sheet on a specific date. For instance, if a firm owns fixed assets valued at $100,000.00 (office building $60,000.00, automobile $40,000.00), the sources of the funding for these assets might have been from cash down-payment from the owners (equity) of $10,000.00 toward purchase of the office building and a mortgage loan from the bank for $50,000.00 (liability), for a total purchase price of $60,000.00 ($10,000.00 + $50,000.00) for office building; cash down-payment from the business owners (equity) on the automobile of $5,000.00 with financing from the car dealer of $35,000.00 (liability) for the total purchase price of $40,000.00 ($5,000.00 + $35,000.00) for the automobile.

The accounting equation would show: **Assets $100,000.00** (building $60,000 + automobile $40,000) = **Liabilities $85,000.00** (mortgage $50,000 + $35,000.00 automobile financing $35,000.00) + **Owners' Equity $15,000.00** (cash down-payment for office building $10,000 + cash down-payment automobile $5,000.00).

Summary Overview of Accounting Activities

Accountants use **Charts of Accounts** when analyzing business transactions to determine which accounts to record them in the general journal and post periodically to the general ledger accounts listed in the chart of accounts. At the end of an accounting period the balances in each general ledger account are listed on a report called a trial balance (TB) and used to determine that the total of all accounts with debit balances equals the total of all accounts with credit balances.

Adjusting entries are also made at the end of the accounting period to a few general ledger (GL) balances to ensure that revenues and expenses and the related assets and liabilities are correctly posted (matched) to the appropriate accounting periods (current or future), and an *adjusted trial balance* created that lists all GL balances *after* the adjustments.

The general ledger accounts for revenues and expenses listed on the adjusted trial balance are then summarized on the *income statement* (IS) to determine the *net income* (or loss) for the period, which is then added to (or subtracted from) the balance for the retained earnings, a balance sheet (BS) account.

The final adjusted retained earnings account balance, along with the other balance sheet (BS) accounts on the adjusted TB, are summarized on the *balance sheet* statement to report the status of the assets, liabilities, and owner's equity on a specific date of the financial period.

Accounting 101: Easy Accounting and Bookkeeping for Beginners

Summary questions of financial activities chapter 1

1) How much cash (value) did the owner invest (capital) to start the business?

   a) Which accounts contain this value?

2) What are the three main sections of the balance sheet?

   a) _____

   b) _____

   c) _____

Practice Journalizing Transactions 1

Reminder of steps: Each transaction would be recorded on three separate lines: (a) Debit entry, followed by (b) Credit entry, then (c) Explanation for the transaction.

1. Paid check for $1,000.00 to landlord for a month's rent of office space.
2. Paid $75.00 for business telephone service to phone service provider.
3. Bought for cash $1,000.00 books to sell to customers.
4. Received $1,500.00 for sale of books to cash customers.
5. Paid $400.00 to local newspaper to advertise business to the public.
6. Paid electric bill for $200.00 to electric utility company.
7. Purchased a used van for cash, $3,000.00

Practice Journalizing Transactions using the chart of accounts

1. GL account _____ is DR and GL account _____ is CR for $
2. GL account _____ is DR and GL account _____ is CR for $
3. GL account _____ is DR and GL account _____ is CR for $
4. GL account _____ is DR and GL account _____ is CR for $
5. GL account _____ is DR and GL account _____ is CR for $
6. GL account _____ is DR and GL account _____ is CR for $
7. GL account _____ is DR and GL account _____ is CR for $

Chapter 1: Must Read Overview of Accounting and Bookkeeping

Answers to Summary questions of financial activities chapter 1

1) How much cash (value) did the owner invest (capital) to start the business? $20,000.00
   a) Which accounts contain this value? Cash account #1010 debit $20,000.00 and Owners Capital account #3010 credit $20,000.00.
2) What are the three main sections of the balance sheet?
   a) Assets
   b) Liabilities
   c) Equity

Solutions to Practice Journalizing Transactions using the chart of accounts

1. GL account 5010 is DR and GL account 1010 is CR for $1,000.00
2. GL account 5040 is DR and GL account 1010 is CR for $75.00
3. GL account 1030 is DR and GL account 1010 is CR for $1,000.00
4. GL account 1010 is DR and GL account 4010 is CR for $1,500.00
5. GL account 5060 is DR and GL account 1010 is CR for $400.00
6. GL account 5040 is DR and GL account 1010 is CR for $200.00
7. GL account 1050 is DR and GL account 1010 is CR for $3,000.00

General Journal

Accounting 101: Easy Accounting and Bookkeeping for Beginners

General Journal — Page No. 1

Date 20xx		Description	GL Ref.	Debit Amount		Credit Amount	
	1	Rent Expense	5010	1,000	00		
		Cash	1010			1,000	00
		Paid Month's rental for office space					
	2	Utilities Expense	5040	75	00		
		Cash	1010			75	00
		Paid for telephone service					
	3	Merchandize Inventory	1030	1,000			
		Cash	1010			1,000	00
		Purchased books for cash					
	4	Cash	1010	1,500	00		
		Sales Revenue	4010			1,500	00
		Cash sales of Books					
	5	Advertising & Promotion Expense	5060	400	00		
		Cash	1010			400	00
		Paid for newspaper advertising					
	6	Utilities Expense	5040	200	00		
		Cash	1010			200	00
		Paid electricity bill for month					
	7	Fixed Asset	1050	3,000	00		
		Cash	1010			3,000	00
		Purchased used van for cash					

Chapter 1: Must Read Overview of Accounting and Bookkeeping

Summary

- Accountants use a systematic step-by-step set of activities taken by the accountant to (1) identify, analyze, and record financial transactions, (2) record the transactions in the journal using a chart of accounts, (3) post the journal entries to the general ledger, (4) prepare a trial balance, (5) record and post end-of-period adjusting and closing entries, and (6) summarize and report on the activities of the firm by compiling financial statements.

- The concepts of the *double-entry system of accounting* and the *accounting equation* are used to record, update, and report on the three main set of *books* used to account for the operations of an organization: (1) *Journal* to record transactions, (2) *General Ledger* to post the journal entries, and (3) *Financial statements* to summarize and report on the balances in the general ledger.

Cumulative Comprehensive Hands-on Example 1

Master Zen started a for-profit business firm, MZ LLC., in the state of Florida, January 1, 2017, with $20,000.00 cash as equity capital. The business used $2,000.00 to purchase office desks and chairs. Show the accounting equation for MZ LLC.

Solutions to Cumulative Hands-On Example 1

Assets $20,000.00 (cash $18,000.00 + office furniture $2,000.00) = Liabilities $0.00 + owners' equity $20,000.00. See effects on the combined COA and TB on the following page.

A Simple Combined Chart of Accounts and Trial Balance MZ LLC.

CHART OF ACCOUNTS	TRIAL BALANCE	
Account #, Classification, and General Ledger Descriptions	Debit $$	Credit $$

Balance Sheet

Assets: 1000
- 1010 Cash — 18,000.00
- 1020 Accounts Receivable — XXXX.XX
- 1021 Allowance for Bad Debts — XXXX.XX (Credit)
- 1030 Merchandise Inventory — XXXX.XX
- 1040 Prepaid Accounts — XXXX.XX
- 1050 Fixed Assets — 2,000.00
- 1051 Accumulated Depreciation — XXXX.XX (Credit)

Liabilities: 2000
- 2010 Accounts Payable — XXXX.XX (Credit)
- 2020 Salaries & Wages Payable — XXXX.XX (Credit)
- 2030 Long-term Payable — XXXX.XX (Credit)
- 2040 Unearned Revenue — XXXX.XX (Credit)

Equity: 3000
- 3010 Owner's Capital/Equity — 20,000.00 (Credit)
- 3020 Drawing — XXXX.XX (Debit)
- 3030 Retained Earnings — XXXX.XX (Credit)

Income Statement

Revenue: 4000
- 4010 Sales Revenue — XXXX.XX (Credit)
- 4020 Other Revenue — XXXX.XX (Credit)
- 4030 Cost of Goods Sold (COGS) — XXXX.XX (Debit)

Expenses: 5000
- 5010 Rent Expense — XXXX.XX
- 5020 Salaries & Wages — XXXX.XX
- 5030 Office Expenses & Supplies — XXXX.XX
- 5040 Utilities Expense — XXXX.XX
- 5050 Insurance Expense — XXXX.XX
- 5060 Advertising & Promotion Expense — XXXX.XX
- 5070 Depreciation Expense — XXXX.XX
- 5080 Vehicle, Travelling & Entertainment Expense — XXXX.XX
- 5090 Bad Debt Expense — XXXX.XX

Totals: $20,000.00 $20,000.00

Chapter 2: Business Transactions, Chart of Accounts, and General Journal

Business Transactions

Question: What is the purpose of this chapter?

Answer: To demonstrate how business transactions are recorded and posted in a typical accounting system.

Business transactions are activities performed on behalf of a firm that are measured or valued by money. Business transactions are expenditures (or expenses) or receipts for goods or services for cash, or contractual obligations to be paid or received at a later date—on terms. These business transactions are recorded by the accountant in the books of the business on journal entries guided by the chart of accounts. Business transactions are usually supported (evidenced) by documents such as invoices, bills, receipts, notes, cash, contracts and written agreements, shipping documents, receiving reports, and paper or digital (computer) statements etc.

It is important to distinguish between personal transactions of the owners, and business transactions on behalf of or by the business as an independent organization (entity) separate from the owners. The business is treated as a separate, non-organic, *person* in the eyes of the law and referred to as a business entity.

Separation of Personal and Business Entity Expenditures and Expenses	
Owner's Personal expenditures/Expenses	**Business Entity Expenditures/Expenses--COA**
Grocery, clothes, travelling, gasoline, rent, telephone, electricity, cable, internet, automobile, mortgage, auto loans, education, entertainment, vacations, personal state and federal taxes etc.	Office and warehouse rental, purchase of inventory for resale, sale of merchandise and services, loans from bank, loan from owner, loan and advances to owners or employees, purchase of office supplies and equipment, insurance, utilities, state and federal taxes, sales taxes, wages and salaries etc.

Business transactions are generally between six main pairs of give/get categories of accounts of a business organization: (1) Assets/Assets (A/ A), (2) Assets/Liabilities (A/ L), (3) Assets/Expenses (A/E), (4) Assets/Revenues (A/R), (5) Liabilities/Expenses (L/E), (6) Assets/Equity (A/OE), or a combination of them. Note that transactions with parties inside or outside of the organization, such as employees, debtors, creditors, banks, and owners, are recorded in the general ledger accounts of the organization (accounts receivable, accounts payable, long-term loans, owner's equity etc.).

SIX PAIRS OF GIVE-GET CATEGORIES OF BUSINESS TRANSACTIONS IN BUSINESS FIRMS					
1. A/A	2. A/L	3. A/E	4. A/R	5. L/E	6. A/OE
Examples include: FA/Cash, Inventory/Cash, Cash/Receivable	Examples include: Inventory/Payable Cash/Creditors FA/Lenders	Examples include: Cash/Rent, Cash/Insurance Cash/Wages & Sal	Example includes: Cash/Revenue, Receivable/Sales	Examples include: Tax Exp./Payable Ins. Exp./Payable Rent Exp./Payable	Examples include: Cash/OE, Cash/Drawings, FA/OE
FA = Fixed Assets, OE = Owners' Equity, A = Assets, L = Liabilities, E = Expenses, R = Revenue, OE = Owners' Equity					

> Important: Only business transactions and activities performed by or on behalf of the business entity are analyzed, recorded, and posted in the books of the business.

The Chart of Accounts (COA)

let us look at the structure of the combined chart of accounts (COA) and trial balance at the end of chapter 1 and imagine moving money (financial transactions) out of (credit) one general ledger account and simultaneously into (debit) another general ledger account. A COA is a list of general ledger accounts set up and used in business firms to identify, record, and post financial transactions conducted on behalf of the organization. Creating and setting up the COA is usually among the first set of activities done by the accountant along with setting up a new bank account for the business.

Notice how the general ledger accounts are numbered and classified in the COA:

- The Balance Sheet (BS) section of the COA contains subcategories listing Asset account numbers beginning with the number 1; Liabilities account numbers starting with the number 2; and Equity account numbers starting with the number 3. The ledger accounts in the balance sheet section are called *permanent* accounts because their balances are carried over from one *financial* period to the next.

- The Income Statement (IS) section of the COA shows subcategories listing Revenue account numbers beginning with the number 4; and Expense account numbers starting with the number 5. The ledger accounts in the income statement section are called *nominal* or *temporary* accounts because their balances are closed out to zero by transferring their totals to an income summary account at the end of each *financial* period. The next financial period begins with zero amounts in these accounts.

Chapter 2: Business Transactions, Chart of Accounts, and General Journal

- The combined COA and Trial Balance (TB) shows the *normal* types of balances—Debit or Credit, found in accounting systems, as demonstrated by "XXXXXX" in the TB columns, with asset accounts (debit); contra-assets (credit); liabilities (credit); equity accounts (credit); expense accounts (debit); revenue accounts (credit).

The General Journal (GJ)

Steps in The Accounting Process					
STEP 1	STEP 2	STEP 3	STEP 4	STEP 5	STEP 6
Analyze Transactions	Record Journal Entries	Post to General Ledger	Prepare Trial Balance	End-of Period Adj. Entries	Compile Financial Statements

The chart of accounts (COA) is used to analyze and record business transactions in the journal (see Steps 1 and 2). The general journal is often called the book of first or prime entry because this is where the business transactions are usually first recorded in the books of the firm. Accountants use the COA to aid in analyzing business transactions, to identify the give-get relationship of the transaction, and determine which general ledger is receiving the value (debit) and its source--where the value is coming from (credit). *Journalizing* a transaction is the accounting jargon used to record entries in the journal and involves *debiting*—recording values in the debit section, and *crediting*—recording values in the credit section of the journal. It is important to remember the double-entry concept to ensure the journal balances.

Recall that Master Zen started his company MZ LLC on January 1, 2017, with $20,000.00 equity capital and purchased office equipment for $2,000.00:

General Journal				Page No. 1	
Date 2017		Description	GL Ref.	Debit	Credit
Jan	1	Cash	1010	20,000.00	
		Owner's Capital/Equity	3010		20,000.00
		Master Zen capital investment			
Jan	1	Fixed Assets	1050	2,000.00	
		Cash	1010		2,000.00
		Chk #001 Demp's Office Desks & Chairs			

Notice in the example: the name and page number of the journal; debits are entered on the first line followed by credits in the second line of the entries; the account descriptions (Description) and related account numbers in the GL Ref.; indentation of the second line for the description of the account credited; the debit and credit amounts are equal; explanation of the journal entries are written on a separate line below the entries; and a blank line between the different entries for readability.

Special Journals

Midsize and large organizations usually have several business transactions daily, and it would be cumbersome to record all transactions using general journals containing multiple lines of information and general ledger (GL) account numbers--especially for repetitive types of transactions. Special journals are journals containing pre-numbered GL account numbers across the *top* of the journal, for the GL accounts to be debited along with the corresponding GL accounts to be credited, in single rows for *each* transaction. Five common types of special journals are (1) *Cash Receipts Journal*, in which *all* receipts of cash and checks are recorded; (2) *Cash Payments Journal*—also called *Cash Disbursements Journal*, in which all payments of cash and checks are recorded; (3) *Purchases Journal*, in which non-cash purchases are recorded; (4) *Sales Journal*, in which non-cash sales are recorded; and (5) Payroll Journal, in which salaries and wages of employees are recorded.

The following demonstrate how *general* journals compare to each type of special journal to show the efficiency of using special journals.

Demonstration Examples

1. Purchased books on account, terms, 5/15/N30, from supplier STU $1,500.00 on Invoice #222.
2. Sold books on account, 2/10/N30, to customer CTU $4,000.00 on Invoice #100.
3. Paid invoice #222 $1,500.00 for supplier STU and deducted $75 for 5 percent early payment discount (5 percent of $1,500.00), with check #5 for $1,425.00.
4. Received check #009 for $3,920.00 from customer CTU for full payment of invoice #100 $4,000.00 less early payment discount of $80.00 (2 percent of $4,000.00).
5. Recorded salary and wage expenses for employees for $5,000.00 Gross, and withholdings for federal tax of $750.00 and F.I.C.A of $382.50 (7.65 percent) to be paid at the end of the pay period.

Note: Terms on account 5/15/N30 means that a 5 percent discount can be deducted from the invoice amount if it is paid within 15 days, or the full amount must be paid within 30 days; likewise, 2/10/N30, means 2 percent discount if paid within 10 days, or the invoice amount must be paid in full within 30 days.

Chapter 2: Business Transactions, Chart of Accounts, and General Journal

The transactions could be recorded in the General Journal *or* the Special Journals using the chart of account as shown in the following tables:

General Journal

General Journal							Page No. 1	
Date 20xx		Description	GL Ref.	Debit		Credit		
				Amount		Amount		
	1	Merchandise Inventory	1030	1,500	00			
		Accounts Payable	2010			1,500	00	
		Purchase books on account from STU Inv. #222						
	2	Accounts Receivable	1020	4,000	00			
		Sales Revenue	4010			4,000	00	
		Sale of Books on account to CTU Inv. # 100						
	3	Accounts Payable	2010	1,500	00			
		Purchases Discount	4031			75	00	
		Cash	1010			1,425	00	
		Paid chk #5 to STU for Inv. 222 less 5% discount						
	4	Cash	1010	3,920	00			
		Sales Discount	4011	80	00			
		Accounts Receivable	1020			4,000	00	
		Chk#009 received from CTU for Inv. #100 less 2%						
	5	Salaries and Wages Expenses	5020	5,000	00			
		Salaries Payable	2020.10			3,867	50	
		Federal Income Tax Payable	2020.20			750	00	
		F.I.C.A. Payable	2020.30			382	50	
		To record salaries and wages expenses for period						

Purchases Journal

				DEBIT				CREDIT	
			Vendor/Supplier Invoice #	Merch. GL AC # 1030		Other GL ACs		Accounts Payable GL AC # 2010	
Date		Vendor/Supplier		Amount		GL AC #	Amount	Subs. AC #	Amount
	1	STU	222	1,500	00				1,500	00

Accounting 101: Easy Accounting and Bookkeeping for Beginners

Sales Journal

Date		Customer Name	Inv. # or CM #	Subs. AC #	DEBIT Accts. Rec. GL AC # 1020 Amount		CREDIT Sales GL AC # 4010 Amount	
	2	CTU	100		4,000	00	4,000	00

Cash Payments Journal

Date	Chk #	Description	DEBIT Accounts Payable GL A/C # 2010 Subs. A/C #	Amount	Merch. GL A/C # 1030 Amount	Other G/L ACs G/L A/C #	Amount	CREDIT Cash GL A/C # 1010 Amount	Purch. Disc. GL A/C # 4031 Amount
	3	5	STU		1,500 00			1,425 00	75 00

Cash Receipts Journal

Date	Chk #	Description	DEBIT Cash GL A/C # 1010 Amount	Sales Disc. GL A/C # 4011 Amount	Accounts Receivable GL A/C # 1020 Subs. A/C #	Amount	CREDIT Sales GL A/C# 4010 Amount	Other G/L G/L A/C	Amount
	4	009	CTU	3,020 00	80 00		4,000 00			

Payroll Journal

Date		Employee Name	GROSS PAY DEBIT Salaries/Wages GL Expense AC # 5020 Amount	FEDERAL DEDUCTIONS CREDIT Federal Tax GL AC # 2020.20 Amount	F.I.C.A. GL AC # 2020.30 Amount	SET UP PAYCHECK CREDIT Net Pay GL AC # 2020.10 Amount	Check Number
	5	Misc. Employee names	5,000 00	750 00	382 00	3,867 00	

Think how many lines of entries would be needed in a general journal if there were multiple activities for each type of transaction in a typical week or month, instead of just one or two!

Denver Pettigrew, Ph.D., C.P.A., M.B.A.

Chapter 2: Business Transactions, Chart of Accounts, and General Journal

Summary questions of financial activities chapter 2

1) What are the three main tools used in recording and posting transactions in the accounting system of the firm?

   a) _____

   b) _____

   c) _____

2) What kind of transactions are recorded in the journals and posted to the general ledger of the firm?

3) What are the common names given to the activities of recording transactions in the journal, and posting transactions in the general ledger accounts?

Practice Journalizing Transactions 2

Reminder of steps: Each transaction would be recorded on three separate lines: (a) Debit entry, followed by (b) Credit entry, then (c) Explanation for the transaction.

1. Received notice from landlord for unpaid rental of office space for $1,000.00.
2. Received bill from telephone service provider for $130.00 for business telephone service.
3. Bought $2,000.00 books on credit terms from XYZ publishers to sell to customers.
4. Sold $3,500.00 on credit terms to customers.
5. Received invoice for $600.00 for advertising to promote new books with local newspaper to be paid in 30 days.
6. Received electric bill for $530.00 from electric utility company to be paid in 15 days.
7. Purchased office equipment on credit terms from YRU Office Equipment Company for $4,300.00.

Practice Journalizing Transactions using the chart of accounts

1. GL account _____ is DR and GL account _____ is CR for $
2. GL account _____ is DR and GL account _____ is CR for $
3. GL account _____ is DR and GL account _____ is CR for $
4. GL account _____ is DR and GL account _____ is CR for $
5. GL account _____ is DR and GL account _____ is CR for $
6. GL account _____ is DR and GL account _____ is CR for $
7. GL account _____ is DR and GL account _____ is CR for $

Accounting 101: Easy Accounting and Bookkeeping for Beginners

Answers to Summary questions of financial activities chapter 2

1) What are the three main tools used in recording and posting transactions in the accounting system of the firm?
   a) The Chart of Accounts (COA)
   b) The Journal
   c) The General Ledger

2) What kind of transactions are recorded in the journals and posted to the general ledger of the firm? Business Transactions.

3) What are the common names given to the acts of recording transactions in the journal, and posting transactions in the general ledger accounts? *Journalizing, debiting,* and *crediting* transactions in the journal and general ledger accounts.

Solutions to Practice Journalizing Transactions using the chart of accounts

1. GL account 5010 is DR and GL account 2010 is CR for $1,000.00
2. GL account 5040 is DR and GL account 2010 is CR for $130.00
3. GL account 1030 is DR and GL account 2010 is CR for $2,000.00
4. GL account 1020 is DR and GL account 4010 is CR for $3,500.00
5. GL account 5060 is DR and GL account 2010 is CR for $600.00
6. GL account 5040 is DR and GL account 2010 is CR for $530.00
7. GL account 1050 is DR and GL account 2010 is CR for $4,300.00

General Journal

Chapter 2: Business Transactions, Chart of Accounts, and General Journal

General Journal — Page No. 1

Date 20xx		Description	GL Ref.	Debit Amount		Credit Amount	
	1	Rent Expense	5010	1,000	00		
		Accounts Payable	2010			1,000	00
		Office rent due to landlord for office space					
	2	Utilities Expense	5040	130	00		
		Accounts Payable	2010			130	00
		Telephone service due for period					
	3	Merchandize Inventory	1030	2,000	00		
		Accounts Payable	2010			2,000	00
		Purchase books on credit from XYZ publishers					
	4	Accounts Receivable	1020	3,500	00		
		Sales Revenue	4010			3,500	00
		Sales of books on credit terms					
	5	Advertising & Promotion Expense	5060	600	00		
		Accounts Payable	2010			600	00
		Newspaper advertising due local newspaper					
	6	Utilities Expense	5040	530	00		
		Accounts Payable	2010			530	00
		Electricity bill due for month					
	7	Fixed Asset	1050	4,300	00		
		Accounts Payable	2010			4,300	00
		Purchased office equipment on credit from YRU					

Summary

Accountants use a Chart of Accounts (COA) to record business transactions following the double-entry accounting concept of debits and corresponding credits. Business transactions are first recorded in the journal therefore the journal is often referred to as the book of prime entry. When journalizing transactions, the general ledger accounts receiving value are first recorded (debited), and then the general ledger accounts giving up corresponding (same) values are recorded (credited) on a separate line, thereby ensuring that the journal is in balance.

Cumulative Comprehensive Hands-On Example 2

Let's now trace a few business transactions and look at how they are recorded in the general journal and effects in the Combined Chart of Accounts and Trial Balance of MZ LLC., during the month of January 2017.

Show the journal entries for the following transactions.

- Jan. 1, paid rent for warehouse space to Hoggspace Inc., for the month using check #002 for $1,500.00
- Jan. 2, paid for advertising for the month of January using check #003 to SocMed Adverts LLC., in the amount of $600.00.
- Jan. 4, paid $2,000.00 for 200 books (merchandise inventory) from BooksRU2 Supplies using check #004.
- Jan. 5, Paid insurance premium for the month of January to Firm Status Insurers in the amount of $200.00 on check #005.
- Jan. 6, paid office manager salary of $800.00 for week ending Jan.7, 2017, on check #006.

> Quick note: Whenever you see a transaction with the words *cash* or *paid* you can immediately identify that one of the accounts affected in the journal is the cash account.

Chapter 2: Business Transactions, Chart of Accounts, and General Journal
Solutions to Cumulative Hands-On Example 2

General Journal				Page No. 1	
Date 2017		Description	GL Ref.	Debit	Credit
Jan	1	Rent Expense	5010	1,500.00	
		Cash	1010		1,500.00
		Chk #002 Hoggspace Inc. Whse. rent Jan.			
Jan	2	Advertising & Promotion	5060	600.00	
		Cash	1010		600.00
		Chk #003 SocMed Adverts Jan. advertising			
Jan	4	Merchandise Inventory	1030	2,000.00	
		Cash	1010		2,000.00
		Chk #004 BooksRU2 Supplies 200 books			
Jan	5	Insurance Expense	5050	200.00	
		Cash	1010		200.00
		Chk #005 Firm Status Ins. Ins. prem Jan			
Jan	6	Salaries & Wages	5020	800.00	
		Cash	1010		800.00
		Chk #006 Office manager salary W/E Jan. 07			

A Simple Combined Chart of Accounts and Trial Balance, MZ LLC 01/07/2017

CHART OF ACCOUNTS	TRIAL BALANCE	
Account #, Classification, and General Ledger Descriptions	Debit $$	Credit $$

Balance Sheet

Assets: 1000
- 1010 Cash — 12,900.00
- 1020 Accounts Receivable — XXXX.XX
- 1021 Allowance for Bad Debts — XXXX.XX (credit)
- 1030 Merchandise Inventory — 2,000.00
- 1040 Prepaid Accounts — XXXX.XX
- 1050 Fixed Assets — 2,000.00
- 1051 Accumulated Depreciation — XXXX.XX (credit)

Liabilities: 2000
- 2010 Accounts Payable — XXXX.XX (credit)
- 2020 Wages & Salaries Payable — XXXX.XX (credit)
- 2030 Long-term Payable — XXXX.XX (credit)
- 2040 Unearned Revenue — XXXX.XX (credit)

Equity: 3000
- 3010 Owner's Capital/Equity — 20,000.00 (credit)
- 3020 Drawing — XXXX.XX (debit)
- 3030 Retained Earnings — XXXX.XX (credit)

Income Statement

Revenue: 4000
- 4010 Sales Revenue — XXXX.XX (credit)
- 4020 Other Revenue — XXXX.XX (credit)
- 4030 Cost of Goods Sold (COGS) — XXXX.XX (debit)

Expenses: 5000
- 5010 Rent Expense — 1,500.00
- 5020 Salaries & Wages — 800.00
- 5030 Office Expenses & Supplies — XXXX.XX
- 5040 Utilities Expense — XXXX.XX
- 5050 Insurance Expense — 200.00
- 5060 Advertising & Promotion Expense — 600.00
- 5070 Depreciation Expense — XXXX.XX
- 5080 Vehicle, Travelling & Entertainment Expense — XXXX.XX
- 5090 Miscellaneous Expense — XXXX.XX

Totals: $20,000.00 / $20,000.00

Chapter 3: The General Ledger and the Trial Balance

The General Ledger (GL)

Steps in The Accounting Process					
STEP 1	**STEP 2**	**STEP 3**	**STEP 4**	**STEP 5**	**STEP 6**
Analyze Transactions	Record Journal Entries	Post to General Ledger	Prepare Trial Balance	End-of Period Adj. Entries	Compile Financial Statements

Question: What is the purpose of this chapter?

Answer: Provide an overview of the makeup of a typical accounting system using general ledger accounts.

The general ledger contains all the firm's ledger accounts listed on the chart of accounts (COA). Business transactions are *posted* to the individual ledger accounts from the entries recorded in the journal on the same sides as recorded in the journal, and the balances in the ledger accounts updated immediately. This type of immediate updating of the general ledger account balances are called *perpetual* updating, as shown in the tables below.

Journal entries relating to general ledger accounts are sometimes totaled and posted *periodically* (weekly or monthly) as one entry in the account instead of individually. Individual postings to the related general ledger accounts recorded in the journal for the first week of January 2017, are as shown in the following tables, notice the perpetually updated balances:

General Ledger							
Account Name: Cash					Account No.: 1010		
				Post JL here		Updated Balance	
Date 2017		Trans. Description	JL Ref.	Debit	Credit	Debit	Credit
Jan.	1	General Journal	J1	20,000.00		20,000.00	
Jan.	1	General Journal	J1		2,000.00	18,000.00	
Jan.	1	General Journal	J1		1,500.00	16,500.00	
Jan.	2	General Journal	J1		600.00	15,900.00	
Jan.	4	General Journal	J1		2,000.00	13,900.00	
Jan.	5	General Journal	J1		200.00	13,700.00	
Jan.	6	General Journal	J1		800.00	12,900.00	

General Ledger

Account Name: Merchandise Inventory   **Account No.: 1030**

Date 2017		Trans. Description	JL Ref.	Post JL here		Updated Balance	
				Debit	Credit	Debit	Credit
Jan.	4	General Journal	J1	2,000.00		2,000.00	

General Ledger

Account Name: Fixed Assets   **Account No.: 1050**

Date 2017		Trans. Description	JL Ref.	Post JL here		Updated Balance	
				Debit	Credit	Debit	Credit
Jan.	1	General Journal	J1	2,000.00		2,000.00	

General Ledger

Account Name: Owner's Capital/Equity   **Account No.: 3010**

Date 2017		Trans. Description	JL Ref.	Post JL here		Updated Balance	
				Debit	Credit	Debit	Credit
Jan.	1	General Journal	J1		20,000.00		20,000.00

General Ledger

Account Name: Rent Expense   **Account No.: 5010**

Date 2017		Trans. Description	JL Ref.	Post JL here		Updated Balance	
				Debit	Credit	Debit	Credit
Jan.	1	General Journal	J1	1,500.00		1,500.00	

General Ledger

Account Name: Salaries & Wages   **Account No.: 5020**

Date 2017		Trans. Description	JL Ref.	Post JL here		Updated Balance	
				Debit	Credit	Debit	Credit
Jan.	6	General Journal	J1	800.00		800.00	

General Ledger

Account Name: Insurance Expense   **Account No.: 5050**

Date 2017		Trans. Description	JL Ref.	Post JL here		Updated Balance	
				Debit	Credit	Debit	Credit
Jan.	5	General Journal	J1	200.00		200.00	

Chapter 3: The General Ledger and the Trial Balance

General Ledger							
Account Name: Advertising & Promotion						Account No.: 5060	
				Post JL here		Updated Balance	
Date 2017		Trans. Description	JL Ref.	Debit	Credit	Debit	Credit
Jan.	2	General Journal	J1	600.00		600.00	

Please note the following in the previous general ledger account examples:

- The dates are the same as on the General Journal.
- The *Trans. Description* section refers to the type of journal—the general journal. This is used when there are large numbers of transactions during the period. Some accountants may use the name of the corresponding account instead to identify the other account involved in the transaction and the explanation provided for the journal entry. For example, the *Trans. Description* column in the preceding Cash ledger account might show instead of *General Journal* on January 1: *Owner's Capital/Equity*; *Fixed Assets*; and *Rent Expense* respectively for the first three lines of entries.
- The JL Ref. section indicates the page number shown at the top of the General Journal containing the transactions, in this case page 1.
- The amounts are posted in the general ledger account in the *same* columns, debit or credit as shown in the General Journal for the account in the "Post JL here" section.
- The "Updated Balance" section shows the latest balance in the ledger accounts *after* each transaction is posted—also called the perpetual balance of the account. Notice in the case of the Cash account, the debit of $10,000.00 increased the *debit* balance in the account on January 1, while the subsequent *credits reduced* the balance remaining in the account.

> **Asset and Expense accounts normally have debit balances that are reducible by credit entries; Liability, Equity, and Revenue accounts normally have credit balances that are reducible by debit entries.**

The Trial Balance (TB)

Steps in The Accounting Process					
STEP 1	**STEP 2**	**STEP 3**	**STEP 4**	**STEP 5**	**STEP 6**
Analyze Transactions	Record Journal Entries	Post to General Ledger	Prepare Trial Balance	End-of Period Adj. Entries	Compile Financial Statements

A Trial Balance (TB) is a tool used by accountants to verify that the total general ledger accounts with debit balances are equal in total to the accounts with credit balances; accounts with zero balances are generally not shown on a TB. The TB does not verify the accuracy of the postings or amounts; only that the total debits equal the total credits of the accounts in the general ledger.

As demonstrated in the Combined Chart of Accounts and Trial Balance shown throughout the book, the TB is a list showing all general ledger accounts and their current balances. The debit column of the TB is totaled at the bottom—called *footing* and compared with the total of the credit column to verify equality (comparison is referred to as *cross-footing* the columns).

If the total amounts do not match, the accountant must locate and correct the reason(s) for the mismatch. This is done by first identifying the difference between the two totals to see if an amount is omitted, posted on the wrong column, or divisible by the number 9 which could indicate a transposition of an amount in the TB. Otherwise, it might be necessary to review and confirm that all journal entries have been recorded and posted correctly in the general ledger accounts in accordance with the double-entry concept.

Even if the total debits and credits cross-foot—have equal amounts, the trial balance (TB) does not confirm that the amounts are correct or correctly posted to the right accounts, as this is not the purpose of the TB; only that the total debit balances equal the total credit balances. If a check is paid to a supplier for $900.00 and is incorrectly recorded in the journal and posted to the general ledger as $90.00, the TB would still be in balance though the records are incorrect. Or, if an amount paid for rent is recorded and posted to insurance expense in error it would not be immediately identified as incorrect in the TB.

Chapter 3: The General Ledger and the Trial Balance

Summary

Business transactions are originally recorded in the general journal in accordance with the chart of accounts (COA) of the firm and the double-entry concept of accounting. The journal entries are then transferred—posted to related general ledger accounts and balances are updated to include the latest transactions. The current, updated (perpetual) balances of the general ledger accounts are listed in a trial balance (TB), a tool showing the list of general accounts and balances used by accountants to verify and confirm that the total of accounts with debit balances are equal to the total of accounts with credit balances. The TB only confirms the double-entry accounting concept that total debits equals total credits in the general ledger account balances.

Accounting 101: Easy Accounting and Bookkeeping for Beginners

Summary questions of financial activities chapter 3

1) Using the Chart of Accounts (COA), indicate in which general ledger account number (GL#); and financial statement, balance sheet (BS) or income statement (IS), you would find the following transactions (account DR and financial statement, then account CR and financial statement):

   a) Investment of cash by owner to start the business.
   b) Cash purchase of office desks and chairs.
   c) Payment of warehouse rental.
   d) Payment for advertising.
   e) Cash purchase of books (merchandise).
   f) Payment of insurance premium.
   g) Payment of salaries and wages.

Practice Journalizing Transactions 3

Reminder of steps: Each transaction would be recorded on three separate lines: (a) Debit entry, followed by (b) Credit entry, then (c) Explanation for the transaction.

1. Paid check for $6,000.00 to landlord in advance 6 month's rent of office space.
2. Borrowed $10,000.00 from the bank on a long-term note to be repaid in 5 years.
3. Journalized the $1,500.00 cost to the firm (purchase) of the books that were sold to customers to reduce the remaining value (cost) of inventory on the books.
4. Received $2,500.00 in advance for pre-orders from customers for upcoming editions of books to be delivered in 3 months.
5. Paid insurance in advance of $2,400 for 2 years of liability insurance coverage.
6. Spent $250 on business expenses--travelling and entertainment with customers.
7. Paid $100.00 for office supplies from Papers 'N Stuff supplies.

Practice Journalizing Transactions using the chart of accounts

1. GL account _____ is DR and GL account _____ is CR for $
2. GL account _____ is DR and GL account _____ is CR for $
3. GL account _____ is DR and GL account _____ is CR for $
4. GL account _____ is DR and GL account _____ is CR for $
5. GL account _____ is DR and GL account _____ is CR for $
6. GL account _____ is DR and GL account _____ is CR for $
7. GL account _____ is DR and GL account _____ is CR for $

Chapter 3: The General Ledger and the Trial Balance
Answers to Summary questions of financial activities chapter 3

1) Using the Chart of Accounts (COA), indicate in which general ledger account number (GL#); and financial statement, balance sheet (BS) or income statement (IS), you would find the following transactions (account DR and financial statement, then account CR and financial statement):

   a) Investment of cash by owner to start the business: GL# 1010 (BS), GL#3010 (BS).
   b) Cash purchase of office desks and chairs: GL# 1050 (BS), GL#1010 (BS).
   c) Payment of warehouse rental: GL# 5010 (IS), GL#1010 (BS).
   d) Payment for advertising: GL# 5060 (IS), GL#1010 (BS).
   e) Cash purchase of books (merchandise): GL# 1030 (BS), GL#1010 (BS).
   f) Payment of insurance premium: GL# 5050 (IS), GL#1010 (BS).
   g) Payment of salaries and wages: GL# 5020 (IS), GL#1010 (BS).

Solutions to Practice Journalizing Transactions using the chart of accounts

1. GL account 1040 is DR and GL account 1010 is CR for $6,000.00
2. GL account 1010 is DR and GL account 2030 is CR for $10,000.00
3. GL account 4030 is DR and GL account 1030 is CR for $1,500.00
4. GL account 1010 is DR and GL account 2040 is CR for $2,500.00
5. GL account 1040 is DR and GL account 1010 is CR for $2,400.00
6. GL account 5080 is DR and GL account 1010 is CR for $250.00
7. GL account 5030 is DR and GL account 1010 is CR for $100.00

General Journal

General Journal							Page No. 1	
Date 20xx		Description	GL Ref.	Debit			Credit	
				Amount			Amount	
	1	Prepaid Accounts-Rental	1040	6,000	00			
		Cash	1010				6,000	00
		Advance payment of 6 month's rent for office space						
	2	Cash	1010	10,000	00			
		Long-term Payable	2030				10,000	00
		Note payable for loan from bank						
	3	Cost of Goods Sold	4030	1,500	00			
		Merchandise Inventory	1030				1,500	00
		Cost of books that were sold						
	4	Cash	1010	2,500	00			
		Unearned Revenue	2040				2,500	00
		Pre-order cash received from customers						
	5	Prepaid Accounts-Insurance	1040	2,400	00			
		Cash	1010				2,400	00
		Advance payment for 2 years liability insurance						
	6	Vehicle, Travelling & Entertainment Expense	5080	250	00			
		Cash	1010				250	00
		Business expenses for entertaining customers						
	7	Office Expense & Supplies	5030	100	00			
		Cash	1010				100	00
		Misc. office supplies purchased and expensed						

Chapter 3: The General Ledger and the Trial Balance

Cumulative Comprehensive Hands-on Example 3

Show the Trial Balance of MZ LLC as at January 7, 2017.

Solutions to Cumulative Hands-On Example 3

A Simple Combined Chart of Accounts and Trial Balance, MZ LLC 01/07/2017			
CHART OF ACCOUNTS Account #, Classification, and General Ledger Descriptions	**TRIAL BALANCE** Debit $$	Credit $$	
Balance Sheet			
Assets: 1000			
• 1010 Cash	12,900.00		BALANCE SHEET
• 1030 Merchandise Inventory	2,000.00		
• 1050 Fixed Assets	2,000.00		
Equity: 3000			
• 3010 Owner's Capital/Equity		20,000.00	
Income Statement			
Expenses: 5000			INCOME STATEMENT
• 5010 Rent Expense	1,500.00		
• 5020 Salaries & Wages	800.00		
• 5050 Insurance Expense	200.00		
• 5060 Advertising & Promotion Expense	600.00		
	$20,000.00	$20,000.00	

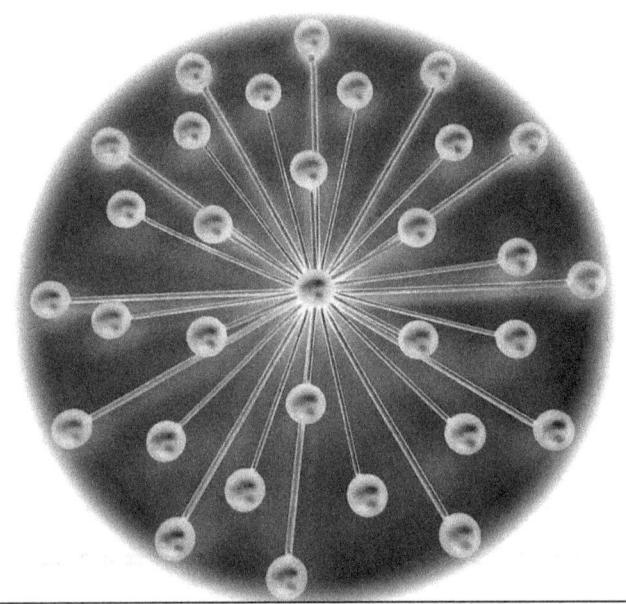

Collaborative learning. "Superior learners seek at least two to six additional sources of information." Dr. Denver Pettigrew

Chapter 4: Elements of the Balance Sheet
Chapter 4: Elements of The Balance Sheet
The Balance Sheet (BS)

Steps in The Accounting Process					
STEP 1	**STEP 2**	**STEP 3**	**STEP 4**	**STEP 5**	**STEP 6**
Analyze Transactions	Record Journal Entries	Post to General Ledger	Prepare Trial Balance	End-of Period Adj. Entries	Compile Financial Statements

Question: What is the purpose of this chapter?
Answer: To identify the permanent accounts in the chart of accounts used in the balance sheet.

The balance sheet summarizes what the organization owns—Assets; what it owes to others—Liabilities; and what is owed to owners of the organization—Equity at the end of a financial period. The balance sheet displays the *Accounting Equation*: Asset = Liability − Equity in detail. We will delay the completion of the balance sheet statement until chapter 6 after closing entries are posted to the income summary account and the net profit or loss for the firm is determined and reported in the income statement report.

In defining the chart of accounts (COA) in chapter 2, general ledger accounts that make up the balance sheet were described as *permanent* accounts because their balances are carried over from one *financial* period to the next. A review of the *Simple Combined Chart of Accounts and Trial Balance* at the end of previous chapters and in Appendix A, shows the categories, description and account numbers that make up the *elements* of the balance sheet. The COA shows the following subcategories: Asset account numbers beginning with number 1; Liabilities account numbers beginning with the number 2; and Equity account numbers, the number 3.

Notice that the chart of accounts (COA) was designed to hold up to 999 different general ledger accounts in each subcategory. The Assets subcategory was designed to accommodate account numbers between 1000 and 1999; the Liability section 2000 to 2999, and the Equities section 3000 to 3999.

Assets

Assets are physical and other valuable resources owned by the organization to be used to support the objectives of the organization. The assets subcategory is generally subdivided into current assets, long-term assets, and intangible assets (not included in this COA). Asset accounts in the general ledger normally have *debit* balances and the number of asset subcategories listed in the balance sheet depends on the reporting requirements of the kind and size of the organization. Many public organizations have many subcategories to provide additional detail to users of the financial statements for decision making and comparative analyses of the organization with other financial periods, or with other organizations and competitors.

Assets are reported on the balance sheet in the order of liquidity, from most liquid to least liquid, with the most liquid asset being cash. The liquidity of an asset refers to how quickly the asset can be converted to cash.

Current Assets

Current assets are expected to be used up within the normal operating cycle of the organization, or one year whichever is more. Most operating periods of organizations are calendar years such as January to December, or other 12—month periods, such as March to the following February. The following are just a few popular classifications of current assets used in most retail organizations.

- *Cash and Cash Equivalents* are money in the bank account, cash on hand, and petty cash. Cash equivalents are things like certificates of deposit and treasury bills that can be easily converted into specific sums of money on short notice as needed.
- *Accounts Receivable* are amounts owed *to* the firm by customers to whom goods were sold on terms—on credit and are still unpaid at the date of the balance sheet. These are non-cash customers allowed to purchase and own the items immediately with the agreement to pay for them later, such as in 30 days from the date of the invoice. The journal entry for recording *sales on terms* to customers is to debit the accounts receivable account for the amounts unpaid—owed *by* customers and credit to the sales or revenue account. *Cash sales* are debited directly to the cash account and credited to sales revenue; no accounts receivable is involved because customers paid in cash and do not owe the firm for these transactions.
- *Allowance for Bad Debts*, also called allowance for doubtful accounts, are amounts in the balance of the accounts receivable that are estimated by the accountant will not be paid by customers when they are due. They are indirectly written off against income for the period. The journal entry to record the estimated bad debt is: debit Bad Debt Expense account and credit the Allowance for Bad Debts account. The balance in this account is a negative (credit) amount, and the account is called a contra-asset account because assets normally have debit balances. Notice that the contra-asset account is a

Chapter 4: Elements of the Balance Sheet

subset of the related asset account in the COA. The amount estimated in the allowance for bad debt account is subtracted from the outstanding amount shown for accounts receivable on the balance sheet to show the *net* accounts receivable expected to be collectible on the date of the balance sheet.

- *Merchandise Inventory* are items purchased by retailers and wholesalers from suppliers, also called vendors, to sell to customers with little or no modification to make a profit. These are not items purchased to be used as supplies for the office or warehouse of the firm, but products to resell to customer in regular business operations.

    Inventory for a firm represents the main "products" the firm sells to its customers, whether the product is a finished item such as a car, or car parts. A car dealer, for instance, might sell both cars and car parts; both are merchandise inventory for the car dealer. Service type organizations do not generally have merchandise accounts because their main *product* is the *service* or expertise they provide for a fee, although some might also sell parts to customers. The journal to record the purchase of merchandise inventory is: debit Merchandise Inventory account, and credit cash (if paid immediately) or credit Accounts Payable if purchased on terms—credit.

    Recall in chapter 2 that MZ LLC purchased 200 books at a *cost* of $10.00 each, totaling $2,000.00, for merchandise inventory. The organization sells the books at a higher sales price at a *markup*, by adding an amount to the cost of each book, called *profit margin*. Hence the selling price (cost plus profit margin) of the books to customers is greater than the amount paid by MZ LLC for the books.

Before finishing the discussion on inventory, I will briefly introduce three cost assumptions—cost concepts of inventory cost which are matched to the related sales for the period on the income statement: First in First out (FIFO); Last in First Out (LIFO); and Weighted average. These are cost assumptions made by accountants to determine gross profit made on revenue (sales) for a specific period; especially when prices for merchandise changes frequently and the firm must pay different prices at different dates for *similar* items.

As an example, suppose that MZ LLC purchases additional books as follows: Jan. 8, 25 books for $12.00 each, totaling $300.00; Jan. 16, 25 books at $9.00, each totaling $225.00; and Jan. 21, 50 books at $8.00 each for a total amount of $400.00. The total cost of the 300 books in inventory available for sale for the period January 1, to January 21, would be $2,925.00 (2,000.00 + 300.00 + 225.00 + 400.00).

If MZ LLC also sold 150 books at $60.00 each (sales price of the firm) during the same period, total revenue would be $9,000.00 (150 x 60.00). The inventory balance at the end of the period is therefore 150 units (200 + 25 + 25 + 50 – 150).

How would the matching cost be determined under each cost flow assumption? Notice there are four different cost layers: $10.00 (Jan. 1), $12.00 (Jan. 8), $9.00 (Jan. 16), and $8.00 (Jan. 21). The valuations shown in the following diagrams are based on the *periodic* costing method of valuing the inventory remaining at the end of the period Jan. 21, 2017, with amounts expensed to C.O.S. in the lighter areas indicated, with the remainder in the inventory account.

	COST OF INVENTORY AVAILABLE FOR SALE			
	JAN. 1	JAN. 8	JAN. 16	JAN. 21
Purch. Unit/cost	200 @ $10.00	25 @ $12.00	25 @ $9.00	50 $8.00
Purchase cost	$2,000.00	$300.00	$225.00	$400.00
Cumulative total	200 $2,000.00	225 $2,300.00	250 $2,525.00	300 $2,925.00

FIFO Inventory value ending balance $1,425.00 and COS $1,500.00

	INVENTORY VALUE & COS UNDER FIRST-IN-FIRST-OUT AFTER SALE OF 150 UNITS				
	JAN. 1	JAN. 1	JAN. 8	JAN. 16	JAN. 21
Purch. Unit/cost	150 @ $10.00	50 @ $10.00	25 @ $12.00	25 @ $9.00	50 $8.00
Purchase cost	$1,500.00	$500.00	$300.00	$225.00	$400.00
Cumulative total	150 $1,500.00	50 $500.00	75 $800.00	100 $1,025.00	150 $1,425.00

LIFO Inventory value ending balance $1,500.00 and COS $1,425.00

	INVENTORY VALUE & COS UNDER LAST-IN-FIRST-OUT AFTER SALE OF 150 UNITS				
	JAN. 1	JAN. 1	JAN. 8	JAN. 16	JAN. 21
Purch. Unit/cost	150 @ $10.00	50 @ $10.00	25 @ $12.00	25 @ $9.00	50 $8.00
Purchase cost	$1,500.00	$500.00	$300.00	$225.00	$400.00
Cumulative total	150 $1,500.00	50 $500.00	75 $800.00	100 $1,025.00	150 $1,425.00

Average Cost Inventory value ending balance $1,462.50 and COS $1,462.50 (150 x 9.75).

	PERIODIC INVENTORY UNIT AVERAGE COST				
	JAN. 1	JAN. 8	JAN. 16	JAN. 21	JAN. 21
Purch. Unit/cost	200 @ $10.00	25 @ $12.00	25 @ $9.00	50 $8.00	
Purchase cost	$2,000.00	$300.00	$225.00	$400.00	
Periodic Average		Total cost/Total Units $2,925.00/300			9.75 each

Long-Term Assets

Long-term assets are expected to be useful to the firm for more than a year and expensed over a period calculated to match revenues directly or indirectly generated by such assets. As with current assets, the number of fixed asset classification will vary depending on the size and scope of the organization. General classifications may include office buildings, office furniture and equipment, computer equipment, land, vehicles, warehouse equipment etc.

Chapter 4: Elements of the Balance Sheet

- *Fixed Assets* are bought to be used by the firm to support the operations of the business over a long period of time—a year or more. Although not immediately obvious to the new learner, the costs of fixed assets will eventually be expensed as part of the operating cost of the business in generating revenues and profits. The initial historical costs of the fixed assets are not expensed immediately in the income statement but spread over current and future operating periods benefitting from the usage of the assets. The operating efficiency of fixed assets deteriorate over time, and some, such as computer equipment, may become outdated or obsolete quickly because of the introduction of new, more efficient technology. The recorded historical costs of fixed assets are reduced—expensed against periodic revenues over time, by a process called depreciation. The historical original purchase price paid for the asset is maintained in the general ledger account and netted against the accumulated depreciation account, a *contra-asset* account with a negative value (credit), to show the reduced or net value of the long-term asset on the balance sheet.

    As described earlier in relation to the account for doubtful account, a contra-asset account carries a negative—credit value in the assets section of the balance sheet instead of the normal, positive, debit values. Notice that this contra-asset account is a subset of the account to which it is related in the chart of accounts. Fixed assets transactions are recorded in the journal by debiting the Fixed Assets account and crediting Cash (if paid for immediately) or credit Long-Term Payable, if payment is postponed for a future date—on terms.

- *Accumulated Depreciation* is the *contra-asset* in the balance sheet for the credit side of the depreciation expense recorded in the income statement to depreciate long-term assets. Depreciation expense is based on estimates for the useful productive life (time) or usage (production) of the related assets, and the calculated amount is debited to the depreciation expense account and credited, not to the long-term asset account, but to the related accumulated depreciation account. The account is called accumulated because it contains the total amount of depreciation expense to the related asset since the date of its purchase.

    Two bases used by accountants to estimate depreciation expense for fixed assets are (1) time, straight-line (most popular) or modified, in number of years; and (2) units of production for a manufacturer such as maximum estimated number of units that can potentially be produced by a machine, or total estimated production hours of usage.

(1) An example of depreciation based on time is straight line depreciation: the value of the asset (the historical price paid less a residual or disposal value) divided by an estimated number of years of useful life such as 5 years. For instance, if a machine was purchased for $5,000.00 with estimated useful life of 5 years and residual value of $1,000.00, the yearly straight-line depreciation would be calculated as $4,000.00 ($5,000.00 - $1,000.00) divided by 5 (yrs.) or $4,000.00/5 = $800.00 per year journalized by debiting depreciation expense account $800.00 and crediting accumulated depreciation—machinery $800.00.

(2) The second depreciation basis used in a manufacturing firm is related to usage of the machine, such as on total number of units to be produced or total estimated production hours, over the useful life of the asset. For instance, if the machine described in the previous section was estimated to produce 40,000 units over its productive life, the depreciation expense would be based on $0.10 per unit of production ($4,000.00 / 40,000). If the number of units produced on the machine *for a period* is 5,000 then the depreciation expense (debit) and accumulated depreciation (credit) amount would be $500.00 (5,000 x $0.10 per unit).

- *Intangible Assets* are not covered in this book or in the chart of accounts (COA). These are assets that cannot be physically touched—intangible but are of economic value to the firm such as copyrights, patents, trade-marks and goodwill.

Liabilities

Liabilities are debts for goods and services incurred by or on behalf of the organization that remain unpaid at the date of the balance sheet. Examples of liabilities include: debts for unpaid merchandise purchased on terms—on credit by the firm; unpaid services provided by employees or other individuals and firms; amounts owed to utility providers; and unpaid amounts due to government agencies. Liability accounts in the general ledger normally contain *credit* balance amounts with categories in the balance sheet subdivided into current liabilities and long-term Liabilities, including unearned Revenue. The different types and numbers of liability accounts and subcategories depend on the operating and reporting needs of the organization and set up in the chart of accounts. Some organizations will have a variety of

Chapter 4: Elements of the Balance Sheet

subcategories for more in-depth analyses to more accurately report on the status and activities of the organization.

Current Liabilities

Like current assets, current liabilities (short-term debts owed by the organization) are expected to be paid within one year or the normal operating cycle of the organization whichever is longer. The operating cycle, also called fiscal year, of organizations can be a calendar year such as January to December, or other 12—month periods, such as March to the following February. Some popular classifications (elements) of current liabilities or debts used by retail organizations are:

- *Accounts Payable* represents operating debts owed by the organization to third parties for goods and services provided to the firm and are expected to be paid in the current fiscal year. One of the largest amounts in this category for retailers and wholesalers are transactions related to the purchase of merchandise inventory from suppliers and vendors on terms—credit. Amounts usually found in this category could include amounts unpaid for utilities, taxes and licenses payable to government agencies, and amounts owed for other operating and office supplies. The journal entry to record an accounts payable transaction is debit the relevant asset or expense account and credit the Accounts Payable account.

- *Salaries & Wages Payable* is a special category for unpaid amounts owed to employees for work performed for the organization. This is a normal category in business because employees are usually paid weekly, bi-weekly, or monthly *after* their services are provided to the firm. In other words, wages and salaries will usually be outstanding—owed to employees at any time for services provided to the organization to be paid on the next payday. This is also called *accrued* wages and salaries. The journal entry to record unpaid salaries and wages, is debit the Salaries & Wages *Expense* account, and credit the Salaries & Wages *Payable* account.

    Employers responsible for withholding certain *statutory* amounts from the wages and salaries of employees on behalf of city, state, and/or federal governments, to be paid over to the government at specific periods. Statutory *employee* withholding amounts include Social Security and Medicare (F.I.C.A.) and Federal Income Tax and may be grouped and shown separately on the balance sheet. Additionally, statutory *employer* tax amounts are additionally owed to the government by firms for federal unemployment taxes (F.U.T.A.) and state unemployment taxes (S.U.T.A.) and shown in the balance sheet.

Long-Term Liabilities

Long-term liabilities are debts incurred by the firm which are agreed to be repaid in over a year—beyond the current fiscal period. These are debts usually incurred to purchase big-ticket items such as buildings, office furniture and equipment, and operating machinery. Long-term liabilities may also include large amounts of cash borrowed to help finance the operations of the firm for several years. Long-term liabilities for large sums of money are generally secured by a mortgage note (land and buildings) or long-term notes payable (furniture and equipment, operating machinery, automobile and trucks etc.), and may also require personal guarantees by owners of the firm to repay the loan when due, especially in small firms.

- *Long-Term Payable* classification is used for debts or loans that are not due to be repaid within the fiscal year. These debts are usually secured by resources of the company and carry interest charges payable in the current period, such as monthly or quarterly and principal payments paid in installments or a lump sum at a specific time in the future. The periodic payments might include amounts for interest *and* reduction of the unpaid debt. The journal entries to record a transaction for long-term debt is generally a debit to Assets (Cash or Fixed Assets) and credit a Long-term Payable account.
- *Unearned Revenue* is not a long-term liability as such, but could be classified as long-term, if customers pay in advance for goods or services to be provided over a year later. Whenever customers pay for goods or services to be received in the future, the firm does not *earn* the related revenues until the goods or services are delivered to the customer—until ownership of the goods passes to the customer. Since the organization has not yet *earned* the revenue, the journal to record such a transaction is to debit the Cash account for the amount advances and credit the Unearned Revenue account.

Equity

The Equity subcategory of the balance sheet is usually subdivided into Owner's Capital, Drawings, and Retained Earnings.

- *Owner's Capital/Equity* represents cash or other resources invested by owners to start and finance the operations of the business as a separate entity. Additional capital resources invested in the business by the owner could include items such as machinery and equipment, office furniture and equipment, merchandise, land and building and

Chapter 4: Elements of the Balance Sheet

trucks or automobiles etc. Journal entries to record the capital resources initially invested in the business by the owner are usually done at the start of the new entity. Additional entries to the account would be recorded if the owners provided additional resources to the business in the future. The journal entries to record these transactions usually involve debits to appropriate asset accounts (such as Cash or Office Furniture) and corresponding credit to the Owner's Capital/Equity account. The transaction is also called *capitalizing* the firm.

- *Drawings* represent *withdrawal* of cash or other resources *from* the business for personal use by owners of the firm, thereby reducing the overall Equity balance of the firm. When an owner withdraws cash or assets from the business for personal use, the related asset account is credited for the reduction, and the Drawings account is debited for the value withdrawn. The Drawing account is a *contra-equity* account because it carries a debit balance against the normal credit balances of the equity accounts on the balance sheet.

- *Retained Earnings* general ledger account contains the accumulated (current and previous) net income or loss amounts of prior and current operating periods not distributed to the owners. At the end of each fiscal period the net income from the Income Statement (Income Summary account) is closed out to the Retained Earnings account.

Expenditure and Expense

A quick note on the usage of the terms expenditure and expense: Accountants refer to the actual spending of cash to purchase or pay for something by the business as an *expenditure*, whereas *expensing* of an amount refers to the allocation of the amount to the expense section of the income statement. For instance, the purchase of an office desk for cash is considered expenditure and reported in the balance sheet, while the periodic depreciation—writing off the cost of the desk in the income statement over time is considered expensing it.

Summary

This chapter provided an overview of the basic structure of an accounting system and general classification, subsections, and elements (accounts) of a typical balance sheet. The accounts are briefly described to provide understanding of how they are used in the business environment and within organizations.

Accounting 101: Easy Accounting and Bookkeeping for Beginners

Summary questions of financial activities chapter 4

1) Using the Chart of Accounts (COA), indicate in which general ledger account number (GL#); and financial statement, balance sheet (BS) or income statement (IS), you would find the following transactions (account DR and financial statement, then account CR and financial statement):

   a) Sold books on account (credit terms) to customer A who promises to pay in 30 days.
   b) Purchased books for inventory (merchandise for resale) on credit terms (on account) from vendor.
   c) Recorded rental expense for month to be paid next period.
   d) Received loan from bank to be repaid in 7 years and signed a promissory note payable.
   e) Recorded salary expense for office manager to be paid bi-weekly in next pay period.
   f) Received advance deposits for pre-paid sale of books from customers to be delivered in 4 months.
   g) Leased vehicle from car dealership to make deliveries and paid for lease in cash.

Practice Journalizing Transactions 4

Reminder of steps: Each transaction would be recorded on three separate lines: (a) Debit entry, followed by (b) Credit entry, then (c) Explanation for the transaction.

1. Received check for $2,000.00 from credit customers on account for prior sales.
2. Paid $1,200 on account to book vendors for prior purchases of inventory.
3. Paid past due rent of $1,000.00 for prior period previously expensed in GL.
4. Paid interest due on long-term loan to bank and recorded pmt to Office Expenses $200.
5. Paid check for $2,400.00 bi-weekly salary to office manager previously recorded in GL.
6. Delivered $2,300 books to pre-paid customers and moved amount to Sales Revenue.
7. Recorded monthly payment of $500 for lease of small truck from dealership.

Practice Journalizing Transactions using the chart of accounts

1. GL account _____ is DR and GL account _____ is CR for $
2. GL account _____ is DR and GL account _____ is CR for $
3. GL account _____ is DR and GL account _____ is CR for $
4. GL account _____ is DR and GL account _____ is CR for $
5. GL account _____ is DR and GL account _____ is CR for $
6. GL account _____ is DR and GL account _____ is CR for $
7. GL account _____ is DR and GL account _____ is CR for $

Chapter 4: Elements of the Balance Sheet

Answers to Summary questions of financial activities chapter 4

1) Using the Chart of Accounts (COA), indicate in which general ledger account number (GL#); and financial statement, balance sheet (BS) or income statement (IS), you would find the following transactions (account DR and financial statement, then account CR and financial statement):

   a) Sold books on account (credit terms) to customer A: GL# 1020 (BS), GL#4010 (IS).
   b) Purchased books for inventory on credit terms: GL# 1030 (BS), GL#2010 (BS).
   c) Recorded rental expense for month not paid: GL# 5010 (IS), GL#2010 (BS).
   d) Received loan from bank to be repaid in 7 years: GL# 1010 (BS), GL#2030 (BS).
   e) Recorded unpaid salary expense for office manager: GL# 5020 (IS), GL#2020 (BS).
   f) Received advance deposits for pre-paid sale of books: GL# 1010 (BS), GL#2040 (BS).
   g) Leased vehicle from car dealership, paid in cash: GL# 5080 (IS), GL#1010 (BS).

Solutions to Practice Journalizing Transactions using the chart of accounts

1. GL account 1010 is DR and GL account 1020 is CR for $2,000.00
2. GL account 2010 is DR and GL account 1010 is CR for $1,200.00
3. GL account 2010 is DR and GL account 1010 is CR for $1,000.00
4. GL account 5030 is DR and GL account 1010 is CR for $200.00
5. GL account 2020 is DR and GL account 1010 is CR for $2,400.00
6. GL account 2040 is DR and GL account 4010 is CR for $2,300.00
7. GL account 5080 is DR and GL account 1010 is CR for $500.00

General Journal

Accounting 101: Easy Accounting and Bookkeeping for Beginners

\	\	General Journal		Debit		Page No. 1	
Date 20xx		Description	GL Ref.	Debit		Credit	
				Amount		Amount	
	1	Cash	1010	2,000	00		
		Accounts Receivable	1020			2,000	00
		Check received on account from credit customers					
	2	Accounts Payable	2010	1,200	00		
		Cash	1010			1,200	00
		Payment on account to vendors					
	3	Accounts Payable	2010	1,000	00		
		Cash	1010			1,000	00
		Rent payment due for previous month					
	4	Office Expenses & Supplies	5030	200	00		
		Cash	1010			200	00
		Interest paid to bank on long-term loan					
	5	Salaries $ Wages payable	2020	2,400	00		
		Cash	1010			2,400	00
		Paid bi-weekly salary to office manager					
	6	Unearned Revenue	2040	2,300	00		
		Sales Revenue	4010			2,300	00
		Revenue earned for books delivered to customers					
	7	Vehicle, Travelling & Entertainment Expense	5080	500	00		
		Cash	1010			500	00
		Payment of lease on truck from dealership					

Denver Pettigrew, Ph.D., C.P.A., M.B.A.

Chapter 4: Elements of the Balance Sheet
Cumulative Comprehensive Hands-on Example 4

Steps in The Accounting Process					
STEP 1	**STEP 2**	**STEP 3**	**STEP 4**	**STEP 5**	**STEP 6**
Analyze Transactions	Record Journal Entries	Post to General Ledger	Prepare Trial Balance	End-of Period Adj. Entries	Compile Financial Statements

This comprehensive example covers (A) journal entries to record transactions and (B) posting of the journal entries to the related general ledger accounts of MZ LLC. See also the revised TB which follows the general ledger accounts.

Transactions:

- January 6, sold 150 books @ $60.00 each for a total of $9,000.00 on 30—day terms to customer A. Customer A promises to pay MZ LLC in 30 days.

- January 8, purchased 25 books @ $12.00 each from BooksRU2 Supplies for $300.00 payable in 30 days for Inventory.

- January 11, paid telephone bill for $175.00 on check #007

- January 13, paid office manager, salary of $800.00 for week ending January 14, 2017, on check #008.

- January 16, purchased 25 books @ $9.00 each from BooksRU2 Supplies for Inventory for $225.00 cash on check #009.

- January 18, purchased office supplies for $85.00 on check #010.

- January 21, purchased 50 books @ $8.00 each from BooksRU2 Supplies for $400.00 on 30—day terms.

- January 23, sold 50 books @ $60.00 each for a total of $3,000.00 cash to walk-in customers.

- January 24, borrowed $15,000.00 on a long-term note from the bank and purchases new packing and sorting machine for the warehouse (paid directly to machine dealer).

- January 27, paid office manager, salary of $1,600.00 for bi-weekly salary w/e Jan.28, 2017, on check #011.

- January 30, received a check for $6,000.00 advance payment from customer B for 100 books to be delivered in February.

- January 30, paid for lease on vehicle to dealership for $560.00 on check #012

Solutions to Cumulative Hands-On Example 4

(A). Journal Entries to record transactions.

		General Journal		Page No. 2	
Date 2017		Description	GL Ref.	Debit	Credit
January	6	Accounts Receivable	1020	9,000.00	
		Sales Revenue	4010		9,000.00
		Sale 150 books to Cust. A 30-day terms			
January	8	Merchandise Inventory	1030	300.00	
		Accounts Payable	2010		300.00
		Purch. 25 books Shana's on account			
January	11	Utilities Expenses	5040	175.00	
		Cash	1010		175.00
		Telephone bill paid on check #007			
January	13	Salaries & Wages	5020	800.00	
		Cash	1010		800.00
		Office manager's salary W/E 1/14 Chk #008			
January	16	Merchandise Inventory	1030	225.00	
		Cash	1010		225.00
		Purch. 25 books Shana's chk #009			
January	18	Office Expense & Supplies	5030	85.00	
		Cash	1010		85.00
		Office supplies chk #010			
January	21	Merchandise Inventory	1030	400.00	
		Accounts Payable	2010		400.00
		Purch. 50 books Shana's 30—day term			
January	23	Cash	1010	3,000.00	
		Sales Revenue	4010		3,000.00
		Cash Sales of 50 books misc. customers			
January	24	Fixed Assets machinery	1050	15,000.00	
		Long-Term Payable	2030		15,000.00
		Bank loan and purchase of machinery			

Chapter 4: Elements of the Balance Sheet

January	27	Salaries & Wages	5020	1,600.00	
		Cash	1010		1,600.00
		Office manager's salary W/E 1/28 Chk #011			
January	30	Cash	1010	6,000.00	
		Unearned Revenue	2040		6,000.00
		Adv. Pmt from Cust. B for 100 books			
January	30	Vehicle, Travelling and Entertainment	5080	560.00	
		Cash	1010		560.00
		Automobile lease payment chk #012			

(B). Posting the Journal entries to the General Ledger accounts

General Ledger							
Account Name: Cash						Account No.: 1010	
				Post JL here		Updated Balance	
Date 2017		Trans. Description	JL Ref.	Debit	Credit	Debit	Credit
Jan.	8	Balance brought forward				12,900.00	
Jan.	11	General Journal	J2		175.00	12,725.00	
Jan.	13	General Journal	J2		800.00	11,925.00	
Jan.	16	General Journal	J2		225.00	11,700.00	
Jan.	18	General Journal	J2		85.00	11,615.00	
Jan.	23	General Journal	J2	3,000.00		14,615.00	
Jan.	27	General Journal	J2		1,600.00	13,015.00	
Jan.	30	General Journal	J2	6,000.00		19,015.00	
Jan.	30	General Journal	J2		560.00	18,455.00	

General Ledger							
Account Name: Accounts Receivable						Account No.: 1020	
				Post JL here		Updated Balance	
Date 2017		Trans. Description	JL Ref.	Debit	Credit	Debit	Credit
Jan.	6	General Journal	J2	9,000.00		9,000.00	

General Ledger

Account Name: Merchandise Inventory **Account No.:** 1030

Date 2017		Trans. Description	JL Ref.	Post JL here		Updated Balance	
				Debit	Credit	Debit	Credit
Jan.	6	Balance brought forward				2,000.00	
	8	General Journal	J2	300.00		2,300.00	
	16	General Journal	J2	225.00		2,525.00	
	21	General Journal	J2	400.00		2,925.00	

General Ledger

Account Name: Fixed Assets **Account No.:** 1050

Date 2017		Trans. Description	JL Ref.	Post JL here		Updated Balance	
				Debit	Credit	Debit	Credit
Jan.	8	Balance brought forward				2,000.00	
	24	General Journal	J2	15,000.00		17,000.00	

General Ledger

Account Name: Accounts Payable **Account No.:** 2010

Date 2017		Trans. Description	JL Ref.	Post JL here		Updated Balance	
				Debit	Credit	Debit	Credit
Jan.	8	General Journal	J2		300.00		300.00
	21	General Journal	J2		400.00		700.00

General Ledger

Account Name: Long-Term Payable **Account No.:** 2030

Date 2017		Trans. Description	JL Ref.	Post JL here		Updated Balance	
				Debit	Credit	Debit	Credit
Jan.	24	General Journal	J2		15,000.00		15,000.00

General Ledger

Account Name: Unearned Revenue **Account No.:** 2040

Date 2017		Trans. Description	JL Ref.	Post JL here		Updated Balance	
				Debit	Credit	Debit	Credit
Jan.	30	General Journal	J2		6,000.00		6,000.00

Chapter 4: Elements of the Balance Sheet

General Ledger						
Account Name: Sales Revenue					Account No.: 4010	
Date 2017		Trans. Description	JL Ref.	Post JL here		Updated Balance	
				Debit	Credit	Debit	Credit
Jan.	6	General Journal	J2		9,000.00		9,000.00
	23	General Journal	J2		3,000.00		12,000.00

General Ledger						
Account Name: Salaries & Wages					Account No.: 5020	
Date 2017		Trans. Description	JL Ref.	Post JL here		Updated Balance	
				Debit	Credit	Debit	Credit
Jan.	7	Balance Brought forward				800.00	
Jan.	13	General Journal	J2	800.00		1,600.00	
Jan.	27	General Journal	J2	1,600.00		3,200.00	

General Ledger						
Account Name: Office Expense & Supplies					Account No.: 5030	
Date 2017		Trans. Description	JL Ref.	Post JL here		Updated Balance	
				Debit	Credit	Debit	Credit
Jan.	18	General Journal	J2	85.00		85.00	

General Ledger						
Account Name: Utilities Expenses					Account No.: 5040	
Date 2017		Trans. Description	JL Ref.	Post JL here		Updated Balance	
				Debit	Credit	Debit	Credit
Jan.	11	General Journal	J2	175.00		175.00	

General Ledger						
Account Name: Vehicle, Travelling and Entertainment					Account No.: 5080	
Date 2017		Trans. Description	JL Ref.	Post JL here		Updated Balance	
				Debit	Credit	Debit	Credit
Jan.	30	General Journal	J2	560.00		560.00	

A Simple Combined Chart of Accounts and Trial Balance, MZ LLC 01/31/2017

CHART OF ACCOUNTS Account #, Classification, and General Ledger Descriptions	TRIAL BALANCE Debit $$	Credit $$
Balance Sheet		
Assets: 1000		
• 1010 Cash	18,455.00	
• 1020 Accounts Receivable	9,000.00	
• 1021 Allowance for Bad Debts		XXXX.XX
• 1030 Merchandise Inventory	2,925.00	
• 1040 Prepaid Accounts	XXXX.XX	
• 1050 Fixed Assets	17,000.00	
• 1051 Accumulated Depreciation		XXXX.XX
Liabilities: 2000		
• 2010 Accounts Payable		700.00
• 2020 Salaries & Wage Payable		XXXX.XX
• 2030 Long-term Payable		15,000.00
• 2040 Unearned Revenue		6,000.00
Equity: 3000		
• 3010 Owner's Capital/Equity		20,000.00
• 3020 Drawing	XXXX.XX	
• 3030 Retained Earnings		XXXX.XX
Income Statement		
Revenue: 4000		
• 4010 Sales Revenue		12,000.00
• 4020 Other Revenue		XXXX.XX
• 4030 Cost of Goods Sold (COGS)	XXXX.XX	
Expenses: 5000		
• 5010 Rent Expense	1,500.00	
• 5020 Salaries & Wages	3,200.00	
• 5030 Office Expenses & Supplies	85.00	
• 5040 Utilities Expense	175.00	
• 5050 Insurance Expense	200.00	
• 5060 Advertising & Promotion Expense	600.00	
• 5070 Depreciation Expense	XXXX.XX	
• 5080 Vehicle, Travelling & Entertainment Expense	560.00 XXXX.XX	
• 5090 Bad Debt Expense		
	$53,700.00	**$53,700.00**

Chapter 5: Elements of the Income Statement

Chapter 5: Elements of the Income Statement

Steps in The Accounting Process					
STEP 1	STEP 2	STEP 3	STEP 4	STEP 5	STEP 6
Analyze Transactions	Record Journal Entries	Post to General Ledger	Prepare Trial Balance	End-of Period Adj. Entries	Compile Financial Statements

The Income Statement AKA the Profit and Loss Statement

Important Summary of Relationship Between Revenues, Expenses, and Net Profit
If *Expenses* (including Cost of Goods Sold) are Greater than Revenues = Net *Loss* for Period
If *Revenues* are Greater than Expenses (including Cost of Goods Sold) = Net *Income* for Period

Question: What is the purpose of this chapter?

Answer: To identify the accounts in the chart of accounts used in the income statement.

The income statement, also known as the profit and loss statement, summarizes the operating activities of the organization over a period called the operating cycle of the organization. In defining the chart of accounts (COA) in chapter 2, general ledger accounts that make up the income statement were described as temporary or nominal accounts because their balances are zeroed out at the end of an operating cycle (or financial period). These accounts begin each financial period with zero balances to account for activities in the new operating cycle.

> Important Note: The **Recognition concept** in accounting is that **revenue** is recognized when **earned**; that is, when the firm has completed its obligation in the transaction. On the other hand, **expenses** are recognized immediately when **incurred** (by the firm) and is related to the **Principle of Conservatism**.

A review of the *Simple Combined Chart of Accounts and Trial Balance* at the end of previous chapters and in Appendix A, shows the categories, descriptions, and account numbers that make up the *elements* of the income statement. The chart of accounts (COA) shows the following subcategories for the income statement: Revenue account numbers beginning with the number 4; and Expense account numbers beginning with the number 5. The original transactions in previous *cumulative comprehensive hands-on examples* at the end of chapter 3 and chapter 4 should be reviewed, as they apply to the concepts and information in this chapter.

The following are descriptions, journal entries, and general ledger account balances reported on the income statement for the period ending January 31, 2017.

Revenue

Sales Revenue: 4010

Sales revenue is the life-blood of for-profit firms and the *main* source of funds used for generating income and sustaining business operations toward the goals of the firm. Revenue, or sales revenue, is derived from the sale of merchandise or services to customers who purchase the firm's products or services. Organizations sell goods or services for more than it pays to acquire the goods or provide the service, to make enough income to cover the expenses of operating the business and turn a profit. MZ LLC, our fictitious firm, sells books (merchandise inventory) to earn enough revenue to cover all expenses of the business and make a net income. Thus, the income earned from the selling of books is the *main* revenue source—sales revenue for MZ LLC.

General Journal					Page No. 2
Date 2017		Description	GL Ref.	Debit	Credit
Jan.	6	Accounts Receivable	1020	9,000.00	
		Sales Revenue	4010		9,000.00
		Sale 150 books to Cust. A 30-day terms			
Jan.	23	Cash	1010	3,000.00	
		Sales Revenue	4010		3,000.00
		Cash Sales of 50 books misc. customers			

General Ledger							
Account Name: Sales Revenue						Account No.: 4010	
				Post JL here		Updated Balance	
Date 2017		Trans. Description	JL Ref.	Debit	Credit	Debit	Credit
Jan.	6	General Journal	J2		9,000.00		9,000.00
	23	General Journal	J2		3,000.00		12,000.00

Other Revenue

An organization might occasionally sell non-inventoried items such as depreciated vehicles or old office equipment. These are not considered sale of merchandise and would be shown as *other revenue* on the income statement because they are not the regular main source of income for the firm.

Chapter 5: Elements of the Income Statement
Cost of Goods Sold (COGS): 4030

Cost of goods sold are the amounts paid by MZ LLC to *purchase* the books from suppliers (vendors) that were sold to customers during the period. Because the FIFO cost technique is used by the firm, we look at the FIFO table in chapter 4 to determine the cost of the 200 books sold for the month. This is an example of the matching principle in accounting, whereby revenue earned by the firm is matched with the associated costs to acquire the items sold; what the firm paid to suppliers for the items it then sold to its customers, *buying low* (at cost) and *selling high* (at sales price to customers). The 200 units were from books purchased by the firm on January 1, 2017, at $10.00 each at a total cost of $2,000.00. We therefore removed (expensed) $2,000.00 from our merchandise inventory account and recorded the expense to Cost of Goods Sold account by journal dated January 31, 2017 by debiting the Cost of Goods Sold account (A/C #4030) and crediting the Merchandise Inventory account (A/C#1030) See *adjusting entries J3* in chapter 6.

General Journal				Page No. 3	
Date 2017		Description	GL Ref.	Debit	Credit
Jan.	31	Cost of Goods Sold (COGS)	4030	2,000.00	
		Merchandise Inventory	1030		2,000.00
		COS for month under FIFO			

General Ledger							
Account Name: Cost of Goods Sold (COGS)						Account No.: 4030	
				Post JL here		Updated Balance	
Date 2017		Trans. Description	JL Ref.	Debit	Credit	Debit	Credit
Jan.	31	General Journal	J3	2,000.00		2,000.00	

Expenses

Expenses are resources used up or paid by the organization in the running of the company toward earning income and to keep the organization going. COGS are considered a special type of expense. A review of the Combined Chart of Accounts and Trial Balance on January 31, 2017, of MZ LLC at the end of chapter 4 shows the elements (G/L accounts) in the income statement of the organization and related amounts to date. Most of the titles in this section are self-explanatory.

- **Rent Expenses: 5010**

The rent expense account is used to keep track of rental expenses incurred by the organization for use of building facilities owned by third parties, such as landlord or property renting agency, usually for monthly periods. The amounts paid or due for the period (accrued) to the landlord or agency at the balance sheet date are journalized by debiting Rent Expense account and crediting the Cash account (if paid) or crediting Accounts Payable account (for unpaid rent). Only journal entries and related expense ledgers related to the sections in the chapter are shown in the tables below because we are discussing elements of the Income Statement.

\multicolumn{2}{c}{}		General Journal		Page No. 1
Date 2017		Description	GL Ref.	Debit	Credit
Jan	1	Rent Expense	5010	1,500.00	
		Cash	1010		1,500.00
		Chk #002 Hoggspace Inc. Whse. rent Jan.			

General Ledger							
Account Name: Rent Expense					Account No.: 5010		
Date 2017		Trans. Description	JL Ref.	Post JL here		Updated Balance	
				Debit	Credit	Debit	Credit
Jan.	1	General Journal	J1	1,500.00		1,500.00	

- **Salaries & Wages: 5020**

This account is used to keep track of amounts incurred by the firm for services provided by employees of the organization, including amounts paid or due (until next paycheck), at the balance sheet date. Only the gross amounts are shown in these examples.

			General Journal		Page No. 1
Date 2017		Description	GL Ref.	Debit	Credit
Jan	6	Salaries & Wages	5020	800.00	
		Cash	1010		800.00
		Chk #006 Office manager salary W/E Jan.07			

			General Journal		Page No. 2
Date 2017		Description	GL Ref.	Debit	Credit
Jan.	13	Salaries & Wages	5020	800.00	
		Cash	1010		800.00
		Office manager salary W/E 1/14 Chk #008			

Chapter 5: Elements of the Income Statement

Jan.	27	Salaries & Wages	5020	1,600.00	
		Cash	1010		1,600.00
		Office manager salary W/E 1/28 Chk #011			

General Ledger						
Account Name: Salaries & Wages						**Account No.: 5020**
Date 2017		Trans. Description	JL Ref.	Post JL here		Updated Balance	
				Debit	Credit	Debit	Credit
Jan.	7	Balance Brought forward				800.00	
Jan.	13	General Journal	J2	800.00		1,600.00	
Jan.	27	General Journal	J2	1,600		3,200	
Jan.	31	General Journal	J2	320.00		3,520.00	

Employees and Independent Contractors

Organizations must distinguish between amounts paid for the services of *employees* of the firm and amounts paid for services provided by *outside* individuals and firms, called *independent contractors*. Briefly, the activities of employees are controlled directly by the human resources guidelines and policies of the firm. Independent contractors are not controlled by the firm and are expected to use their own expertise, judgement, and methods to perform services to the organization.

The distinction is important because firms are accountable to the Internal Revenue Service (IRS) for additional federal employer's payroll expenses by having employees and withhold statutory deductions from their paychecks on behalf of federal, state, and local governments. Payments to employees are recorded in the salaries and wages expense accounts.

Firms are not required to withhold statutory amounts from checks paid to independent contractors and these payments are generally recorded in the office expenses or miscellaneous expenses accounts. An IRS form 1099 is required to be sent to the independent contractor and to the Internal Revenue Service (IRS) showing the amounts paid for the year.

- **Office Expenses & Supplies: 5030**

This expense account is used to record amounts paid for small everyday office supplies such as paper and ink toner for printers, paper clips and file folders, pens and pencils used in the office etc. Office supplies are usually expensed immediately when purchased. Some organizations might use a separate asset account for Office Supplies and transfer amounts to Office Expense periodically to record amounts used up during the period. These are not mixed with regular Merchandise Inventory available for sale to customers. The journal entries to record Office Expenses and Supplies when purchased for cash are as follows:

General Journal				Page No. 2	
Date 2017		Description	GL Ref.	Debit	Credit
Jan.	18	Office Expense & Supplies	5030	85.00	
		Cash	1010		85.00
		Office supplies chk #010			

General Ledger							
Account Name: Office Expense & Supplies						Account No.: 5030	
Date 2017		Trans. Description	JL Ref.	Post JL here		Updated Balance	
				Debit	Credit	Debit	Credit
Jan.	18	General Journal	J2	85.00		85.00	

- **Utilities Expense: 5040**

Monthly payments to telephone service companies for office telephone and fax services are charged to this account. Mobile phones used strictly for business purposes by office managers and senior executives may also be charged to this account.

General Journal				Page No. 2	
Date 2017		Description	GL Ref.	Debit	Credit
Jan.	11	Utilities Expenses	5040	175.00	
		Cash	1010		175.00
		Telephone bill paid on check #007			

General Ledger							
Account Name: Utilities Expenses						Account No.: 5040	
Date 2017		Trans. Description	JL Ref.	Post JL here		Updated Balance	
				Debit	Credit	Debit	Credit
Jan.	11	General Journal	J2	175.00		175.00	

- **Insurance Expense: 5050**

Premiums for insurance policies on business property and liability insurance against damage to private individuals and other organizations are recorded in this account. Premiums paid on life insurance policies on the lives of senior executives are also usually recorded to this account,

Chapter 5: Elements of the Income Statement

although a separate account may be created for this. Workers' compensation insurance payments are usually recorded in a separate Workers' Compensation Insurance Expense account.

General Journal					Page No. 1
Date 2017		Description	GL Ref.	Debit	Credit
Jan	5	Insurance Expense	5050	200.00	
		Cash	1010		200.00
		Chk #005 Firm Status Ins. Ins. prem Jan			

General Ledger							
Account Name: Insurance Expense						Account No.: 5050	
Date 2017		Trans. Description	JL Ref.	Post JL here		Updated Balance	
				Debit	Credit	Debit	Credit
Jan.	5	General Journal	J1	200.00		200.00	

- **Advertising & Promotion Expense: 5060**

Amounts paid or due to advertising agencies for advertising or promoting the firm and its products in newspapers and electronic media, including social media, are recorded in this account.

General Journal					Page No. 1
Date 2017		Description	GL Ref.	Debit	Credit
Jan	2	Advertising & Promotion	5060	600.00	
		Cash	1010		600.00
		Chk #003 SocMed Adverts Jan. advertising			

General Ledger							
Account Name: Advertising & Promotion						Account No.: 5060	
Date 2017		Trans. Description	JL Ref.	Post JL here		Updated Balance	
				Debit	Credit	Debit	Credit
Jan.	2	General Journal	J1	600.00		600.00	

- **Depreciation Expense: 5070**

The recorded, historical value, of fixed assets is reduced systematically over time by a process called depreciation and charged to the depreciation expense account. Depreciation is essentially the systematic spreading of the historical cost of the firm's fixed assets over current and future operating periods, matching the cost of fixed assets with periodic revenues earned while the assets are in service. It is important to recognize that assets are combined with other resources, including the expertise of employees, toward the profitable goals of an organization. As explained in chapter 4 in describing *Fixed Assets*, the depreciation concept also includes deterioration of fixed assets over time due to deteriorating operating efficiency of equipment, machines, buildings or vehicles; or items such as computer software and equipment becoming outdated or obsolete because of the introduction of new, more efficient technology.

Depreciation expense is based on estimates of the useful productive life (time) or usage (production) of an asset over which it contributes toward the earning of income for the firm (an example of the matching principle mentioned earlier for COGs). The amount calculated is recorded in the journal by debiting the depreciation expense account and crediting the related accumulated depreciation account for the period using the accumulation method.

General Journal				Page No. 3	
Date 2017		Description	GL Ref.	Debit	Credit
Jan.	31	Depreciation Expense	5070	33.33	
		Accumulated Depreciation	1051		33.33
		Month's depreciation office furniture			

General Ledger							
Account Name: Depreciation Expense					Account No.: 5070		
				Post JL here		Updated Balance	
Date 2017		Trans. Description	JL Ref.	Debit	Credit	Debit	Credit
Jan.	31	General Journal	J3	33.33		33.33	

- **Vehicle Travelling & Entertainment Expense: 5080**

Amounts posted to this account would include lease payments for company vehicles, gas, and tolls paid by the firm; travelling expenses paid for business trips such as airline, ship and train tickets; and business meals and entertainment expenses allowable by the IRS.

General Journal				Page No. 2	
Date 2017		Description	GL Ref.	Debit	Credit
Jan.	30	Vehicle, Travelling and Entertainment	5080	560.00	
		Cash	1010		560.00
		Automobile lease payment chk #012			

Chapter 5: Elements of the Income Statement

General Ledger							
Account Name: Vehicle, Travelling and Entertainment					Account No.: 5080		
				Post JL here		Updated Balance	
Date 2017		Trans. Description	JL Ref.	Debit	Credit	Debit	Credit
Jan.	30	General Journal	J2	560.00		560.00	

- **Bad Debt Expenses: 5090**

Sales to customers on terms—also called credit sales, are a major source of revenue for many organizations. These sales are usually on 30-day terms, meaning that the customer has 30 days in which to pay for goods sold and delivered to them. Credit sales are recorded in the Accounts Receivable general ledger account. Over time, some of these customers run into financial difficulties and are unable to pay amounts when they become due. Accountants estimate that a percentage of the accounts receivable balance or a percentage of the monthly sales on credit will not eventually be paid by customers and records an estimated amount to the bad debt expense account each period. See also the related definition of the *Allowance for Bad Debts* in chapter 4.

General Journal				Page No. 3	
Date 2017		Description	GL Ref.	Debit	Credit
Jan.	31	Bad Debt Expense	5090	450.00	
		Allowance for Bad Debts	1021		450.00
		Est. 5% of credit sales of $9,000.00			

General Ledger							
Account Name: Bad Debt Expense					Account No.: 5090		
				Post JL here		Updated Balance	
Date 2017		Trans. Description	JL Ref.	Debit	Credit	Debit	Credit
Jan.	31	General Journal	J3	450.00		450.00	

Summary

An overview of the basic structure of an accounting system and general classification, subsections, and elements (accounts) of a typical income statement was covered in this chapter. Some popular general ledger accounts found in a typical income statement were briefly described to provide understanding of how they are used in the business environment by organizations.

In the discussion of the salary and wages expense category of the income statement, a brief introduction of the characteristics and importance of distinguishing between employees and independent contractors who provide services to the organization was included.

Accounting 101: Easy Accounting and Bookkeeping for Beginners

Summary questions of financial activities chapter 5

1) Using the Chart of Accounts (COA), indicate in which general ledger account number (GL#); and financial statement, balance sheet (BS) or income statement (IS), you would find the following transactions (account DR and financial statement, then account CR and financial statement):

   a) Delivered books to prepaid customers and recognized the revenue now earned.
   b) Record the reduction in inventory for the cost of books sold during the period.
   c) Record rent (expense) due for the current period out of a prepaid rent balance.
   d) Record depreciation expenses on equipment for the period using accumulation method.
   e) Record estimate for bad debts in accounts receivable based on the allowance method.
   f) Record salary expense for current period to be paid in next period's payroll.
   g) Payment of salaries and wages earned in previous period.

Practice Journalizing Transactions 5

Reminder of steps: Each transaction would be recorded on three separate lines: (a) Debit entry, followed by (b) Credit entry, then (c) Explanation for the transaction.

1. Shipped $600.00 books to prepaid customers cash recorded in prior periods.
2. Made adjustment to inventory for cost of books sold during period for $700.00.
3. Recorded $1,000.00 rent for period out of the prepaid rent account balance.
4. Recorded $200.00 for depreciation on fixed assets using allowance method.
5. Recorded an estimated allowance of $600.00 for potential bad accounts receivable.
6. Paid salaries and wages including $3,000.00 expensed in previous period.
7. Expensed $700.00 current month's insurance premium out of prepaid account balance.

Practice Journalizing Transactions using the chart of accounts

1. GL account _____ is DR and GL account _____ is CR for $
2. GL account _____ is DR and GL account _____ is CR for $
3. GL account _____ is DR and GL account _____ is CR for $
4. GL account _____ is DR and GL account _____ is CR for $
5. GL account _____ is DR and GL account _____ is CR for $
6. GL account _____ is DR and GL account _____ is CR for $
7. GL account _____ is DR and GL account _____ is CR for $

Chapter 5: Elements of the Income Statement
Answers to Summary questions of financial activities chapter 5

1) Using the Chart of Accounts (COA), indicate in which general ledger account number (GL#); and financial statement, balance sheet (BS) or income statement (IS), you would find the following transactions (account DR and financial statement, then account CR and financial statement):

   a) Shipped pre-ordered books to prepaid customers: GL# 2040 (BS), GL#4010 (IS).
   b) Reduction in inventory for the cost of books sold: GL# 4030 (IS), GL#1030 (BS).
   c) Record rent for the current period out of prepaid rent: GL# 5010 (IS), GL#1040 (BS).
   d) Record depreciation using accumulation method: GL# 5070 (IS), GL#1051 (BS).
   e) Estimate bad debts using allowance method: GL# 5090 (IS), GL#1021 (BS).
   f) Record (accrue) salary expense to be paid next period: GL# 5020 (IS), GL#2020 (BS).
   g) Payment of salaries and wages accrued in prior period: GL# 2020 (BS), GL#1010 (BS).

Solutions to Practice Journalizing Transactions using the chart of accounts

1. GL account 2040 is DR and GL account 4010 is CR for $600.00
2. GL account 4030 is DR and GL account 1030 is CR for $700.00
3. GL account 5010 is DR and GL account 1040 is CR for $1,000.00
4. GL account 5070 is DR and GL account 1051 is CR for $200.00
5. GL account 5090 is DR and GL account 1021 is CR for $600.00
6. GL account 2020 is DR and GL account 1010 is CR for $3,000.00
7. GL account 5050 is DR and GL account 1040 is CR for $700.00

General Journal

Date 20xx		Description	GL Ref.	Debit Amount		Credit Amount	
	1	Unearned Revenue	2040	600	00		
		Sales Revenue	4010			600	00
		Shipped books to prepaid customer					
	2	Cost of Goods Sold (COGS)	4030	700	00		
		Merchandise Inventory	1030			700	00
		Record cost of books sold for period					
	3	Rent Expenses	5010	1,000	00		
		Prepaid Accounts	1040			1,000	00
		Rent expenses for period from prepaid rent amount					

General Journal — Page No. 1

Accounting 101: Easy Accounting and Bookkeeping for Beginners

	4	Depreciation Expense	5070	200	00		
		Accumulated Depreciation	1051			200	00
		Record depreciation on equipment					
	5	Bad Debt Expense	5090	600	00		
		Allowance for Bad Debts	1021			600	00
		Estimated doubtful accounts in AR					
	6	Salaries & Wages Payable	2020	3,000	00		
		Cash	1010			3,000	00
		Check paid for salaries and wages for prior month					
	7	Insurance Expense	5050	700	00		
		Prepaid Accounts	1040			700	00
		Insurance premium due current period					

Chapter 6: Adjusting Entries, Post-Adj. TB, Closing Entries, and Net Income
Chapter 6: Adjusting Entries, Post-Adj. TB, Closing Entries, and Net Income

Steps in The Accounting Process					
STEP 1	**STEP 2**	**STEP 3**	**STEP 4**	**STEP 5**	**STEP 6**
Analyze Transactions	Record Journal Entries	Post to General Ledger	Prepare Trial Balance	End-of Period Adj. Entries	Compile Financial Statements

Question: What is the purpose of this chapter?

Answer: To determine the net profit or loss for the period, by summarizing and closing out the balances in the temporary accounts in the income statement.

Adjusting Entries

At the end of an operating, accountants make adjusting journal entries for unrecorded revenue and expenses to determine the *true* operating results for the period. This is necessary because payment for some resources used by the firm might not have been made or paid in advance, or transfers from unearned revenues to recognize actual revenues earned, might need to be recorded to determine the true profit or loss for the period. Examples of such adjustments include: payments made in advance for insurance and rent, called prepaid expense (technically prepaid assets); accruals for unpaid wages and salaries of employees; depreciation expense, estimate for bad debts; interest accrued on long-term debts; reclass from unearned revenue to revenue; and inventory adjustments and cost of sales.

The following adjusting entries were made on January 31, 2017, for MZ LLC, and the resulting effects on the general ledger accounts shown below the entries.

- Jan. 31 Estimated 5% of sales on *terms* for the month will eventually not be paid and recorded the appropriate allowance for bad debts. Recorded $450.00 ($9,000.00 x 0.05) to bad debt expense.
- Jan. 31 Recorded accrued Wages and Salaries payable of $320.00 (2/5 x $800.00) for period ending January 31 which will be included in the next bi-weekly paycheck.
- Jan. 31 Estimated and recorded one month's straight-line depreciation expense on office desks and chairs purchased on January 1, depreciable over 5 years (60 months) with no residual value. 1/60 x $2,000.00 = $33.33.
- Adjust Merchandise Inventory to Cost of Sales amounting to $2,000.00 for merchandise sold during month using FIFO (see FIFO table earlier in chapter), using the *periodic*

inventory adjustment method, whereby the balance in the inventory account is adjusted at the end of an operating period instead of *perpetually* after each transaction.

Adjusting General Journal					Page No. 3
Date 2017		Description	GL Ref.	Debit	Credit
Jan.	31	Cost of Goods Sold (COGS)	4030	2,000.00	
		Merchandise Inventory	1030		2,000.00
		COS for month under FIFO			
Jan.	31	Salaries & Wages Expense	5020	320.00	
		Salaries & Wages Payable	2020		320.00
		2 days wages accrued for office manager.			
Jan.	31	Depreciation Expense	5070	33.33	
		Accumulated Depreciation	1051		33.33
		Month's depreciation office furniture			
Jan.	31	Bad Debt Expense	5090	450.00	
		Allowance for Bad Debts	1021		450.00
		Est. 5% of credit sales of $9,000.00			

Adjustments for Cost of Goods Sold

General Ledger							
Account Name: Cost of Goods Sold (COGS)					Account No.: 4030		
Date 2017		Trans. Description	JL Ref.	Post JL here		Updated Balance	
				Debit	Credit	Debit	Credit
Jan.	31	General Journal	J3	2,000.00		2,000.00	

General Ledger							
Account Name: Merchandise Inventory					Account No.: 1030		
Date 2017		Trans. Description	JL Ref.	Post JL here		Updated Balance	
				Debit	Credit	Debit	Credit
Jan.	6	Balance brought forward				2,000.00	
Jan.	8	General Journal	J2	300.00		2,300.00	
Jan.	16	General Journal	J2	225.00		2,525.00	
Jan.	21	General Journal	J2	400.00		2,925.00	
Jan.	31	General journal	J3		2,000.00	925.00	

Chapter 6: Adjusting Entries, Post-Adj. TB, Closing Entries, and Net Income

Adjustments for Accrual of Unpaid Salaries and Wages: 5020

General Ledger						
Account Name: Salaries & Wages					Account No.: 5020	
Date 2017		Trans. Description	JL Ref.	Post JL here		Updated Balance	
				Debit	Credit	Debit	Credit
Jan.	7	Balance Brought forward				800.00	
Jan.	13	General Journal	J2	800.00		1,600.00	
Jan.	27	General Journal	J2	1,600.00		3,200.00	
Jan.	31	General Journal	J3	320.00		3,520.00	

General Ledger						
Account Name: Salaries & Wages Payable					Account No.: 2020	
Date 2017		Trans. Description	JL Ref.	Post JL here		Updated Balance	
				Debit	Credit	Debit	Credit
Jan.	31	General Journal	J3		320.00		320.00

Adjustments for Estimated Depreciation

General Ledger						
Account Name: Depreciation Expense					Account No.: 5070	
Date 2017		Trans. Description	JL Ref.	Post JL here		Updated Balance	
				Debit	Credit	Debit	Credit
Jan.	31	General Journal	J3	33.33		33.33	

General Ledger						
Account Name: Accumulated Depreciation					Account No.: 1051	
Date 2017		Trans. Description	JL Ref.	Post JL here		Updated Balance	
				Debit	Credit	Debit	Credit
Jan.	31	General Journal	J3		33.33		33.33

Adjustments for Estimated Bad Debts

General Ledger						
Account Name: Bad Debt Expense					Account No.: 5090	
Date 2017		Trans. Description	JL Ref.	Post JL here		Updated Balance	
				Debit	Credit	Debit	Credit
Jan.	31	General Journal	J3	450.00		450.00	

General Ledger						
Account Name: Allowance for Bad Debts				Account No.: 1021		
				Post JL here		Updated Balance	
Date 2017		Trans. Description	JL Ref.	Debit	Credit	Debit	Credit
Jan.	31	General Journal	J3		450.00		450.00

After the adjusting entries are completed and posted to the general ledger accounts, a *post-adjustment* trial balance is prepared, and the debit and credit columns totaled to check that they are equal in accordance with the double-entry accounting concept discussed earlier. A review of the Post-Adjustment Chart of Accounts and Trial Balance on the next page shows the totals of the Debit and Credit columns are equal (also referred to as footing the TB). After the accountant has reviewed the TB and is satisfied that it is in order, he or she proceeds to the next phase of the systematic steps: *closing the books*.

Closing the books refers to closing out all the nominal or temporary revenue and expense accounts by transferring their balances to another temporary, transitionary account, the income summary account, which is then closed out to the retained earnings account.

New General Ledger Account: Income Summary Account

I waited until the new learner was introduced and exposed to other major types of general ledger accounts found in a typical chart of accounts (COA), especially the revenue and expense (temporary accounts), to introduce the *Income Summary* general ledger account. This account is not a typical general ledger account and is used temporarily at the end of the accounting period to close all amounts in the nominal or temporary accounts in the income statement and determine the net profit or loss for the period. The account, 3900 Income Summary, will be added to the COA as a *clearing account* for revenues and expenses, and the ending balance in this account subsequently closed out to the Retained Earnings account #3030 in the balance sheet.

Chapter 6: Adjusting Entries, Post-Adj. TB, Closing Entries, and Net Income

Post-Adjustment Chart of Accounts and Trial Balance, MZ LLC 01/31/2017

CHART OF ACCOUNTS — Account #, Classification and General Ledger Descriptions	TRIAL BALANCE Debit $$	Credit $$
Balance Sheet		
Assets: 1000		
• 1010 Cash	18,455.00	
• 1020 Accounts Receivable	9,000.00	
• 1021 Allowance for Bad Debts		450.00
• 1030 Merchandise Inventory	925.00	
• 1040 Prepaid Accounts	XXXX.XX	
• 1050 Fixed Assets	17,000.00	
• 1051 Accumulated Depreciation		33.33
Liabilities: 2000		
• 2010 Accounts Payable		700.00
• 2020 Salaries & Wage Payable		320.00
• 2030 Long-term Payable		15,000.00
• 2040 Unearned Revenue		6,000.00
Equity: 3000		
• 3010 Owner's Capital/Equity		20,000.00
• 3020 Drawing	XXXX.XX	
• 3030 Retained Earnings		XXXX.XX
Income Statement		
Revenue: 4000		
• 4010 Sales Revenue		12,000.00
• 4020 Other Revenue		XXXX.XX
• 4030 Cost of Goods Sold (COGS)	2,000.00	
Expenses: 5000		
• 5010 Rent Expense	1,500.00	
• 5020 Salaries & Wages	3,520.00	
• 5030 Office Expenses & Supplies	85.00	
• 5040 Utilities Expense	175.00	
• 5050 Insurance Expense	200.00	
• 5060 Advertising & Promotion Expense	600.00	
• 5070 Depreciation Expense	33.33	
• 5080 Vehicle, Travelling & Entertainment Expense	560.00	
• 5090 Bad Debt Expense	450.00	
	$54,503.33	$54,503.33

Accounting 101: Easy Accounting and Bookkeeping for Beginners

The following tables show the closing entries for the nominal (temporary accounts) to the income summary account; the balances in the nominal general ledger accounts; and the income statement of MZ LLC for the period ending January 31, 2017.

End of Period Closing Entries

\multicolumn{3}{c	}{}	Closing Journal		Page No. 4	
Date 2017		Description	GL Ref.	Debit	Credit
Jan.	31	Sales Revenue	4010	12,000.00	
		Income Summary	3900		12,000.00
		Close Sales Revenue to Income Summary			
Jan.	31	Income Summary	3900	2,000.00	
		Cost of Goods Sold	4030		2,000.00
		Close COGS to Income Summary			
Jan.	31	Income Summary	3900	1,500.00	
		Rent Expense	5010		1,500.00
		Close Rent Expense to Income Summary			
Jan.	31	Income Summary	3900	3,520.00	
		Salaries & Wages Expense	5020		3,520.00
		Close Sal. & Wages to Income Summary			
Jan.	31	Income Summary	3900	85.00	
		Office Expenses & Supplies	5030		85.00
		Close Of. Expenses to Income Summary			
Jan.	31	Income Summary	3900	175.00	
		Utilities Expense	5040		175.00
		Close Sales Revenue to Income Summary			
Jan.	31	Income Summary	3900	200.00	
		Insurance Expense	5050		200.00
		Close Ins. Exps. to Income Summary			
Jan.	31	Income Summary	3900	600.00	
		Advertising & Promotion	5060		600.00
		Close Adv. & Prom. to Income Summary			

Chapter 6: Adjusting Entries, Post-Adj. TB, Closing Entries, and Net Income

Jan.	31	Income Summary	3900	33.33	
		Depreciation Expense	5070		33.33
		Close Depr. Exp. to Income Summary			
Jan.	31	Income Summary	3900	560.00	
		Vehicle, Travelling & Entertainment	5080		560.00
		Close Trav. & Ent. to Income Summary			
Jan.	31	Income Summary	3900	450.00	
		Bad Debt Expense	5090		450.00
		Close Bad Debt Exp. to Income Summary			
Jan.	31	Income Summary	3900	2,867.67	
		Retained Earnings	3030		2,876.67
		Close Income Summary to Retained Earn.			

Note: The final entry closes out a credit balance (Net Income) in the income summary account (3900) to the retained earnings account (3030).

General Ledger							
Account Name: Retained Earnings						Account No.: 3030	
				Post JL here		Updated Balance	
Date 2017		Trans. Description	JL Ref.	Debit	Credit	Debit	Credit
Jan.	31	Closing Journal	J4		2,876.67		2,876.67

General Ledger							
Account Name: Income Summary						Account No.: 3900	
				Post JL here		Updated Balance	
Date 2017		Trans. Description	JL Ref.	Debit	Credit	Debit	Credit
Jan.	31	Closing Journal	J4		12,000.00		12,000.00
Jan.	31	Closing Journal	J4	2,000.00			10,000.00
Jan.	31	Closing Journal	J4	1,500.00			8,500.00
Jan.	31	Closing Journal	J4	3,520.00			4,980.00
Jan.	31	Closing Journal	J4	85.00			4,895.00
Jan.	31	Closing Journal	J4	175.00			4,720.00
Jan.	31	Closing Journal	J4	200.00			4,520.00
Jan.	31	Closing Journal	J4	600.00			3,920.00
Jan.	31	Closing Journal	J4	33.33			3,886.67

Date		Trans. Description	JL Ref.	Debit	Credit	Debit	Credit
Jan.	31	Closing Journal	J4	560.00			3,326.67
Jan.	31	Closing Journal	J4	450.00			2,876.67
Jan.	31	Closing Journal	J4	2,876.67			0.00

General Ledger

Account Name: Sales Revenue   **Account No.: 4010**

Date 2017		Trans. Description	JL Ref.	Post JL here Debit	Credit	Updated Balance Debit	Credit
Jan.	6	General Journal	J2		9,000.00		9,000.00
	23	General Journal	J2		3,000.00		12,000.00
Jan.	31	Closing Journal	J4	12,000.00			0.00

General Ledger

Account Name: Cost of Goods Sold (COGS)   **Account No.: 4030**

Date 2017		Trans. Description	JL Ref.	Post JL here Debit	Credit	Updated Balance Debit	Credit
Jan.	31	General Journal	J2	2,000.00		2,000.00	
Jan.	31	Closing Journal	J4		2,000.00	0.00	

General Ledger

Account Name: Rent Expense   **Account No.: 5010**

Date 2017		Trans. Description	JL Ref.	Post JL here Debit	Credit	Updated Balance Debit	Credit
Jan.	1	General Journal	J1	1,500.00		1,500.00	
Jan.	31	Closing Journal	J4		1,500.00	0.00	

General Ledger

Account Name: Salaries & Wages   **Account No.: 5020**

Date 2017		Trans. Description	JL Ref.	Post JL here Debit	Credit	Updated Balance Debit	Credit
Jan.	7	Balance Brought forward				800.00	
Jan.	13	General Journal	J2	800.00		1,600.00	
Jan.	27	General Journal	J2	1,600		3,200	
Jan.	31	General Journal	J2	320.00		3,520.00	
Jan.	31	Closing Journal	J4		3,520.00	0.00	

Chapter 6: Adjusting Entries, Post-Adj. TB, Closing Entries, and Net Income

General Ledger							
Account Name: Office Expense & Supplies						Account No.: 5030	
Date 2017		Trans. Description	JL Ref.	Post JL here		Updated Balance	
				Debit	Credit	Debit	Credit
Jan.	18	General Journal	J2	85.00		85.00	
Jan.	31	Closing Journal	J4		85.00	0.00	

General Ledger							
Account Name: Utilities Expenses						Account No.: 5040	
Date 2017		Trans. Description	JL Ref.	Post JL here		Updated Balance	
				Debit	Credit	Debit	Credit
Jan.	11	General Journal	J2	175.00		175.00	
Jan.	31	Closing Journal	J4		175.00	0.00	

General Ledger							
Account Name: Insurance Expense						Account No.: 5050	
Date 2017		Trans. Description	JL Ref.	Post JL here		Updated Balance	
				Debit	Credit	Debit	Credit
Jan.	5	General Journal	J1	200.00		200.00	
Jan.	31	Closing Journal	J4		200.00	0.00	

General Ledger							
Account Name: Advertising & Promotion						Account No.: 5060	
Date 2017		Trans. Description	JL Ref.	Post JL here		Updated Balance	
				Debit	Credit	Debit	Credit
Jan.	2	General Journal	J1	600.00		600.00	
Jan.	31	Closing Journal	J4		600.00	0.00	

General Ledger							
Account Name: Depreciation Expense						Account No.: 5070	
Date 2017		Trans. Description	JL Ref.	Post JL here		Updated Balance	
				Debit	Credit	Debit	Credit
Jan.	31	General Journal	J2	33.33		33.33	
Jan.	31	Closing Journal	J4		33.33	0.00	

General Ledger

Account Name: Vehicle, Travelling and Entertainment					Account No.: 5080	
Date 2017		Trans. Description	JL Ref.	Post JL here		Updated Balance	
				Debit	Credit	Debit	Credit
Jan.	30	General Journal	J2	560.00		560.00	
Jan.	31	Closing Journal	J4		560.00	0.00	

General Ledger

Account Name: Bad Debt Expense					Account No.: 5090	
Date 2017		Trans. Description	JL Ref.	Post JL here		Updated Balance	
				Debit	Credit	Debit	Credit
Jan.	31	General Journal	J2	450.00		450.00	
Jan.	31	Closing Journal	J4		450.00	0.00	

The Income Statement

MZ LLC. Income Statement
For Period Ended January 31, 2017

	$	$
Sales Revenue		
Sales:		12,000.00
Less Cost of Goods Sold:		(2,000.00)
Gross Profit		10,000.00
Expenses	$	$
Rent Expense	1,500.00	
Salaries & Wages	3,520.00	
Office Expenses & Supplies	85.00	
Utilities Expense	175.00	
Insurance Expense	200.00	
Advertising & Promotion Expense	600.00	
Depreciation Expense	33.33	
Vehicle, Trav. & Ent. Expenses	560.00	
Bad Debt Expenses	450.00	
Total Expenses		7,123.33
Net Income		2,876.67

Notice how the temporary (nominal) accounts are displayed in the income statement.

MZ LLC made net income of $2,876.67 during the first month of operation: The $10,000.00 Gross profit of $10,000.00 was more than the $7,123.33 Expenses.

Chapter 6: Adjusting Entries, Post-Adj. TB, Closing Entries, and Net Income

The $12,000.00 credit balance in the Sales Revenue account was greater than the combined debit balances in the expense accounts of 7,123.33 and cost of sales account of $2,000.00.

> **Important Summary of Relationship Between Revenues, Expenses, and Net Profit**
> If *Revenues* are Greater than *Expenses* (including Cost of Goods Sold) = Net Income for Period
> *Revenues* $12,000.00 are Greater than Expenses $9,123.33 (including Cost of Goods Sold) =
> Net *Income* $2,876.33 for Period

Summary

In this chapter, we demonstrated the systematic steps taken by accountants to record, post, adjust, and close out the ending balances in the temporary general ledger accounts for revenue and expenses to the income summary account. We then closed the ending balance amount in the income summary account (Acct. #3900) to the retained earnings account (Acct. #3030)—a permanent account reported in the equity section of the balance sheet. The chapter ended with a preview of the income statement of MZ LLC, and how the closed temporary accounts are categorized and shown on the statement. We will discuss the main financial statements in the next chapter and show the next step in the systematic step-by-step accounting procedures to *report* the results of the operating activities for the period, and show the resources owned and owed by the firm at the end of the fiscal period.

Summary questions of financial activities chapter 6

1) Using the Chart of Accounts (COA), indicate the groups of general ledger account numbers (GL#) are used in the income statement and why.

2) Using the Chart of Accounts (COA), indicate (a) which groups of account numbers are closed out at the end of the fiscal year and why; (b) what they are called (temporary or permanent); and (c) to which account in the balance sheet are the amounts in the temporary accounts in the income statement ultimately closed at the end of the fiscal period.

Chapter 6: Adjusting Entries, Post-Adj. TB, Closing Entries, and Net Income

Answers to Summary questions of financial activities chapter 1

1) Using the Chart of Accounts (COA), indicate the groups of general ledger account numbers (GL#) are used in the income statement and why.

   Revenue account numbers—4####, and Expense account numbers—5####. They are used to determine the net profit or loss of the operating activities of the business for the period.

2) Using the Chart of Accounts (COA), indicate (a) Revenue account numbers—4####, and Expense account numbers—5#### are closed out at the end of the fiscal year to determine profit or loss for the period and to start the subsequent period with zero balances; (b) they are called temporary or nominal accounts; and (c) the ending balances in the temporary accounts are first closed out to and interim income summary account; the income summary account is then closed out to the retained earnings account, a permanent account, in the balance sheet at the end of the fiscal period.

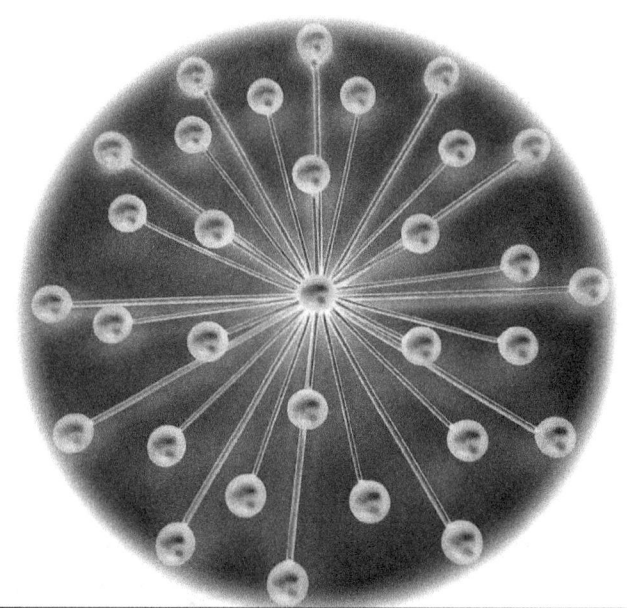

Collaborative learning. "Superior learners seek at least two to six additional sources of information." Dr. Denver Pettigrew

Chapter 7: Income Statement, Balance Sheet, Changes in Owner's Equity

Steps in The Accounting Process					
STEP 1	**STEP 2**	**STEP 3**	**STEP 4**	**STEP 5**	**STEP 6**
Analyze Transactions	Record Journal Entries	Post to General Ledger	Prepare Trial Balance	End-of Period Adj. Entries	Compile Financial Statements

Question: What is the purpose of this chapter?

Answer: To introduce the main financial statement reports of a firm and learn the relationships between them.

We have completed the activities shown in steps 1 to 5 of the accounting process to record and post business transactions in the journal and related general ledger accounts; closed the temporary accounts and prepared the income statement; and determined and transfer net income to the retained earnings in the balance sheet, we will now look at the financial statement reports of our hypothetical business, MZ LLC, as at January 31, 2017. The income statement is shown in the following table:

The Income Statement

MZ LLC. Income Statement For Period Ended January 31, 2017		
Sales Revenue	$	$
Sales:		12,000.00
Less Cost of Goods Sold:		(2,000.00)
Gross Profit		10,000.00
Expenses	$	$
Rent Expense	1,500.00	
Salaries & Wages	3,520.00	
Office Expenses & Supplies	85.00	
Utilities Expense	175.00	
Insurance Expense	200.00	
Advertising & Promotion Expense	600.00	
Depreciation Expense	33.33	
Vehicle, Trav. & Ent. Expenses	560.00	
Bad Debt Expenses	450.00	
Total Expenses		7,123.33
Net Income		2,876.67

The net income for the period is transferred to the retained earnings account balance and shown in the equity section of the balance sheet, and all temporary accounts now contain zero balances in preparation for the next accounting period. This is depicted in the following diagram:

Relationship Between Income Statement and The Balance Sheet

1 — **Income Statement Containing Temporary Expense and Revenue Accounts**

+ Expense Accounts And -Revenue Accounts

+4030+5010+5020+5030+5040+5050+5060+5070+5080+5090   -4010-4020

These temporary accounts are closed out to the Income Summary account as Net Income or Net Loss for the period

If Expenses > Revenues = Net Loss; If Expenses < Revenues = Net Income for the Period

The temporary Income Summary account is closed out to the Retained Earnings account, a Permanent account in the Balance Sheet

2 — **Net Income to Retained Earnings Account—Permanent Account in Balance Sheet**

Net Income/Loss is added to/subtracted from the beginning amount in the Retained Earnings account, 3030, to determine the ending balance of Retained Earnings shown in the Equity section of the Balance Sheet

3 — **Balance Sheet – Permanent Accounts**

Assets: 1010+1020-1021+1030+1040+1050-1051 = **Liabilities:** 2010+2020+2030+2040 Plus **Equity:** 3010-3020+3030

The Statement of Retained Earnings

Some organizations account for changes in the balance of the retained earnings account, a permanent account reported in the balance sheet, by combining the information in the income statement, after arriving at the net income for the period. It is common, however, to prepare a separate statement of retained earnings to indicate the intermediary relationship between the income statement and the balance sheet. The structure of the statement of retained earnings is like the Statement of Changes in Owner's Equity described later in the chapter.

MZ LLC Statement of Retained Earnings Jan. 1 to Jan. 31, 2017

	$$
Retained Earnings	
Balance December 31, 2016	0.00
Add Net income or Less Net Loss from Income Statement for period	2,876.67
Balance in Retained Earnings January 31, 2017	$2,876.67

Chapter 7: Income Statement, Balance Sheet, Changes in Owner's Equity

The statement of retained earnings is sometimes included with the income statement in a combined statement of income and retained earnings.

MZ LLC. Combined Income Statement & Retained Earnings
For Period Ended January 31, 2017

	$	$
Sales Revenue		
Sales:		12,000.00
Less Cost of Goods Sold:		(2,000.00)
Gross Profit		**10,000.00**
Expenses	$	$
Rent Expense	1,500.00	
Salaries & Wages	3,520.00	
Office Expenses & Supplies	85.00	
Utilities Expense	175.00	
Insurance Expense	200.00	
Advertising & Promotion Expense	600.00	
Depreciation Expense	33.33	
Vehicle, Trav. & Ent. Expenses	560.00	
Bad Debt Expenses	450.00	
Total Expenses		7,123.33
Net Income		**2,876.67**
Retained Earnings		
Balance December 31, 2016		0.00
Add Net income or Less Net Loss from Income Statement for period		2,876.67
Balance in Retained Earnings January 31, 2017		**$2,876.67**

Review the balance sheet section of the *Post-Adjustment Chart of Accounts and Trial Balance* in the previous chapter and the Combined Statement of Income & Retained Earnings shown above. We can now show the final balance of $2,876.67 from the statement of retained earnings account 3030 in the equity section of the balance sheet. The completed balance sheet report and statement of changes in owner's equity report are as shown on the next page.

Accounting 101: Easy Accounting and Bookkeeping for Beginners

The Balance Sheet

MZ LLC Balance Sheet as at Period Ending January 31, 2017

	$$	$$
Assets		
Cash		18,455.00
Accounts Receivable	9,000.00	
Less Allowance for Bad Debts	(450.00	
Net Accounts Receivable		8,550.00
Merchandise Inventory		925.00
Total Current Assets		27,930.00
Fixed Assets	17,000.00	
Less Accumulated Depreciation	(33.33)	
Net Fixed Assets		16,966.67
Total Assets (A)		$44,896.67
Liabilities		
Accounts Payable		700.00
Salaries & Wages Payable		320.00
Unearned Revenue		6,000.00
Total Current Liabilities		7,020.00
Long-term Payable		15,000.00
Total Liabilities (L)		$22,020.00
Owners' Equity		
Owners' Capital/Equity		20,000.00
Retained Earnings		2,876.67
Total Equity (E)		$22,876.67
Total Liabilities + Equity (L+E) = (A)		$44,896.67

The Statement of Changes in Owner's Equity/Stockholder's Equity

MZ LLC Statement of Changes in Owner's Equity Jan. 1 to Jan. 31, 2017

	$$
Owners' Equity	
January 1, Beginning Owners' Capital/Equity	0.00
Add Capital Contributed Master Zen	20,000.00
Loss for Period Posted to Retained Earnings	2,876.67
Less Drawings by Owners for the Period	0.00
Total Equity (E) January 31, 2017	$22,876.67

Chapter 7: Income Statement, Balance Sheet, Changes in Owner's Equity

The statement of changes in owner's equity is a report showing in detail why the balance of the equity account of the organization increased, or decreased, from the beginning to the end of the current reporting period. The report shows (a) there was no balance in the account at the start of the period, January 1, 2017; (b) that Master Zen, the owner of the business, invested $20,000.00 to capitalize the organization; (c) there was no withdrawal for personal use by the owner; and (d) the organization made net operating income of $2,876.67 for the month, to arrive at the ending balance of $22,876.67 in the owner's equity account.

Summary

In this chapter, we reviewed four financial statements for MZ LLC for the period ending January 31, 2017: (1) Income Statement, (2) Statement of Retained Earnings, (3) Balance Sheet, and (4) Statement of Changes in Owner's Equity. You should study how the financial statements are interrelated: the net income or loss for the period in the income statement is closed out to the retained earnings account and reported in the owner's equity section of the balance sheet. We will explore another important financial statement, the cash flows statement, along with the bank reconciliation statement in chapter 9.

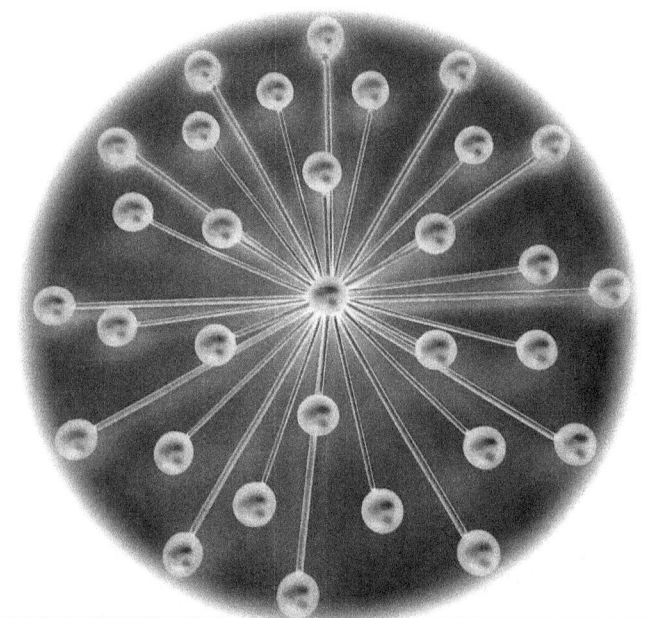

Collaborative learning. "Superior learners seek at least two to six additional sources of information." Dr. Denver Pettigrew

Chapter 8: Simple Payroll and Payroll Expenses

> **Net Take-home Pay = Gross Earnings Less Federal, State, and Other Withholdings**

Question: What is the purpose of this chapter?
Answer: To demonstrate a typical payroll system and related journal entries for a firm.

Simple payroll bookkeeping activities are introduced in this chapter to assist beginners in understanding basic payroll functions in firms; not human resources functions. Actual, real-world situations will be different due to several factors beyond the scope of this book, including: different state rules and regulations; changing federal and state withholding requirements and rates; and different additional personal withholdings. The basic payroll concepts, calculations, and recordings are like the simple examples provided in this chapter, although the quantities and types of withholdings from the gross wages and salaries on the paychecks of individual employees may be different. Additional payroll information and resources can be found on the IRS website, WWW.IRS.gov, and in more advanced accounting textbooks.

Payroll expenses for the organization consist of two major parts (1) Wages and Salaries paid to employees, and (2) additional payroll charges payable to the State and Federal government by the organization:

Wages and Salaries

Payroll expenses of an organization consist mainly of the wages and salaries paid to employees of the organization for their services (labor) to the organization. Although the terms salary and wages are often used interchangeably, most firms use the term *salary* for pay to administrative and managerial employees, and *wages* for pay to other employees. By law, firms must withhold certain amounts from the employee paychecks on behalf of the Federal and State Governments, such as Federal Income Tax, and Federal Insurance Contributions Act (FICA) toward Social Security and Medicare benefits. Employees may also request that the payroll department withhold voluntary additional amounts from their paychecks for things such as health insurance, contributions to 401(k) retirement plans, and charitable donations.

> **Net Take-home Pay = Gross Earnings Less Federal, State, and Other Withholdings**

See example of a simple paycheck statement and table summarizing gross earnings (total compensation), withholdings, and net amount paid to an employee.

TYPICAL PAYSTUB

PAYROLL STATEMENT OF EARNINGS				
Employee Name: First_____ MI____ Last_____			Check No:_____	
Address: Street/No._____ APT____ City_____ State___ Zip_____				
Social Security Number: ___-__-____		Pay Period Ending:_____		
		AMOUNT		AMOUNT
GROSS EARNINGS				
WITHHOLDING DEDUCTIONS				
FEDERAL INCOME TAX				
STATE INCOME TAX				
SOCIAL SECURITY				
MEDICARE				
401(k)				
OTHER				
OTHER				
TOTAL WITHHOLDINGS/DEDUCTIONS				
NET EARNINGS				

    Withholding of Federal income taxes is based on the information provided to the human resources department (HR) by the employee on IRS form W4, which the firm uses to determine the amount of federal taxes to withhold from the employee's salary according to IRS *Pub. 15, Employer's Tax Guide* and IRS *Notice 1036 Withholding Tables*. Social Security tax rate is 6.2% and the Medicare tax rate is 1.45%. Free copies of publications containing detailed instructions for calculating, withholding, recording, and submitting federal taxes to the Internal Revenue Service (IRS) and the Social Security Administration (SSA) can be found on the IRS website WWW.IRS.gov.

The average Social Security and Medicare Tax rates for the previous three years can be seen in Table 3, copied from the IRS Pub. 15, Employer's Tax Guide on the IRS.gov website.

Chapter 8: Simple Payroll and Payroll Expenses

Table 3. Social Security and Medicare Tax Rates *(for 3 prior years)*

Calendar Year	Wage Base Limit (each employee)	Tax Rate on Taxable Wages and Tips
2017–Social Security	$127,200	12.4%
2017–Medicare	All Wages	2.9%
2016–Social Security	$118,500	12.4%
2016–Medicare	All Wages	2.9%
2015–Social Security	$118,500	12.4%
2015–Medicare	All Wages	2.9%

The following list are names of IRS publications copied from the IRS website and can be seen at the end of this chapter and in the Appendix:

- Publication 15: (Circular E), Employer's Tax Guide
- Form W-4: Employee's Withholding Allowance Certificate
- General Instructions for Forms W-2 and W-3
- Form W-2: Wage and Tax Statement
- Form W-3: Transmittal of Wage and Tax Statements
- Form 940: Employer's Annual Federal Unemployment (FUTA) Tax Return
- Form 941: Employer's Quarterly Federal Tax Return
- Wage Bracket Method Tables for Income Tax Withholding
- Percentage Method Tables for Income Tax Withholding

We will use a simple payroll example to demonstrate how to calculate the monthly pay for a salaried employee, Mr. G. Mann, who is single and earns $5,000.00 per month. Mr. Mann completed and provided a signed Form W-4, Employee's Withholding Allowance Certificate claiming 4 withholding allowances, along with other employment documents to the human resources department when he was hired. Mr. Mann contributed 5 percent of his pay toward the firm's 401(k) plan, $150.00 for health insurance, and $50.00 for charitable contribution to the *Keep Fish Free Charity Organization*. We will ignore any non-taxable or pre-tax effects of items such as the 401(k)-plan deduction for this simple example; although amounts withheld for participating in a firm's 401(k) plan is usually deducted from gross pay *before* calculating federal income tax withholding. Refer to IRS *Pub. 15, Employer's Tax Guide* for information and instructions on federal withholdings. The IRS publishes a W-4 IRS Withholding Calculator on their website to help taxpayers to calculate the number of withholding allowances to put on their Form W-4 Withholding Allowance certificate.

Accounting 101: Easy Accounting and Bookkeeping for Beginners

The calculations are as follows:

1. Gross Pay $5,000.00
2. Federal Income Tax using the *IRS Wage Bracket Method Tables* from "*at least 4,965 but less than 5,005*" in the left columns, and 4 in the "*number of withholding allowances claimed is*" for 4 allowances in the middle columns, amounts to withholding amount of $386.00. You can also use the *Percentage Method Tables* to arrive at an approximately similar amount using the monthly taxable salary $5,000 less total monthly Withholding Allowances of $1,350.00 ($4,050/12 = $337.50 each x 4) per month or taxable salary of $3,650.00 ($5,000.00-$1,350.00). The IRS website also provides a *Withholding Calculator* you can use to calculate the federal income tax withholding amount.
3. F.I.C.A (combined) $5,000.00 x 6.2% = $310.00 for Social Security, and $5,000.00 x 1.45% or $72.50 for Medicare, for a combined total of $382.50
4. 401(k) plan $5,000.00 x 5.0% = $250.00
5. Health Insurance $150.00
6. Charitable contribution $50.00

PAYROLL STATEMENT OF EARNINGS					
Employee Name: First_Girlie_____MI_____Last_Mann_____Check No:_____					
Address: Street/No._____APT_____City_____State____Zip_____					
Social Security Number: ### – ## - ####		Pay Period Ending:_____			
	AMOUNT			AMOUNT	
GROSS EARNINGS				$5,000	00
WITHHOLDING DEDUCTIONS					
FEDERAL INCOME TAX	386	00			
STATE INCOME TAX					
SOCIAL SECURITY	310	00			
MEDICARE	72	50			
401(k)	250	00			
OTHER- HEALTH INSURANCE	150	00			
OTHER- CHARITABLE CONTRIBUTION	50	00			
TOTAL WITHHOLDINGS/DEDUCTIONS			1,218	50	
NET EARNINGS				$3,781	50

Chapter 8: Simple Payroll and Payroll Expenses

Journalizing the payroll for Mr. Mann's payroll expense:

General Journal						Page No. __ _	
Date 20xx		Description	GL Ref.	Debit		Credit	
				Amount		Amount	
xxxxx	xx	Salaries and Wages Expenses	5020	5,000	00		
		Salaries Payable	2020.10			3,781	50
		Federal Income Tax Payable	2020.20			386	00
		F.I.C.A. Payable	2020.30			382	50
		401(k) Contributions	2020.40			250	00
		Other Voluntary Withholdings	2020.50			200	00
		To record salary of Mr. G. Mann for period					

Journalizing the checks paid for Mr. Mann's salary and withholdings:

General Journal						Page No. __ _	
Date 20xx		Description	GL Ref.	Debit		Credit	
				Amount		Amount	
xxxxx	xx	Salaries Payable	2020.10	3,781	50		
		Federal Income Tax Payable	2020.20	386	00		
		F.I.C.A. Payable	2020.30	382	50		
		401(k) Contributions	2020.40	250	00		
		Other Voluntary Withholdings	2020.50	200	00		
		Cash (separate checks would be used for each amt.)	1010			5,000	00
		Payroll checks for salary of Mr. G. Mann for period					

Note if, as is usually the case, 401(k) deductions are pre-taxed, then the gross salary becomes gross *taxable* salary after deducting the amount withheld for 401(k), and Federal income tax would be based on the lower taxable amount. In this case the amount used to determine Federal income tax would be $4,750.00 ($5,000.00-$250.00), and the tax using the IRS Wage Bracket Method Tables, would be $351.00, with the other withholding amounts remaining the same as before.

His paycheck would be $35.00 more calculated as follows:

PAYROLL STATEMENT OF EARNINGS						
Employee Name: First_Girlie_____MI_____Last_Mann_____					Check No:_____	
Address: Street/No._____APT_____City_____State____Zip_____						
Social Security Number: ### – ## - ####		Pay Period Ending:_____				
		AMOUNT			AMOUNT	
GROSS EARNINGS					$5,000	00
WITHHOLDING DEDUCTIONS						
FEDERAL INCOME TAX		351	00			
STATE INCOME TAX						
SOCIAL SECURITY		310	00			
MEDICARE		72	50			
401(k)		250	00			
OTHER- HEALTH INSURANCE		150	00			
OTHER- CHARITABLE CONTRIBUTION		50	00			
TOTAL WITHHOLDINGS/DEDUCTIONS				1,183	50	
NET EARNINGS					$3,816	50

The journal entries to record the payroll and to record the paycheck and withholdings would be the same as before, except for the change in the amount withheld and paid for federal taxes.

Additional Employer's Payroll Expenses

Additional employer's payroll expenses consist of FICA, SUTA, and FUTA and are payable *only by employers* to the Federal and State governments. The combined rate for FICA (Social Security Tax 6.2% and Medicare Tax 1.45%) is 7.65%, matching the amounts withheld from the employee paychecks; Although the Federal Unemployment tax (FUTA) is around 6.2 %; State (Florida) unemployment tax (SUTA) averages around 5.4%; and the *net* federal unemployment tax rate is 0.8% (FUTA 6.2% less SUTA 5.4%). SUTA and FUTA are limited to the *first* $7,000.00 (annual) of employees' wages or salaries.

The additional payroll expenses that the firm would pay based on our earlier example for Mr. G. Mann' salary of $5,000.00, assuming this was also his year-to-date amount, would be:

Gross Salary	F.I.C.A (7.65%) GL A/C #5020.30	FUTA (6.2%-5.4%) GL GL A/C # 5020.60	SUTA (5.4%) GL A/C # 5020.70	Total Addl. Tax Exp.
5,000.00	382.50	40.00	270.00	692.50

Chapter 8: Simple Payroll and Payroll Expenses

Journalizing the *additional employer's* payroll tax expense based on the salary for Mr. Mann:

General Journal				Debit		Page No.___ Credit	
Date 20xx		Description	GL Ref.	Amount		Amount	
xxxxxx	xx	Employer's F.I.C.A. Payroll Tax Expenses	5020.30	382	50		
		Employer's FUTA Payroll Tax Expenses	5020.60	40	00		
		Employer's SUTA Payroll Tax Expenses	5020.70	270	00		
		F.I.C.A. Payable	2020.30			382	50
		FUTA Payable	2020.60			40	00
		SUTA Payable	2020.70			270	00
		To record Employer payroll tax expenses					

Journalizing the checks paid for additional employer's Federal and State taxes:

General Journal				Debit		Page No.___ Credit	
Date 20xx		Description	GL Ref.	Amount		Amount	
xxxxx	xx	F.I.C.A. Payable	2020.30	382	50		
		FUTA Payable	2020.60	40	00		
		SUTA Payable	2020.70	270	00		
		Cash (separate checks would be used for each amt.)	1010			692	50
		Checks paid for Employer's payroll tax expenses					

Paying and Reporting Withholding and Employer Payroll Taxes to the Government

Firms are responsible for timely payments to the government for withholdings from employees' paycheck Federal income tax, F.I.C.A, and Medicare; and for the additional employer's payroll taxes. Forms as IRS Form W-3, Form 940, Form 941 etc. must be submitted as instructed on IRS Pub. 15 and the IRS website.

IRS Wage Bracket Method Tax Withholding

Wage Bracket Method Tables for Income Tax Withholding
SINGLE Persons—MONTHLY Payroll Period
(For Wages Paid through December 31, 2018)

And the wages are—		And the number of withholding allowances claimed is—										
At least	But less than	0	1	2	3	4	5	6	7	8	9	10
		The amount of income tax to be withheld is—										
$2,765	$2,805	$261	$240	$198	$157	$115	$75	$40	$8	$0	$0	$0
2,805	2,845	266	245	203	162	120	79	44	10	0	0	0
2,845	2,885	291	249	208	166	125	83	48	14	0	0	0
2,885	2,925	296	254	213	171	130	88	52	18	0	0	0
2,925	2,965	301	259	218	176	135	93	56	22	0	0	0
2,965	3,005	305	264	222	181	139	98	60	26	0	0	0
3,005	3,045	310	269	227	186	144	103	64	30	0	0	0
3,045	3,085	315	273	232	190	149	107	68	34	0	0	0
3,085	3,125	320	278	237	195	154	112	72	38	3	0	0
3,125	3,165	325	283	242	200	159	117	76	42	7	0	0
3,165	3,205	329	288	246	205	163	122	80	46	11	0	0
3,205	3,245	334	293	251	210	168	127	85	50	15	0	0
3,245	3,285	339	297	256	214	173	131	90	54	19	0	0
3,285	3,325	344	302	261	219	178	136	95	58	23	0	0
3,325	3,365	349	307	266	224	183	141	100	62	27	0	0
3,365	3,405	353	312	270	229	187	146	104	66	31	0	0
3,405	3,445	358	317	275	234	192	151	109	70	35	0	0
3,445	3,485	363	321	280	238	197	155	114	74	39	4	0
3,485	3,525	368	326	285	243	202	160	119	78	43	8	0
3,525	3,565	374	331	290	248	207	165	124	82	47	12	0
3,565	3,605	382	336	294	253	211	170	128	87	51	16	0
3,605	3,645	391	341	299	258	216	175	133	92	55	20	0
3,645	3,685	400	345	304	262	221	179	138	96	59	24	0
3,685	3,725	409	350	309	267	226	184	143	101	63	28	0
3,725	3,765	418	355	314	272	231	189	148	106	67	32	0
3,765	3,805	426	360	318	277	235	194	152	111	71	36	2
3,805	3,845	435	365	323	282	240	199	157	116	75	40	6
3,845	3,885	444	369	328	286	245	203	162	120	79	44	10
3,885	3,925	453	377	333	291	250	208	167	125	84	48	14
3,925	3,965	462	386	338	296	255	213	172	130	89	52	18
3,965	4,005	470	394	342	301	259	218	176	135	93	56	22
4,005	4,045	479	403	347	306	264	223	181	140	98	60	26
4,045	4,085	488	412	352	310	269	227	186	144	103	64	30
4,085	4,125	497	421	357	315	274	232	191	149	108	68	34
4,125	4,165	506	430	362	320	279	237	196	154	113	72	38
4,165	4,205	514	438	366	325	283	242	200	159	117	76	42
4,205	4,245	523	447	371	330	288	247	205	164	122	81	46
4,245	4,285	532	456	380	334	293	251	210	168	127	85	50
4,285	4,325	541	465	389	339	298	256	215	173	132	90	54
4,325	4,365	550	474	398	344	303	261	220	178	137	95	58
4,365	4,405	558	482	406	349	307	266	224	183	141	100	62
4,405	4,445	567	491	415	354	312	271	229	188	146	105	66
4,445	4,485	576	500	424	358	317	275	234	192	151	109	70
4,485	4,525	585	509	433	363	322	280	239	197	156	114	74
4,525	4,565	594	518	442	368	327	285	244	202	161	119	78
4,565	4,605	602	526	450	374	331	290	248	207	165	124	82
4,605	4,645	611	535	459	383	336	295	253	212	170	129	87
4,645	4,685	620	544	468	392	341	299	258	216	175	133	92
4,685	4,725	629	553	477	401	346	304	263	221	180	138	97
4,725	4,765	638	562	486	409	351	309	268	226	185	143	102
4,765	4,805	646	570	494	418	355	314	272	231	189	148	106
4,805	4,845	655	579	503	427	360	319	277	236	194	153	111
4,845	4,885	664	588	512	436	365	323	282	240	199	157	116
4,885	4,925	673	597	521	445	370	328	287	245	204	162	121
4,925	4,965	682	606	530	453	377	333	292	250	209	167	126
4,965	5,005	690	614	538	462	386	338	296	255	213	172	130
5,005	5,045	699	623	547	471	395	343	301	260	218	177	135

Image copied from Circular E, Pub. 15, IRS Employer Tax Guide 2018 published on the IRS website WWW.IRS.gov

Chapter 8: Simple Payroll and Payroll Expenses

IRS Percentage Method Tax Withholding

Percentage Method Tables for Income Tax Withholding

(For Wages Paid in 2018)

TABLE 1—WEEKLY Payroll Period

(a) SINGLE person (including head of household)—
If the amount of wages (after subtracting withholding allowances) is:
Not over $71 . . . . The amount of income tax to withhold is: $0

Over—	But not over—			of excess over—
$71	—$254	. .	$0.00 plus 10%	—$71
$254	—$815	. .	$18.30 plus 12%	—$254
$815	—$1,658	. .	$85.62 plus 22%	—$815
$1,658	—$3,100	. .	$271.08 plus 24%	—$1,658
$3,100	—$3,917	. .	$617.16 plus 32%	—$3,100
$3,917	—$9,687	. .	$878.60 plus 35%	—$3,917
$9,687		. .	$2,898.10 plus 37%	—$9,687

(b) MARRIED person—
If the amount of wages (after subtracting withholding allowances) is:
Not over $222 . . . . The amount of income tax to withhold is: $0

Over—	But not over—			of excess over—
$222	—$588	. .	$0.00 plus 10%	—$222
$588	—$1,711	. .	$36.60 plus 12%	—$588
$1,711	—$3,395	. .	$171.36 plus 22%	—$1,711
$3,395	—$6,280	. .	$541.84 plus 24%	—$3,395
$6,280	—$7,914	. .	$1,234.24 plus 32%	—$6,280
$7,914	—$11,761	. .	$1,757.12 plus 35%	—$7,914
$11,761		. .	$3,103.57 plus 37%	—$11,761

TABLE 2—BIWEEKLY Payroll Period

(a) SINGLE person (including head of household)—
If the amount of wages (after subtracting withholding allowances) is:
Not over $142 . . . . The amount of income tax to withhold is: $0

Over—	But not over—			of excess over—
$142	—$509	. .	$0.00 plus 10%	—$142
$509	—$1,631	. .	$36.70 plus 12%	—$509
$1,631	—$3,315	. .	$171.34 plus 22%	—$1,631
$3,315	—$6,200	. .	$541.82 plus 24%	—$3,315
$6,200	—$7,835	. .	$1,234.22 plus 32%	—$6,200
$7,835	—$19,373	. .	$1,757.42 plus 35%	—$7,835
$19,373		. .	$5,795.72 plus 37%	—$19,373

(b) MARRIED person—
If the amount of wages (after subtracting withholding allowances) is:
Not over $444 . . . . The amount of income tax to withhold is: $0

Over—	But not over—			of excess over—
$444	—$1,177	. .	$0.00 plus 10%	—$444
$1,177	—$3,421	. .	$73.30 plus 12%	—$1,177
$3,421	—$6,790	. .	$342.58 plus 22%	—$3,421
$6,790	—$12,560	. .	$1,083.76 plus 24%	—$6,790
$12,560	—$15,829	. .	$2,468.56 plus 32%	—$12,560
$15,829	—$23,521	. .	$3,514.64 plus 35%	—$15,829
$23,521		. .	$6,206.84 plus 37%	—$23,521

TABLE 3—SEMIMONTHLY Payroll Period

(a) SINGLE person (including head of household)—
If the amount of wages (after subtracting withholding allowances) is:
Not over $154 . . . . The amount of income tax to withhold is: $0

Over—	But not over—			of excess over—
$154	—$551	. .	$0.00 plus 10%	—$154
$551	—$1,767	. .	$39.70 plus 12%	—$551
$1,767	—$3,592	. .	$185.62 plus 22%	—$1,767
$3,592	—$6,717	. .	$587.12 plus 24%	—$3,592
$6,717	—$8,488	. .	$1,337.12 plus 32%	—$6,717
$8,488	—$20,988	. .	$1,903.84 plus 35%	—$8,488
$20,988		. .	$6,278.84 plus 37%	—$20,988

(b) MARRIED person—
If the amount of wages (after subtracting withholding allowances) is:
Not over $481 . . . . The amount of income tax to withhold is: $0

Over—	But not over—			of excess over—
$481	—$1,275	. .	$0.00 plus 10%	—$481
$1,275	—$3,706	. .	$79.40 plus 12%	—$1,275
$3,706	—$7,356	. .	$371.12 plus 22%	—$3,706
$7,356	—$13,606	. .	$1,174.12 plus 24%	—$7,356
$13,606	—$17,148	. .	$2,674.12 plus 32%	—$13,606
$17,148	—$25,481	. .	$3,807.56 plus 35%	—$17,148
$25,481		. .	$6,724.11 plus 37%	—$25,481

TABLE 4—MONTHLY Payroll Period

(a) SINGLE person (including head of household)—
If the amount of wages (after subtracting withholding allowances) is:
Not over $308 . . . . The amount of income tax to withhold is: $0

Over—	But not over—			of excess over—
$308	—$1,102	. .	$0.00 plus 10%	—$308
$1,102	—$3,533	. .	$79.40 plus 12%	—$1,102
$3,533	—$7,183	. .	$371.12 plus 22%	—$3,533
$7,183	—$13,433	. .	$1,174.12 plus 24%	—$7,183
$13,433	—$16,975	. .	$2,674.12 plus 32%	—$13,433
$16,975	—$41,975	. .	$3,807.56 plus 35%	—$16,975
$41,975		. .	$12,557.56 plus 37%	—$41,975

(b) MARRIED person—
If the amount of wages (after subtracting withholding allowances) is:
Not over $963 . . . . The amount of income tax to withhold is: $0

Over—	But not over—			of excess over—
$963	—$2,550	. .	$0.00 plus 10%	—$963
$2,550	—$7,413	. .	$158.70 plus 12%	—$2,550
$7,413	—$14,713	. .	$742.26 plus 22%	—$7,413
$14,713	—$27,213	. .	$2,348.26 plus 24%	—$14,713
$27,213	—$34,296	. .	$5,348.26 plus 32%	—$27,213
$34,296	—$50,963	. .	$7,614.82 plus 35%	—$34,296
$50,963		. .	$13,448.27 plus 37%	—$50,963

Image copied from Circular E, Pub. 15, IRS Employer Tax Guide 2018 published on the IRS website WWW.IRS.gov

Accounting 101: Easy Accounting and Bookkeeping for Beginners

Federal Tax Reporting and Payment Forms Available on the IRS.gov Website

IRS.gov Publication 15 (Circular E) Employer's Tax Guide

Department of the Treasury
Internal Revenue Service

Publication 15
Cat. No. 10000W

(Circular E), Employer's Tax Guide

For use in **2018**

Get forms and other Information faster and easier at:
- *IRS.gov* (English)
- *IRS.gov/Spanish* (Español)
- *IRS.gov/Chinese* (中文)
- *IRS.gov/Korean* (한국어)
- *IRS.gov/Russian* (Русский)
- *IRS.gov/Vietnamese* (TiếngViệt)

Jan 25, 2018

Contents

What's New	1
Reminders	2
Calendar	8
Introduction	9
1. Employer Identification Number (EIN)	11
2. Who Are Employees?	11
3. Family Employees	13
4. Employee's Social Security Number (SSN)	14
5. Wages and Other Compensation	15
6. Tips	18
7. Supplemental Wages	19
8. Payroll Period	20
9. Withholding From Employees' Wages	21
10. Required Notice to Employees About the Earned Income Credit (EIC)	26
11. Depositing Taxes	26
12. Filing Form 941 or Form 944	31
13. Reporting Adjustments to Form 941 or Form 944	33
14. Federal Unemployment (FUTA) Tax	36
15. Special Rules for Various Types of Services and Payments	38
16. Third-Party Payer Arrangements	43
17. How To Use the Income Tax Withholding Tables	44
How To Get Tax Help	68
Index	70

Future Developments

For the latest information about developments related to Pub. 15, such as legislation enacted after it was published, go to *IRS.gov/Pub15*.

What's New

2018 federal income tax withholding. This publication includes the 2018 Percentage Method Tables and Wage Bracket Method Tables for Income Tax Withholding. The 2018 withholding tables incorporate changes to the individual tax rates based on tax legislation enacted on December 22, 2017 (P.L. 115-97). Employers should

Chapter 8: Simple Payroll and Payroll Expenses
IRS.gov Form W-4

Form W-4 (2018)

Future developments. For the latest information about any future developments related to Form W-4, such as legislation enacted after it was published, go to www.irs.gov/FormW4.

Purpose. Complete Form W-4 so that your employer can withhold the correct federal income tax from your pay. Consider completing a new Form W-4 each year and when your personal or financial situation changes.

Exemption from withholding. You may claim exemption from withholding for 2018 if **both** of the following apply.

- For 2017 you had a right to a refund of **all** federal income tax withheld because you had **no** tax liability, **and**
- For 2018 you expect a refund of **all** federal income tax withheld because you expect to have **no** tax liability.

If you're exempt, complete **only** lines 1, 2, 3, 4, and 7 and sign the form to validate it. Your exemption for 2018 expires February 15, 2019. See Pub. 505, Tax Withholding and Estimated Tax, to learn more about whether you qualify for exemption from withholding.

General Instructions

If you aren't exempt, follow the rest of these instructions to determine the number of withholding allowances you should claim for withholding for 2018 and any additional amount of tax to have withheld. For regular wages, withholding must be based on allowances you claimed and may not be a flat amount or percentage of wages.

You can also use the calculator at www.irs.gov/W4App to determine your tax withholding more accurately. Consider using this calculator if you have a more complicated tax situation, such as if you have a working spouse, more than one job, or a large amount of nonwage income outside of your job. After your Form W-4 takes effect, you can also use this calculator to see how the amount of tax you're having withheld compares to your projected total tax for 2018. If you use the calculator, you don't need to complete any of the worksheets for Form W-4.

Note that if you have too much tax withheld, you will receive a refund when you file your tax return. If you have too little tax withheld, you will owe tax when you file your tax return, and you might owe a penalty.

Filers with multiple jobs or working spouses. If you have more than one job at a time, or if you're married and your spouse is also working, read all of the instructions including the instructions for the Two-Earners/Multiple Jobs Worksheet before beginning.

Nonwage income. If you have a large amount of nonwage income, such as interest or dividends, consider making estimated tax payments using Form 1040-ES, Estimated Tax for Individuals. Otherwise, you might owe additional tax. Or, you can use the Deductions, Adjustments, and Other Income Worksheet on page 3 or the calculator at www.irs.gov/W4App to make sure you have enough tax withheld from your paycheck. If you have pension or annuity income, see Pub. 505 or use the calculator at www.irs.gov/W4App to find out if you should adjust your withholding on Form W-4 or W-4P.

Nonresident alien. If you're a nonresident alien, see Notice 1392, Supplemental Form W-4 Instructions for Nonresident Aliens, before completing this form.

Specific Instructions
Personal Allowances Worksheet

Complete this worksheet on page 3 first to determine the number of withholding allowances to claim.

Line C. Head of household please note: Generally, you can claim head of household filing status on your tax return only if you're unmarried and pay more than 50% of the costs of keeping up a home for yourself and a qualifying individual. See Pub. 501 for more information about filing status.

Line E. Child tax credit. When you file your tax return, you might be eligible to claim a credit for each of your qualifying children. To qualify, the child must be under age 17 as of December 31 and must be your dependent who lives with you for more than half the year. To learn more about this credit, see Pub. 972, Child Tax Credit. To reduce the tax withheld from your pay by taking this credit into account, follow the instructions on line E of the worksheet. On the worksheet you will be asked about your total income. For this purpose, total income includes all of your wages and other income, including income earned by a spouse, during the year.

Line F. Credit for other dependents. When you file your tax return, you might be eligible to claim a credit for each of your dependents that don't qualify for the child tax credit, such as any dependent children age 17 and older. To learn more about this credit, see Pub. 505. To reduce the tax withheld from your pay by taking this credit into account, follow the instructions on line F of the worksheet. On the worksheet, you will be asked about your total income. For this purpose, total income includes all of

---

Separate here and give Form W-4 to your employer. Keep the worksheet(s) for your records.

Form W-4 Department of the Treasury Internal Revenue Service

Employee's Withholding Allowance Certificate

► Whether you're entitled to claim a certain number of allowances or exemption from withholding is subject to review by the IRS. Your employer may be required to send a copy of this form to the IRS.

OMB No. 1545-0074

2018

1. Your first name and middle initial | Last name | 2. Your social security number

Home address (number and street or rural route)

3. ☐ Single ☐ Married ☐ Married, but withhold at higher Single rate.
Note: If married filing separately, check "Married, but withhold at higher Single rate."

City or town, state, and ZIP code

4. If your last name differs from that shown on your social security card, check here. You must call 800-772-1213 for a replacement card. ► ☐

5. Total number of allowances you're claiming (from the applicable worksheet on the following pages) ... **5**
6. Additional amount, if any, you want withheld from each paycheck ... **6 $**
7. I claim exemption from withholding for 2018, and I certify that I meet **both** of the following conditions for exemption.
   - Last year I had a right to a refund of **all** federal income tax withheld because I had **no** tax liability, **and**
   - This year I expect a refund of **all** federal income tax withheld because I expect to have **no** tax liability.
   If you meet both conditions, write "Exempt" here ... ► **7**

Under penalties of perjury, I declare that I have examined this certificate and, to the best of my knowledge and belief, it is true, correct, and complete.

Employee's signature
(This form is not valid unless you sign it.) ►   Date ►

8. Employer's name and address (Employer: Complete boxes 8 and 10 if sending to IRS and complete boxes 8, 9, and 10 if sending to State Directory of New Hires.) | 9. First date of employment | 10. Employer identification number (EIN)

For Privacy Act and Paperwork Reduction Act Notice, see page 4.   Cat. No. 10220Q   Form **W-4** (2018)

2018 General Instructions for Forms W-2 and W-3

(Including Forms W-2AS, W-2CM, W-2GU, W-2VI, W-3SS, W-2c, and W-3c)

Department of the Treasury
Internal Revenue Service

Section references are to the Internal Revenue Code unless otherwise noted.

Contents — Page

- Future Developments 1
- What's New 1
- Reminders 2
- Need Help? 4
- How To Get Forms and Publications 4
- Common Errors on Forms W-2 5
- General Instructions for Forms W-2 and W-3 5
- Special Reporting Situations for Form W-2 7
- Penalties 13
- Specific Instructions for Form W-2 15
- Specific Instructions for Form W-3 22
- General Instructions for Forms W-2c and W-3c 24
- Special Situations for Forms W-2c and W-3c 25
- Specific Instructions for Form W-2c 26
- Specific Instructions for Form W-3c 27
- Form W-2 Reference Guide for Box 12 Codes 30
- Form W-2 Box 13 Retirement Plan Checkbox Decision Chart 30
- Nonqualified Deferred Compensation Reporting Example Chart 31
- Index 33

Future Developments

For the latest information about developments related to Forms W-2 and W-3 and their instructions, such as legislation enacted after they were published, go to IRS.gov/FormW2.

What's New

Leave-based donation programs to aid victims of Hurricanes and Tropical Storms Harvey, Irma, and Maria, and the 2017 California Wildfires. Under these programs, employees may donate their vacation, sick, or personal leave in exchange for employer cash payments made before January 1, 2019, to qualified tax-exempt organizations providing relief for the victims of Hurricane Harvey and Tropical Storm Harvey, Hurricane Irma and Tropical Storm Irma, Hurricane Maria and Tropical Storm Maria, and the California Wildfires that began on October 8, 2017. The donated leave need not be included in the income or wages of the employee. The employer may deduct the cash payments as business expenses or charitable contributions. For more information, impacted taxpayers should see the following:

- For Hurricane Harvey and Tropical Storm Harvey, see Notice 2017-48, 2017-39 I.R.B. 254 at IRS.gov/irb/2017-39_IRB#NOT-2017-48.
- For Hurricane Irma and Tropical Storm Irma, see Notice 2017-52, 2017-40 I.R.B. 262 at IRS.gov/irb/2017-40_IRB#NOT-2017-52.
- For Hurricane Maria and Tropical Storm Maria, see Notice 2017-62, 2017-44 I.R.B. 460 at IRS.gov/irb/2017-44_IRB#NOT-2017-62, and
- For the California Wildfires, see Notice 2017-70, 2017-48 I.R.B. 543 at IRS.gov/irb/2017-48_IRB#NOT-2017-70.

Suspension of exclusion for qualified moving expense reimbursements. The Tax Cuts and Jobs Act (Public Law 115-97) temporarily suspends the exclusion for qualified moving expense reimbursements under section 132(a)(6) and (g). However, the exclusion still applies for a member of the Armed Forces of the United States on active duty who moves under a military order to a permanent change of station. This change is effective for taxable years beginning after December 31, 2017, and before January 1, 2026. See P.L. 115-97, section 11048 and Code P—Excludable moving expense reimbursements paid directly to a member of the U.S. Armed Forces for more information.

Combat pay of members of the Armed Forces performing services in the Sinai Peninsula of Egypt. The Tax Cuts and Jobs Act also temporarily makes the Sinai Peninsula of Egypt a qualified hazardous duty area. Treat this hazardous duty area as a combat zone for the exclusion from income of certain combat pay under section 112 and exclusion from wages under section 3401(a)(1). For purposes of withholding, this change generally applies to remuneration paid during the period December 22, 2017 through December 31, 2017, and taxable years 2018 through 2025. For more information, including a special rule for non-calendar year tax years for the period that includes December 22, 2017, see P.L. 115-97, section 11026.

New qualified equity grants under section 83(i). The Tax Cuts and Jobs Act added section 83(i) for "qualified equity grants." The law also added new Form W-2 reporting requirements for these grants. Employers with employees who have qualified equity grants must report the amount includible in gross income under section 83(i) for an event which occurs in the calendar year in box 12 using code GG. Also, employers must report the aggregate amount of income which employees elect to defer under section 83(i) as of the close of the calendar year in box 12, using code HH. See P.L. 115-97, section 13603 for more information. See also Code GG—Income from qualified equity grants under section 83(i) and Code

Jul 13, 2018   Cat. No. 25979S

Chapter 8: Simple Payroll and Payroll Expenses

IRS.gov Form W-2

Accounting 101: Easy Accounting and Bookkeeping for Beginners
IRS.gov Form W-3

DO NOT STAPLE

33333	a Control number
	For Official Use Only ▶ OMB No. 1545-0008

b Kind of Payer (Check one): 941 / Military / 943 / 944 / CT-1 / Hshld. emp. / Medicare govt. emp.

Kind of Employer (Check one): None apply / 501c non-govt. / State/local non-501c / State/local 501c / Federal govt. / Third-party sick pay (Check if applicable)

- c Total number of Forms W-2
- d Establishment number
- e Employer Identification number (EIN)
- f Employer's name
- g Employer's address and ZIP code
- h Other EIN used this year
- 15 State — Employer's state ID number
- 16 State wages, tips, etc.
- 17 State income tax
- 1 Wages, tips, other compensation
- 2 Federal income tax withheld
- 3 Social security wages
- 4 Social security tax withheld
- 5 Medicare wages and tips
- 6 Medicare tax withheld
- 7 Social security tips
- 8 Allocated tips
- 9
- 10 Dependent care benefits
- 11 Nonqualified plans
- 12a Deferred compensation
- 13 For third-party sick pay use only
- 12b
- 14 Income tax withheld by payer of third-party sick pay
- 18 Local wages, tips, etc.
- 19 Local income tax
- Employer's contact person
- Employer's telephone number
- For Official Use Only
- Employer's fax number
- Employer's email address

Under penalties of perjury, I declare that I have examined this return and accompanying documents and, to the best of my knowledge and belief, they are true, correct, and complete.

Signature ▶   Title ▶   Date ▶

Form W-3 Transmittal of Wage and Tax Statements   2018   Department of the Treasury Internal Revenue Service

Send this entire page with the entire Copy A page of Form(s) W-2 to the Social Security Administration (SSA). Photocopies are not acceptable. Do not send Form W-3 if you filed electronically with the SSA.
Do not send any payment (cash, checks, money orders, etc.) with Forms W-2 and W-3.

Reminder
Separate Instructions. See the 2018 General Instructions for Forms W-2 and W-3 for information on completing this form. Do not file Form W-3 for Form(s) W-2 that were submitted electronically to the SSA.

Purpose of Form
Complete a Form W-3 Transmittal only when filing paper Copy A of Form(s) W-2, Wage and Tax Statement. Don't file Form W-3 alone. All paper forms **must** comply with IRS standards and be machine readable. Photocopies are **not** acceptable. Use a Form W-3 even if only one paper Form W-2 is being filed. Make sure both the Form W-3 and Form(s) W-2 show the correct tax year and Employer Identification Number (EIN). Make a copy of this form and keep it with Copy D (For Employer) of Form(s) W-2 for your records. The IRS recommends retaining copies of these forms for four years.

E-Filing
The SSA strongly suggests employers report Form W-3 and Forms W-2 Copy A electronically instead of on paper. The SSA provides two free e-filing options on its Business Services Online (BSO) website:

- **W-2 Online.** Use fill-in forms to create, save, print, and submit up to 50 Forms W-2 at a time to the SSA.
- **File Upload.** Upload wage files to the SSA you have created using payroll or tax software that formats the files according to the SSA's *Specifications for Filing Forms W-2 Electronically (EFW2)*.

W-2 Online fill-in forms or file uploads will be on time if submitted by **January 31, 2019.** For more information, go to *www.SSA.gov/bso*. First time filers, select "Register"; returning filers select "Log in."

When To File Paper Forms
Mail Form W-3 with Copy A of Form(s) W-2 by **January 31, 2019.**

Where To File Paper Forms
Send this entire page with the entire Copy A page of Form(s) W-2 to:

Social Security Administration
Direct Operations Center
Wilkes-Barre, PA 18769-0001

Note: If you use "Certified Mail" to file, change the ZIP code to "18769-0002." If you use an IRS-approved private delivery service, add "ATTN: W-2 Process, 1150 E. Mountain Dr." to the address and change the ZIP code to "18702-7997." See Publication 15 (Circular E), Employer's Tax Guide, for a list of IRS-approved private delivery services.

For Privacy Act and Paperwork Reduction Act Notice, see the separate instructions.

Cat. No. 10159Y

Chapter 8: Simple Payroll and Payroll Expenses

IRS.gov Form 940

Form 940 for 2017: Employer's Annual Federal Unemployment (FUTA) Tax Return
Department of the Treasury — Internal Revenue Service

850113
OMB No. 1545-0028

Employer identification number (EIN)

Name (not your trade name)

Trade name (if any)

Address: Number, Street, Suite or room number, City, State, ZIP code, Foreign country name, Foreign province/county, Foreign postal code

Type of Return (Check all that apply.)
- a. Amended
- b. Successor employer
- c. No payments to employees in 2017
- d. Final: Business closed or stopped paying wages

Go to www.irs.gov/Form940 for instructions and the latest information.

Read the separate instructions before you complete this form. Please type or print within the boxes.

Part 1: Tell us about your return. If any line does NOT apply, leave it blank. See instructions before completing Part 1.

1a. If you had to pay state unemployment tax in one state only, enter the state abbreviation . . . 1a [ ]
1b. If you had to pay state unemployment tax in more than one state, you are a multi-state employer . . . 1b [ ] Check here. Complete Schedule A (Form 940).
2. If you paid wages in a state that is subject to CREDIT REDUCTION . . . 2 [ ] Check here. Complete Schedule A (Form 940).

Part 2: Determine your FUTA tax before adjustments. If any line does NOT apply, leave it blank.

3. Total payments to all employees . . . 3
4. Payments exempt from FUTA tax . . . 4
   Check all that apply: 4a [ ] Fringe benefits   4c [ ] Retirement/Pension   4e [ ] Other
   4b [ ] Group-term life insurance   4d [ ] Dependent care
5. Total of payments made to each employee in excess of $7,000 . . . 5
6. Subtotal (line 4 + line 5 = line 6) . . . 6
7. Total taxable FUTA wages (line 3 – line 6 = line 7). See instructions . . . 7
8. FUTA tax before adjustments (line 7 x 0.006 = line 8) . . . 8

Part 3: Determine your adjustments. If any line does NOT apply, leave it blank.

9. If ALL of the taxable FUTA wages you paid were excluded from state unemployment tax, multiply line 7 by 0.054 (line 7 × 0.054 = line 9). Go to line 12 . . . 9
10. If SOME of the taxable FUTA wages you paid were excluded from state unemployment tax, OR you paid ANY state unemployment tax late (after the due date for filing Form 940), complete the worksheet in the instructions. Enter the amount from line 7 of the worksheet . . . 10
11. If credit reduction applies, enter the total from Schedule A (Form 940) . . . 11

Part 4: Determine your FUTA tax and balance due or overpayment. If any line does NOT apply, leave it blank.

12. Total FUTA tax after adjustments (lines 8 + 9 + 10 + 11 = line 12) . . . 12
13. FUTA tax deposited for the year, including any overpayment applied from a prior year . . . 13
14. Balance due. If line 12 is more than line 13, enter the excess on line 14.
    - If line 14 is more than $500, you must deposit your tax.
    - If line 14 is $500 or less, you may pay with this return. See instructions . . . 14
15. Overpayment. If line 13 is more than line 12, enter the excess on line 15 and check a box below . . . 15
    ▶ You MUST complete both pages of this form and SIGN it.   Check one: [ ] Apply to next return.   [ ] Send a refund.

Next ▶

For Privacy Act and Paperwork Reduction Act Notice, see the back of the Payment Voucher.   Cat. No. 11234O   Form **940** (2017)

850212

Name (not your trade name) | Employer Identification number (EIN)

Part 5: Report your FUTA tax liability by quarter only if line 12 is more than $500. If not, go to Part 6.

16 Report the amount of your FUTA tax liability for each quarter; do NOT enter the amount you deposited. If you had no liability for a quarter, leave the line blank.

    16a 1st quarter (January 1 – March 31) . . . . 16a [.   ]

    16b 2nd quarter (April 1 – June 30) . . . . 16b [.   ]

    16c 3rd quarter (July 1 – September 30) . . . . 16c [.   ]

    16d 4th quarter (October 1 – December 31) . . . . . . 16d [.   ]

17 Total tax liability for the year (lines 16a + 16b + 16c + 16d = line 17) 17 [.   ] Total must equal line 12.

Part 6: May we speak with your third-party designee?

Do you want to allow an employee, a paid tax preparer, or another person to discuss this return with the IRS? See the instructions for details.

☐ Yes. Designee's name and phone number [   ]   [   ]

Select a 5-digit Personal Identification Number (PIN) to use when talking to IRS [ ][ ][ ][ ][ ]

☐ No.

Part 7: Sign here. You MUST complete both pages of this form and SIGN it.

Under penalties of perjury, I declare that I have examined this return, including accompanying schedules and statements, and to the best of my knowledge and belief, it is true, correct, and complete, and that no part of any payment made to a state unemployment fund claimed as a credit was, or is to be, deducted from the payments made to employees. Declaration of preparer (other than taxpayer) is based on all information of which preparer has any knowledge.

X Sign your name here [   ]   Print your name here [   ]

                                                   Print your title here [   ]

Date [/ /]   Best daytime phone [   ]

Paid Preparer Use Only   Check if you are self-employed ☐

Preparer's name [   ]   PTIN [   ]

Preparer's signature [   ]   Date [/ /]

Firm's name (or yours if self-employed) [   ]   EIN [   ]

Address [   ]   Phone [   ]

City [   ] State [   ]   ZIP code [   ]

Page 2   Form **940** (2017)

Chapter 8: Simple Payroll and Payroll Expenses

Form 940-V, Payment Voucher

Purpose of Form

Complete Form 940-V if you're making a payment with Form 940. We will use the completed voucher to credit your payment more promptly and accurately, and to improve our service to you.

Making Payments With Form 940

To avoid a penalty, make your payment with your 2017 Form 940 **only if** your FUTA tax for the fourth quarter (plus any undeposited amounts from earlier quarters) is $500 or less. If your total FUTA tax after adjustments (Form 940, line 12) is more than $500, you must make deposits by electronic funds transfer. See *When Must You Deposit Your FUTA Tax?* in the Instructions for Form 940. Also see sections 11 and 14 of Pub. 15 for more information about deposits.

 Use Form 940-V when making any payment with Form 940. However, if you pay an amount with Form 940 that should've been deposited, you may be subject to a penalty. See *Deposit Penalties* in section 11 of Pub. 15.

Specific Instructions

Box 1—Employer Identification Number (EIN). If you don't have an EIN, you may apply for one online by visiting the IRS website at *www.irs.gov/EIN*. You may also apply for an EIN by faxing or mailing Form SS-4 to the IRS. If you haven't received your EIN by the due date of Form 940, write "Applied For" and the date you applied in this entry space.

Box 2—Amount paid. Enter the amount paid with Form 940.

Box 3—Name and address. Enter your name and address as shown on Form 940.

- Enclose your check or money order made payable to "United States Treasury." Be sure to enter your EIN, "Form 940," and "2017" on your check or money order. Don't send cash. Don't staple Form 940-V or your payment to Form 940 (or to each other).

- Detach Form 940-V and send it with your payment and Form 940 to the address provided in the Instructions for Form 940.

Note: You must also complete the entity information above Part 1 on Form 940.

▼ Detach Here and Mail With Your Payment and Form 940. ▼

Form **940-V**
Department of the Treasury
Internal Revenue Service

Payment Voucher
► Don't staple or attach this voucher to your payment.

OMB No. 1545-0028

2017

| 1 Enter your employer identification number (EIN). | 2 Enter the amount of your payment. ► Make your check or money order payable to "United States Treasury" | Dollars | Cents |

3 Enter your business name (individual name if sole proprietor).

Enter your address.

Enter your city, state, and ZIP code or your city, foreign country name, foreign province/county, and foreign postal code.

Accounting 101: Easy Accounting and Bookkeeping for Beginners

IRS.gov Form 941

Form 941 for 2018: Employer's QUARTERLY Federal Tax Return
(Rev. January 2018) — Department of the Treasury — Internal Revenue Service

950117
OMB No. 1545-0029

Employer identification number (EIN): ☐☐ – ☐☐☐☐☐☐☐

Name (not your trade name): _____

Trade name (if any): _____

Address:
- Number, Street, Suite or room number
- City, State, ZIP code
- Foreign country name, Foreign province/county, Foreign postal code

Report for this Quarter of 2018
(Check one.)
- ☐ 1: January, February, March
- ☐ 2: April, May, June
- ☐ 3: July, August, September
- ☐ 4: October, November, December

Go to www.irs.gov/Form941 for instructions and the latest information.

Read the separate instructions before you complete Form 941. Type or print within the boxes.

Part 1: Answer these questions for this quarter.

1. Number of employees who received wages, tips, or other compensation for the pay period including: Mar. 12 (Quarter 1), June 12 (Quarter 2), Sept. 12 (Quarter 3), or Dec. 12 (Quarter 4) ..... 1 _____

2. Wages, tips, and other compensation ..... 2 _____

3. Federal income tax withheld from wages, tips, and other compensation ..... 3 _____

4. If no wages, tips, and other compensation are subject to social security or Medicare tax ☐ Check and go to line 6.

		Column 1		Column 2
5a	Taxable social security wages	_____	× 0.124 =	_____
5b	Taxable social security tips	_____	× 0.124 =	_____
5c	Taxable Medicare wages & tips	_____	× 0.029 =	_____
5d	Taxable wages & tips subject to Additional Medicare Tax withholding	_____	× 0.009 =	_____

5e. Add Column 2 from lines 5a, 5b, 5c, and 5d ..... 5e _____

5f. Section 3121(q) Notice and Demand—Tax due on unreported tips (see instructions) ..... 5f _____

6. Total taxes before adjustments. Add lines 3, 5e, and 5f ..... 6 _____

7. Current quarter's adjustment for fractions of cents ..... 7 _____

8. Current quarter's adjustment for sick pay ..... 8 _____

9. Current quarter's adjustments for tips and group-term life insurance ..... 9 _____

10. Total taxes after adjustments. Combine lines 6 through 9 ..... 10 _____

11. Qualified small business payroll tax credit for increasing research activities. Attach Form 8974 ..... 11 _____

12. Total taxes after adjustments and credits. Subtract line 11 from line 10 ..... 12 _____

13. Total deposits for this quarter, including overpayment applied from a prior quarter and overpayments applied from Form 941-X, 941-X (PR), 944-X, or 944-X (SP) filed in the current quarter ..... 13 _____

14. Balance due. If line 12 is more than line 13, enter the difference and see instructions ..... 14 _____

15. Overpayment. If line 13 is more than line 12, enter the difference _____ Check one: ☐ Apply to next return. ☐ Send a refund.

▶ You MUST complete both pages of Form 941 and SIGN it.   **Next ▶**

For Privacy Act and Paperwork Reduction Act Notice, see the back of the Payment Voucher.   Cat. No. 17001Z   Form **941** (Rev. 1-2018)

Chapter 8: Simple Payroll and Payroll Expenses

950217

Name (not your trade name) _____   Employer Identification number (EIN) _____

Part 2: Tell us about your deposit schedule and tax liability for this quarter.

If you are unsure about whether you are a monthly schedule depositor or a semiweekly schedule depositor, see section 11 of Pub. 15.

16 Check one: ☐ Line 12 on this return is less than $2,500 or line 12 on the return for the prior quarter was less than $2,500, and you didn't incur a $100,000 next-day deposit obligation during the current quarter. If line 12 for the prior quarter was less than $2,500 but line 12 on this return is $100,000 or more, you must provide a record of your federal tax liability. If you are a monthly schedule depositor, complete the deposit schedule below; if you are a semiweekly schedule depositor, attach Schedule B (Form 941). Go to Part 3.

☐ You were a monthly schedule depositor for the entire quarter. Enter your tax liability for each month and total liability for the quarter, then go to Part 3.

Tax liability: Month 1 _____ .
               Month 2 _____ .
               Month 3 _____ .

Total liability for quarter _____ .   Total must equal line 12.

☐ You were a semiweekly schedule depositor for any part of this quarter. Complete Schedule B (Form 941), Report of Tax Liability for Semiweekly Schedule Depositors, and attach it to Form 941.

Part 3: Tell us about your business. If a question does NOT apply to your business, leave it blank.

17 If your business has closed or you stopped paying wages . . . . ☐ Check here, and
    enter the final date you paid wages __/__/__ .

18 If you are a seasonal employer and you don't have to file a return for every quarter of the year . . . ☐ Check here.

Part 4: May we speak with your third-party designee?

Do you want to allow an employee, a paid tax preparer, or another person to discuss this return with the IRS? See the instructions for details.

☐ Yes. Designee's name and phone number _____   _____

Select a 5-digit Personal Identification Number (PIN) to use when talking to the IRS. ☐☐☐☐☐

☐ No.

Part 5: Sign here. You MUST complete both pages of Form 941 and SIGN it.

Under penalties of perjury, I declare that I have examined this return, including accompanying schedules and statements, and to the best of my knowledge and belief, it is true, correct, and complete. Declaration of preparer (other than taxpayer) is based on all information of which preparer has any knowledge.

X Sign your name here _____

Print your name here _____
Print your title here _____

Date __/__/__   Best daytime phone _____

Paid Preparer Use Only   Check if you are self-employed . . . ☐

Preparer's name		PTIN	
Preparer's signature		Date	__/__/__
Firm's name (or yours if self-employed)		EIN	
Address		Phone	
City		State ___ ZIP code	

Page 2   Form **941** (Rev. 1-2018)

Form 941-V, Payment Voucher

Purpose of Form

Complete Form 941-V if you're making a payment with Form 941. We will use the completed voucher to credit your payment more promptly and accurately, and to improve our service to you.

Making Payments With Form 941

To avoid a penalty, make your payment with Form 941 **only if**:

- Your total taxes after adjustments and credits (Form 941, line 12) for either the current quarter or the preceding quarter are less than $2,500, you didn't incur a $100,000 next-day deposit obligation during the current quarter, and you're paying in full with a timely filed return; or

- You're a monthly schedule depositor making a payment in accordance with the Accuracy of Deposits Rule. See section 11 of Pub. 15 for details. In this case, the amount of your payment may be $2,500 or more.

Otherwise, you must make deposits by electronic funds transfer. See section 11 of Pub. 15 for deposit instructions. Don't use Form 941-V to make federal tax deposits.

⚠ Use Form 941-V when making any payment with Form 941. However, if you pay an amount with Form 941 that should've been deposited, you may be subject to a penalty. See Deposit Penalties in section 11 of Pub. 15.

Specific Instructions

Box 1—Employer identification number (EIN). If you don't have an EIN, you may apply for one online by visiting the IRS website at *www.irs.gov/EIN*. You may also apply for an EIN by faxing or mailing Form SS-4 to the IRS. If you haven't received your EIN by the due date of Form 941, write "Applied For" and the date you applied in this entry space.

Box 2—Amount paid. Enter the amount paid with Form 941.

Box 3—Tax period. Darken the circle identifying the quarter for which the payment is made. Darken only one circle.

Box 4—Name and address. Enter your name and address as shown on Form 941.

- Enclose your check or money order made payable to "United States Treasury." Be sure to enter your EIN, "Form 941," and the tax period ("1st Quarter 2018," "2nd Quarter 2018," "3rd Quarter 2018," or "4th Quarter 2018") on your check or money order. Don't send cash. Don't staple Form 941-V or your payment to Form 941 (or to each other).

- Detach Form 941-V and send it with your payment and Form 941 to the address in the Instructions for Form 941.

Note: You must also complete the entity information above Part 1 on Form 941.

✂ ▼ Detach Here and Mail With Your Payment and Form 941. ▼ ✂

Form 941-V Department of the Treasury Internal Revenue Service

Payment Voucher

► Don't staple this voucher or your payment to Form 941.

OMB No. 1545-0029

2018

1 Enter your employer identification number (EIN).

2 Enter the amount of your payment. ►
Make your check or money order payable to "United States Treasury"

Dollars | Cents

3 Tax Period
○ 1st Quarter
○ 2nd Quarter
○ 3rd Quarter
○ 4th Quarter

4 Enter your business name (individual name if sole proprietor).

Enter your address.

Enter your city, state, and ZIP code or your city, foreign country name, foreign province/county, and foreign postal code.

Chapter 9: The Cash Flows and Bank Reconciliation Statements

Steps in The Accounting Process					
STEP 1	**STEP 2**	**STEP 3**	**STEP 4**	**STEP 5**	**STEP 6**
Analyze Transactions	Record Journal Entries	Post to General Ledger	Prepare Trial Balance	End-of Period Adj. Entries	Compile Financial Statements

Question: What is the purpose of this chapter?

Answer: To demonstrate how direct and indirect cash flows methods and bank reconciliation statements are constructed.

Two statements that appear to provide great challenges to new learners are (1) cash flows statement, and (2) the bank reconciliation statement. The cash flows statement is sometimes called the statement of *sources and uses* of cash.

The Cash Flows Statement

The cash flows statement is a report summarizing the *changes* in the balance of the *cash account* between the start and the end of a firm's operating cycle or financial period, showing the sources and usage of cash by the firm for the period. The *change* in the cash account balance is classified as financing, investing, and operating cash flows in the statement of cash flows. In other words, the purpose of cash flows statements is to identify what caused the cash account balance to change for the period and classify the reasons. Identifying the causes is done by analyzing the non-cash accounts (assets, liabilities, and equity accounts) in the balance sheet along with items from the income statement for the period. To prepare the cash flows statements we will need to study the financial statements to find the following:

- By what amount did the cash account change between the start and end of the period? Simply deduct the beginning balance from the ending balance to identify the *change* in the cash account.
- What was the net income for the period as shown in the Income Statement?
- Use a comparative Balance Sheet to identify the non-cash accounts—all other accounts except the cash account—and calculate the changes in their balances for the period (between the start and end of the current period).

   Note: the *start* of the *current* period is also the *end* of the *previous* period.
- Summarize and classify the changes in the non-cash account into three groups, (1) Financing cash flows, which includes receipt and payments of major sources of cash for

funding the business such as obtaining and repaying major bank loans and equity funding and drawings; (2) Investing cash flows, which entail purchase and disposal of long-term fixed assets; and (3) Operating cash flows are the remaining cash flows other than those in financing and investing cash flows. The operating cash flows are listed first in the cash flows statements, followed by investing cash flows, and then financing cash flows.

Operating cash flows represent the bulk of cash activities of a business because it involves the receipts and payments for the main value-creating activities for earning revenue and increasing profits for the firm. Operating cash flows are directly or indirectly related to the income statement and the current assets and liabilities of the balance sheet and include: receipts from, and sales to customers—cash and on terms (receivable); purchases from, and payments to suppliers for merchandize, services of employees, rent, insurance etc.

We will use the Comparative Balance Sheet to identify the cash and non-cash accounts and the Income Statement to prepare the cash flows statements.

INCOME STMT. & STMT OF RET. EARNINGS

MZ LLC. Combined Income Statement & Statement of Retained Earnings
For Period Ended January 31, 2017

	$	$
Sales Revenue		
Sales:		12,000.00
Less Cost of Goods Sold:		(2,000.00)
Gross Profit		10,000.00
Expenses	$	$
Rent Expense	1,500.00	
Salaries & Wages	3,520.00	
Office Expenses & Supplies	85.00	
Utilities Expense	175.00	
Insurance Expense	200.00	
Advertising & Promotion Expense	600.00	
Depreciation Expense	33.33	
Vehicle, Trav. & Ent. Expenses	560.00	
Bad Debt Expenses	450.00	
Total Expenses		(7,123.33)
Net Income/(Loss)		2,876.67
Add Previous Retained Earnings Balance		0.00
Less Drawings by Owner for Period		0.00
Current Y/E Retained Earnings Balance		2,876.67

Chapter 9: The Cash Flows and Bank Reconciliation Statements

COMPARATIVE BALANCE SHEET

MZ LLC Comparative Balance Sheet as at January 31, 2017

		January 31, 2017	December 31, 2016	
Assets	$$	$$	$$	
Cash		18,455.00	0.00	*Cash AC*
Accounts Receivable	9,500.00			
Less Allowance for Bad Debts	(450.00			
Net Accounts Receivable		8,550.00	0.00	
Merchandise Inventory		925.00	0.00	
Total Current Assets		27,930.00	0.00	
Fixed Assets	17,000.00			
Less Accumulated Depreciation	(33.33)			
Net Fixed Assets		16,966.67	0.00	
Total Assets (A)		$44,896.67	$0.00	
Liabilities				
Accounts Payable		700.00	0.00	
Salaries & Wages Payable		320.00	0.00	
Unearned Revenue		6,000.00	0.00	
Total Current Liabilities		7,020.00	0.00	
Long-term Payable		15,000.00	0.00	
Total Liabilities (L)		$22,020.00	$0.00	
Owners' Equity				
Owners' Capital/Equity		20,000.00	0.00	
Retained Earnings		2,876.67	0.00	
Total Equity (E)		$22,876.67	$0.00	
Total Liabilities + Equity (L+E) = (A)		$44,896.67	$0.00	

(Right margin annotation spanning the non-cash rows: *-------NON-CASH ACCOUNTS-------*)

The first step in preparing the cash flows statement is to identify the change in the cash account balance for the period ending January 31. The amount in MZ LLC's cash account on December 31, 2016, was zero before the owner's capital contribution of $20,000.00 on 1st January 2017, and on January 31, 2017 the balance was, $18,455.00. Therefore, the net *change* is $18,455.00.00 ($00.00 - $18,455.00) for the period. This change will be analyzed and summarized by using the non-cash accounts to identify the sources and uses into three categories: *operating*, *investing*, and *financing*. See the transactions recorded previously in the journals in chapters 2, 3 and 4.

Accounting 101: Easy Accounting and Bookkeeping for Beginners

> **Important Reminder:** The Cash Flows Statement is used to analyze the _**change**_ in the cash account for the period and summarize the _**change**_ into three categories: (1) Operating, (2) Investing, and (3) Financing.

There are two methods used for statements of cash flows: the *direct* method and the *indirect* method.

Direct method

The direct method for cash flows statements analyzes the transactions posted to the cash account ledger and categorizes them as operating, investing, or financing *directly* on the cash flows statement. Two approaches to the direct method are (a) analyzing and classifying each transaction posted in the cash account for the period; and (b) analyzing and classifying transactions posted to the *non-cash accounts* on the balance sheet and income statement for the cash components for the period. Both approaches achieve the same results: identifying the receipts and payments (sources and uses) of cash for the period and categorizes them as operating, investing, and financing *directly* on the cash flows statement.

To understand the cash flows statements, study the following diagrams:

The Direct Cash Flows Method

Direct Method: Statement of Cash Flows Cash Account 1010 for Period Ending January 31, 2017							
Bal. Jan. 1, 2017	Plus (+) or minus (-)	Net Operating flows	Plus (+) or minus (-)	Net Investing flows	Plus (+) or minus (-)	Net Financing flows	Bal. Jan. 31, 2017
$0.00		$455.00		-$17,000.00		+$35,000.00	$18,455.00
Sources—inflows (deposits) of cash (+) and *Uses*—outflows (payments) of cash went (-) for the period							
		Operating flows		Investing flows		Financing flows	
Details of operating, investing, and financing deposits and payments in the cash account.		Merch. -$2,225.00, Sales +$3,000.00, Sales Adv. +$6,000.0 Expenses -$6,320.00		Off. Furn. -$2,000.00, mach. -$15,000.00,		Capital/Equity from Owner +$20,000.00 plus Bank loan $15,000.00	

Chapter 9: The Cash Flows and Bank Reconciliation Statements

The Statement of Cash Flows using the direct method:

Net Operating Cash Flows
Receipts from Sales	3,000.00	
Advance receipts from customers	6,000.00	9,000.00
Payments to suppliers	-2,225.00	
Payments to employees	-3,200.00	
Payments to telephone co.	-175.00	
Payments for office supplies	-85.00	
Payments to auto dealership	-560.00	
Payments to landlord	-1,500.00	
Payments to insurance Co.	-200.00	
Payments to advertising Co.	-600.00	-8,545.00
		455.00

Net Investing Cash Flows
Payments for office equipment	-2000.00	
Payment for sorting machine	-15,000	**-17,000.00**

Net Financing Cash Flows
Cash investment from owner	20,000.00	
Receipt of long-term loan from bank	15,000.00	**35,000.00**

Total Change in Cash Position		**18,455.00**

Note: In the *direct* method, the sources and uses of receipts and payments posted in the cash account for the period are identified and displayed directly in the appropriate sections of the statement as operating, investing, or financing cash flows. This can be cumbersome for firms with large amounts of cash transactions in operating the business for the period.

The Indirect Method

Instead of analyzing every transaction in each non-cash balance sheet account to identify the cash received or used in the operating section of the cash flows statement as in the direct method, the *indirect* method identifies the *changes* in the current assets and current liabilities sections of the balance sheet to determine the sources and uses of cash in the operating activities for the period. This method uses comparative balance sheets to calculate the changes in the ending balances of the non-cash the accounts in consecutive balance sheets, along with the net income or loss from the income statement and adding back depreciation expenses for the period. This is shown in the table below. Notice the totals are identical to the summarized operating, investing, and financing sections in the direct method. The indirect cash flows method is much quicker and easier to complete and is the method used by most organizations to report the sources and uses of cash for the period, especially to identify if the business operations for the period brought in more cash than was spent.

The Indirect Cash Flows Method

Indirect Method: Statement Cash Flows Cash Account 1010 for Period Ending January 31, 2017									
		BALANCE SHEETS							
GL Accts	Flow Types	January 31, 2017 A		December 31, 2016 B		Period Changes A - B		Statement of Cash Flows	
	O, I, F	Debit	Credit	Debit	Credit	Debit	Credit	Operating Activities: (O)	
ASSETS								N. Inc./-Loss	2,876.67
1010. Cash	Not used in the indirect method as this is the account being analyzed							Add deprec.	+33.33
1020 Accounts Receivable	O	9,000.00		0.00		9,000.00		Net Current Assets	-9,475.00
1021 Allowance for Bad Debts	O		450.00		0.00		450.00	Net Current Liabilities	+7,020.00
1030 Merch. Inventory	O	925.00		0.00		925.00		Operating cash flows	455.00
1040 Prepaid Accounts	O	0.00		0.00		0.00			
								Investing Activities (I)	
1050 Fixed Assets	I	17,000.00		0.00		17,000.00		Net Fixed Assets	-17,000.00
1051 Accum. Depreciation	O		33.33		0.00		33.33	Investing cash flows	-17,000.00
LIABILITIES								Financing Activities (F)	
2010 Accounts Payable	O		700.00		0.00		700.00	Capital + LT Loan	+35,000.00
2020 Salaries & Wage Payable	O		320.00		0.00		320.00	Financing cash flows	+35,000.00
2030 Long-term Payable	F		15,000.00		0.00		15,000.00		
2040 Unearned Revenue	O		6,000.00		0.00		6,000.00	Cash flows (O+I+F)	+18,455.00
								Cash Jan. 1	0.00
EQUITY									

Chapter 9: The Cash Flows and Bank Reconciliation Statements

3010 Owner's Capital/Equity	F		20,000.00		0.00		20,000	Cash Bal. Jan. 31, 2017	+18,455.00
3020 Drawing	F								

The Statement of Cash Flows using the Indirect method:

Net Operating Cash Flows
    Net Income from Income Statement   2,876.67
    Add Depreciation non-Cash expense   33.33

    Change in Net Current Assets   -9,475.00
    Change in Net Current Liabilities   7,020.00   -2,455.00
             455.00

Net Investing Cash Flows
    Purchase of Office Furniture   -2000.00
    Purchase of Machinery   -15,000   -17,000.00

Net Financing Cash Flows
    Capital invested by owner   20,000.00
    Long Term Bank Loan   15,000.00   35,000.00

Total Change in Cash Position   **18,455.00**

Notes regarding the *indirect* cash flows method:

- The idea behind the indirect method is that, in accordance with the double-entry system of accounting, we can mathematically, indirectly determine the *changes* in the cash account by summing the changes in all the other (non-cash) accounts in the balance sheet for the period. *Changes* in the *cash* account represent opposite changes in the non-cash accounts: (a) *inflows* or receipt of cash from the *reduction* of the other assets and *increases* in liabilities; and (b) *outflows* or payment of cash to *increase* the non-cash asset amounts or *reduce* the balances in liability accounts.

    It might sound confusing at first, but if you think of the accounting equation, A = L + E, as *related to the cash account only* in simple arithmetic terms it might be easier to understand. Providing the liability and equity accounts in the balance sheet are held constant (unchanged), if the non-cash asset accounts were *reduced* (cash source), the *cash* account must be *increased* (cash used to increase cash balance) to keep the accounting equation in balance. It then follows, that an *increase* in the value of the *non-cash* asset accounts, would need a reduction in the *cash* account (cash source) for the accounting equation to remain in balance.

Similar reasoning using the accounting equation and simple arithmetic could also be applied to the (non-cash) liability accounts by holding the non-assets and equity accounts constant: if the amount in the *liabilities* accounts increased (increased debt as cash source), the *cash* account must also be increased (cash used to increase cash balance) to maintain the balance in the accounting equation.

A decrease in the value of the liabilities accounts would also need a in the cash account, all other non-cash and equity accounts remaining unchanged (constant). By combining the changes to the non-cash assets and liabilities accounts we can calculate the overall change in the cash account. This is what was meant earlier by "as related to the cash account only."

- The statement begins with the operating cash flows section starting with the net income (NI) or loss for the period under review.
- The net income (NI) amount includes non-cash expenses such as depreciation. This amount must be added back to the NI because they have no effect on *cash* for the period.
- Note that the amount for bad debt is also added back to NI only if the change to the accounts receivable (gross, not net receivable) is used in the calculation of total changes in the current assets; otherwise, using the changes in both accounts receivable and the allowance for bad debts for the period has the same effect as adding the bad debt expense for the period back to the NI.
- Depreciation expense is added back to NI because it is a non-cash item for the period.

The Bank Reconciliation Statement

The bank reconciliation is a tool used to provide detailed information about how much cash resources are legally owned by the organization on a specific date. Let me repeat this statement because it is extremely important for learners to grasp:

> The bank reconciliation statement is used to provide detailed information about how much cash resources on hand or in the bank is legally owned by the organization on a specific date.

Chapter 9: The Cash Flows and Bank Reconciliation Statements

The major question the reconciliation answers is: how much money does the business still legally own at the end of the month if all checks issued and bank service fees were paid, and the bank had recorded all deposits in the business' account, including any interest earned? When an individual or company opens an account with a financial institution, such as a bank or credit union, the individual or company receives a check book, deposit slips, and a *check register* to be used to keep track of the checks paid out and deposits made on a day to day basis.

A typical check register looks like the following table with a few minor changes: the author switched the *ADDITIONS* and *SUBTRACTIONS* sections and inserted reference letters (a) to (g) to make it easier for beginners to understand how the register is used.

PLEASE MAKE SURE TO DEDUCT CHARGES THAT AFFECT YOUR ACCOUNT							
ITEM NO. OR TRANS. CODE (a)	DATE (b)	TRANSACTION DESCRIPTION (c)	ADDITIONS: AMT OF DEPOSITS OR INTEREST (+) (d)	✓ T	FEE IF ANY (-) (e)	SUBTRACTIONS: AMT OF PAYMENTS OR WITHDRAWALS (-) (f)	BALANCE (g)

A reconciliation of the balance in the cash general ledger account in the books of the firm with the amount shown on the monthly statement sent by the bank, or digitally downloaded from and online-bank account, is called a bank reconciliation, and details are shown on a document called a Bank Reconciliation Statement as at a certain date.

As an example, MZ LLC uses the local bank, Sharks & Loans LLC, for the firm's daily banking business to deposit funds and make check payments.

We will need three documents to prepare a bank reconciliation statement as at January 31, 2017 for MZ LLC: (1) Previous bank reconciliation statement (since this is the first one, none is available), (2) printout of the general ledger cash account for the period, and (3) the current bank statement.

Accounting 101: Easy Accounting and Bookkeeping for Beginners

Printout of the General Ledger Cash Account

\multicolumn{5}{c}{General Ledger}			
\multicolumn{3}{l}{Account Name: Cash}		\multicolumn{4}{l}{Account No.: 1010}
				Post JL here		Updated Balance	
Date 2017		Trans. Description	JL Ref.	Debit	Credit	Debit	Credit
Jan.	1	General Journal	J1	20,000.00		20,000.00	
Jan.	1	General Journal	J1		2,000.00	18,000.00	
Jan.	1	General Journal	J1		1,500.00	16,500.00	
Jan.	2	General Journal	J1		600.00	15,900.00	
Jan.	4	General Journal	J1		2,000.00	13,900.00	
Jan.	5	General Journal	J1		200.00	13,700.00	
Jan.	6	General Journal	J1		800.00	12,900.00	
Jan.	11	General Journal	J2		175.00	12,725.00	
Jan.	13	General Journal	J2		800.00	11,925.00	
Jan.	16	General Journal	J2		225.00	11,700.00	
Jan.	18	General Journal	J2		85.00	11,615.00	
Jan.	23	General Journal	J2	3,000.00		14,615.00	
Jan.	27	General Journal	J2		1,600.00	13,015.00	
Jan.	30	General Journal	J2	6,000.00		19,015.00	
Jan.	30	General Journal	J2		560.00	18,455.00	

Chapter 9: The Cash Flows and Bank Reconciliation Statements

Copy of the Bank Statement from Sharks & Loans LLC for January 31, 2017

STATEMENT OF ACCOUNT	SHARKS & LOANS LLC YOUR CITY, YOUR STATE, ZIP 99998			STATEMENT NO. 00004567
ACCOUNT NO.	**MONTH**			
999100	January 21, 2017			
	MZ LLC 20 Anywhere Ave. Florida Town. Florida City, FL. 12345			
PREV. BALANCE	**TOTAL CHECK AMT.**	**TOTAL DEPOSIT AMT.**	**BANK FEES**	**CLOSING BALANCE**
0.00	8,300.00	23,000.00	0.00	14,700.00
MIN. BALANCE	**NUMBER OF CHECKS**	**NUMBER OF DEPOSITS**	**AVERAGE BAL.**	
11,700.00	9	2	14,765.63	

CHECKING ACCOUNT ACTIVITIES RECORDED FOR THE MONTH				
DATE	**CHECK AMOUNTS**	**CHECK AMOUNTS**	**DEPOSITS**	**BALANCE**
January 1			20,000.00	20,000.00
January 3	2,000.00	1,500.00		16,500.00
January 5	600.00			15,900.00
January 8	200.00	2,000.00		13,700.00
January 10	800.00			12,900.00
January 14	175.00			12,725.00
January 19	800.00	225.00		11,700.00
January 24			3,000.00	14,700.00
		January 31, 2017 Ending Balance		14,700.00

Using the printout of the cash account from the general ledger and the bank statement, all transactions for the month are compared and transactions appearing in both documents are crossed out. Transactions not crossed out on the printout of the general ledger cash account are

Accounting 101: Easy Accounting and Bookkeeping for Beginners

then used to adjust the ending balance amount on the bank statement in the reconciliation statement: outstanding deposits (called deposit in transit) are added and check outstanding are deducted from the *bank statement balance*. The results would look like the following:

Printout of general ledger and bank statement showing the amounts deposited and checks paid for the period which appeared in both statements crossed out.

				Post JL here		Updated Balance	
Date 2017		Trans. Description	JL Ref.	Debit	Credit	Debit	Credit
Jan.	1	General Journal	J1	~~20,000.00~~		20,000.00	
Jan.	1	General Journal	J1		~~2,000.00~~	18,000.00	
Jan.	1	General Journal	J1		~~1,500.00~~	16,500.00	
Jan.	2	General Journal	J1		~~600.00~~	15,900.00	
Jan.	4	General Journal	J1		~~2,000.00~~	13,900.00	
Jan.	5	General Journal	J1		~~200.00~~	13,700.00	
Jan.	6	General Journal	J1		~~800.00~~	12,900.00	
Jan.	11	General Journal	J2		~~175.00~~	12,725.00	
Jan.	13	General Journal	J2		~~800.00~~	11,925.00	
Jan.	16	General Journal	J2		~~225.00~~	11,700.00	
Jan.	18	General Journal	J2		85.00	11,615.00	
Jan.	23	General Journal	J2	~~3,000.00~~		14,615.00	
Jan.	27	General Journal	J2		1,600.00	13,015.00	
Jan.	30	General Journal	J2	6,000.00		19,015.00	
Jan.	30	General Journal	J2		560.00	18,455.00	

General Ledger
Account Name: Cash   **Account No.: 1010**

Chapter 9: The Cash Flows and Bank Reconciliation Statements

STATEMENT OF ACCOUNT	SHARKS & LOANS LLC YOUR CITY, YOUR STATE, ZIP 99998			STATEMENT NO. 00004567
ACCOUNT NO.	**MONTH**			
999100	January 21, 2017			
	MZ LLC 20 Anywhere Ave. Florida Town. Florida City, FL. 12345			
PREV. BALANCE	**TOTAL CHECK AMT.**	**TOTAL DEPOSIT AMT.**	**BANK FEES**	**CLOSING BALANCE**
0.00	8,300.00	23,000.00	0.00	14,700.00
MIN. BALANCE	**NUMBER OF CHECKS**	**NUMBER OF DEPOSITS**	**AVERAGE BAL.**	
11,700.00	9	2	14,765.63	
CHECKING ACCOUNT ACTIVITIES RECORDED FOR THE MONTH				
DATE	**CHECK AMOUNTS**	**CHECK AMOUNTS**	**DEPOSITS**	**BALANCE**
January 1			20,000.00	20,000.00
January 3	2,000.00	1,500.00		16,500.00
January 5	600.00			15,900.00
January 8	200.00	2,000.00		13,700.00
January 10	800.00			12,900.00
January 14	175.00			12,725.00
January 19	800.00	225.00		11,700.00
January 24			3,000.00	14,700.00
		January 31, 2017 Ending Balance		14,700.00

The bank reconciliation statement for January 31, 2017, showing the adjusted balances in the general ledger and the adjusted bank statement amount showing deposits in transit and outstanding check not yet recorded at the bank, would appear as follows:

Bank Reconciliation of MZ LLC for Month Ending January 31, 2017			
	C/O	General Ledger	Bank Statement
Balances as at January 31, 2017		$18,455.00	$14,700.00
Add Deposits in Transit:			
Jan. 30 $6,000.00	O		+ $6,000.00
Less Checks Outstanding:			
Jan. 18 check #010 $85.00	O		
Jan. 27 check #011 $1,600.00	O		
Jan. 30 check #012 $560.00	O		-2,245.00
Less bank service charges not posted to GL to be JL			
Reconciled Balances showing actual cash owned		$18,455.00	$18,455.00

Notes: C/O = items cleared or outstanding—not yet presented or posted at the bank. The strikethrough of the amounts signifies that the amounts have been presented and posted to both systems.

Summary

We have now completed coverage of the main financial statements: Income Statement, Changes in Owner's Equity, and Balance Sheet in chapter 7; and the Cash Flows Statement in this chapter. The cash flows statement can be presented in two formats: direct, and indirect. The statement of cash flows provides a summary of the sources and uses of cash for a business, categorized as operating, financing, and investing. The reason and mechanics of completing bank reconciliation for an organization was also discussed in this chapter. The bank reconciliation is used to determine the amount of cash legally available to be used by the firm at the end of the period.

Chapter 10: Basic Introduction to Financial Ratios and Trend Analysis

Chapter 10: Basic Introduction to Financial Ratios and Trend Analysis

Question: What is the purpose of this chapter?

Answer: Introduction to popular accounting tools used to analyze the results of a firm's operating systems and managerial results compared to competitors and industry metrics.

This book is written for new learners of accounting and bookkeeping therefore only a brief introduction and description of financial ratios and trend analysis will be presented. Detailed analyses and explanations can be found in more advanced accounting books. Financial ratios and trend analyses are tools used by accountants in analyzing and reporting on the performance of the organization over time and compared with ratios of competitors and the industry in which the organization operates. The ratios and trend analyses are calculated from data shown on comparative balance sheets and income statements of the firm and its competitors.

The information derived from the ratios and trend analyses are used by individuals within and outside of the firm, and other organizations, for various decision-making purposes. Information provided by financial analyses are usually grouped into three main areas: (1) profitability (how profitable is the business?), (2) solvency (will the firm be able to continue in the foreseeable future?), and (3) liquidity (will the firm be able to pay its debts when due?). Individuals such as, managers, employees, creditors, loan officers of banks, the government, and owners and investors are collectively referred to in accounting as *stakeholders*. The following is an overview of vertical and horizontal analysis of few of the more common ratios used for comparison, decision-making, and strategic purposes used for decision making.

Trend Analysis

Trend analyses look at changes in the amounts (balances) of the elements or general ledger accounts in the income statement and balance sheet over time to assess the possible effects on the operating performance and profitability of the organization. Two types of trend analyses are (1) Vertical analysis and (2) Horizontal analysis.

Vertical Analysis

Trend comparisons using the balance sheet and income statement are usually done by first converting them to percentages: the elements (accounts) of the *balance sheet* are converted to percentages based on total assets for each period, with *total assets* representing 100 percent; whereas the accounts (elements) of the *income statement* are converted to percentages of *net sales*, with net sales representing 100 percent for the period. This conversion of balance sheet and income statement accounts to percentages for comparison purposes is referred to as converting them to *similar sizes* of 100 percent. By using similar-sized comparative balance sheets and income statements trends can be identified and comparisons can be made between organizations of different types and sizes, or between organizations in different industries.

Converting the Income Statement and Balance Sheet to similar-sized statements entail adding columns to show the percentages next to the related amounts as shown below. The following amounts were created and used for illustration purposes only.

COMPARATIVE BALANCE SHEET

Comparative Balance Sheet as at December 31, 2017

		Dec. 31, 2017		Dec. 31, 2016	
Assets	%	$$	$$	%	$$
Cash	19.76		7,000.00	18.86	6275.00
Accounts Receivable	16.94	6,000.00			
Less Allowance for Bad Debts	-0.64	-225.00			
Net Accounts Receivable	16.30		5,775.00	15.03	5000.00
Merchandise Inventory	16.94		6000.00	21.04	7000.00
Total Current Assets	53.00		18,775.00	54.92	18,275.00
Fixed Assets	47.99	17,000.00			
Less Accumulated Depreciation	-0.99	-350.00			
Net Fixed Assets	47.00		16,650.00		15000.00
Total Assets (A)	100.00		$35,425.00	100.00	$33,275.00
Liabilities					
Accounts Payable	7.76		2750.00	10.22	3401.00
Salaries & Wages Payable	2.48		880.00	1.95	650.00
Unearned Revenue	7.06		2,500.00	4.51	1500.00
Total Current Liabilities	17.30		6,130.00	16.68	5,551.00
Long-term Payable	33.87		12,000.00	36.06	12000.00
Total Liabilities (L)	51.18		$18,130.00	52.75	$17,551.00
Owners' Equity					
Owners' Capital/Equity	28.23		10,000.00	30.05	10000.00
Retained Earnings	20.59		7,295.00	17.20	5724.00
Total Equity (E)	48.82		$17,295.00	47.25	$15,724.00
Total Liabilities + Equity (L+E) = (A)	100.00		$35,425.00	100.00	$33,275.00

Chapter 10: Basic Introduction to Financial Ratios and Trend Analysis

COMPARATIVE INCOME STATEMENT

Comparative Income Statement
For Period Ended December 31, 2017

	2017 %	2017 $	2016 %	2016 $
Sales Revenue				
Sales:	100.00	18,000.00	100.00	14,000.00
Less Cost of Goods Sold:	33.33	6,000.00	33.33	4,666.20
Gross Profit	66.67	12,000.00	66.67	9,333.80
Expenses	%	$	%	$
Rent Expense	9.44	1,700.00	10.71	1,500.00
Salaries & Wages	19.44	3,500.00	21.43	3,000.00
Office Expenses & Supplies	1.25	225.00	1.07	150.00
Utilities Expense	3.06	550.00	2.32	325.00
Insurance Expense	6.67	1,200.00	7.14	1,000.00
Advertising & Promotion Expense	5.00	900.00	5.36	750.00
Depreciation Expense	3.61	650.00	2.50	350.00
Vehicle, Trav. & Ent. Expenses	5.44	980.00	5.50	770.00
Bad Debt Expenses	4.03	725.00	3.75	525.00
Total Expenses	57.94	10,430.00	59.79	8,370.00
Net Income/(Loss)	8.73	1,570.00	6.88	963.80

Horizontal Analysis

Horizontal analysis looks at changes in the elements of the financial statements over time and usually between two consecutive operating periods. The first step in horizontal analysis is the construction of two additional columns in the comparative financial statements, one to show the dollar change of each major element in the statement, and the other to calculate the percentage of the change based on the previous period amount. First, we subtract the amount in the previous period from the equivalent in the most current period. For example, in the illustrations that follow, the amounts in the 2016 column are subtracted from the amounts in the 2017 column to create the amounts in the column titled $ Change. Next, we divide the $ Change amounts by the 2016 $ amounts and convert them to percentages, to populate the percentages in the % Change column.

The following tables and amounts are used for our demonstration of horizontal analysis of financial statements and created for illustration purposes only.

COMPARATIVE BALANCE SHEET

Comparative Balance Sheet as at December 31, 2017

	% Change	$ Change	Dec. 2017 $$	Dec. 2016 $$
Assets				
Cash	11.55	725.00	7,000.00	6275.00
Accounts Receivable				
Less Allowance for Bad Debts				
Net Accounts Receivable	15.50	775.00	5,775.00	5000.00
Merchandise Inventory	-14.29	-1,000.00	6000.00	7000.00
Total Current Assets	2.74	500.00	18,775.00	18,275.00
Fixed Assets				
Less Accumulated Depreciation				
Net Fixed Assets	11.00	1,650.00	16,650.00	15000.00
Total Assets (A)	6.46	2,150.00	$35,425.00	$33,275.00
Liabilities				
Accounts Payable	-19.14	-651.00	2750.00	3401.00
Salaries & Wages Payable	35.38	230.00	880.00	650.00
Unearned Revenue	66.67	1,000.00	2,500.00	1500.00
Total Current Liabilities	10.43	579.00	6,130.00	5,551.00
Long-term Payable	0.00	0.00	12,000.00	12000.00
Total Liabilities (L)	3.30	579.00	$18,130.00	$17,551.00
Owners' Equity				
Owners' Capital/Equity	0.00	0.00	10,000.00	10000.00
Retained Earnings	27.45	1,571.00	7,295.00	5724.00
Total Equity (E)	9.99	1,571.00	$17,295.00	$15,724.00
Total Liabilities + Equity (L+E) = (A)	6.46	2,150.00	$35,425.00	$33,275.00

Summary of steps taken to create the data to be used for horizontal analysis of financial statements:

1. Insert two additional columns to the left of the 2017 amounts in the financial statements to be used for (a) change in the dollar amounts for each element of the statement between 2016 and 2017 ($ Change column), and (b) conversion of the changes to percentages (% Change column);
2. Deduct the amounts in the 2016 column from the amounts in the 2017 column to fill the $ Change column;
3. Divide the amounts in the $ Change column by the amounts in the 2016 column and convert the ratio to percentages to fill the % column.

Chapter 10: Basic Introduction to Financial Ratios and Trend Analysis

COMPARATIVE INCOME STATEMENT

Comparative Income Statement
For Period Ended December 31, 2017

	% Change	$ Change	2017 $	2016 $
Sales Revenue				
Sales:	28.57	4,000.00	18,000.00	14,000.00
Less Cost of Goods Sold:	28.57	1,333.80	6,000.00	4,666.20
Gross Profit	28.57	2,666.20	12,000.00	9,333.80
Expenses			$	$
Rent Expense	13.33	200.00	1,700.00	1,500.00
Salaries & Wages	16.67	500.00	3,500.00	3,000.00
Office Expenses & Supplies	50.00	75.00	225.00	150.00
Utilities Expense	69.23	225.00	550.00	325.00
Insurance Expense	20.00	200.00	1,200.00	1,000.00
Advertising & Promotion Expense	20.00	150.00	900.00	750.00
Depreciation Expense	85.71	300.00	650.00	350.00
Vehicle, Trav. & Ent. Expenses	27.27	210.00	980.00	770.00
Bad Debt Expenses	38.10	200.00	725.00	525.00
Total Expenses	24.61	2,060.00	10,430.00	8,370.00
Net Income/(Loss)	62.90	606.20	1,570.00	963.80

Financial Ratios

Examples of some common ratios for 2017 are shown below and identified as profitability (P), liquidity (L), and solvency (S), and the financial statements associated with their calculations.

- Working capital (L) is the difference between current assets and current liabilities as shown on the balance sheet. Source balance sheet. 18,775 – 6,130 = 12,645
- Current ratio (L) is current assets divided by current liabilities. Source balance sheet. 18,775 / 6,130 = 3.06
- Quick ratio (L) is the current assets minus the merchandise inventory, divided by current liabilities. Source balance sheet (18,775 – 6,000) / 6,130 = 2.08
- Gross Profit margin (P) is net sales minus cost of goods sold (COGS) to provide a gross profit amount which is then divided by the net sales. This is also called contribution margin. Source income statement (12,000 / 18,000) x 100 = 66.67%
- Net Income ratio (P) to net sales is net income divided by net sales. Source Income Statement (1,570 /18,000) x 100 = 8.73%

- Return on assets (P) is net income divided by average total assets for the period. Sources income statement and balance sheet 1,570 / ((35,425 + 33,275)/2) x 100 = (1,570 / 34,350) x 100 = 4.57%
- Asset turnover (L) is net sales divided by the average total assets for the period. Sources income statement and balance sheet 18,000 / ((35,425 + 33,275)/2) = (18,000 / 34,350 = 0.52
- Accounts receivable turnover (L) is net sales on terms (credit) divided by the average net accounts receivable for the period. Sources income statement and balance sheet 18,000 / ((5,775 + 5000)/2) = 18,000 / 5,387.50 = 3.34
- Merchandise inventory turnover (L) ratio is cost of goods sold divided by the average merchandise inventory for the period. income statement and balance sheet 6,000 / ((6,000 + 7,000)/2) = 6,000 / 6,500 = 0.92
- Debt to Assets ratio (S) is total liabilities divided by total Assets (notice the accounting equation). Source balance sheet 18,130 / 35,425 = 0.51
- Debt to Equity ratio (S) is total liabilities divided by total owner's equity (notice the accounting equation). Source balance sheet 18,130 / 17,295 = 1.05

Notice that some of the ratios are converted to percentages.

Summary

Financial analyses are activities done by experienced accountants and financial analysts to provide information useful for decision-making by users of financial statements. The basic concepts related to trend analyses, including vertical and horizontal analyses, and financial ratios were introduced in this chapter. Learners interested in learning more about these concepts and interpretations are encouraged to seek more advanced books on accounting and finance.

Chapter 11: Final Thoughts and Encouragement

Steps in The Accounting Process					
STEP 1	**STEP 2**	**STEP 3**	**STEP 4**	**STEP 5**	**STEP 6**
Analyze Transactions	Record Journal Entries	Post to General Ledger	Prepare Trial Balance	End-of Period Adj. Entries	Compile Financial Statements

I wish to express my appreciation and thanks for taking this journey with me. I hope you learned a great deal from this trip.

General journals were used in the examples in the book because many computerized accounting software systems available for business use require a good understanding of how to journalize business transactions. Many transaction entries in computerized accounting systems are created by the creating, recording, and posting documents such as invoices, cash receipts and checks. This is important to know because when transactions are recorded and saved in a computerized accounting system, the other steps, except for the end-of-period manual adjustments in the accounting process, can be automatically generated by the program.

In chapter 1 we learned that accounting is both a process and a means of recording, posting, summarizing and reporting financial transactions and activities of a business for specific periods; that accounting is a systematic step-by-step set of activities taken by the accountant to (1) identify, analyze and record financial transactions, (2) record the transactions in the journal using a chart of accounts, (3) post the journal entries to the general ledger, (4) prepare a trial balance of the general ledger accounts, (5) make adjustments at the end of accounting periods, and (6) summarize and report on the activities of the firm. *Accounting* is also referred to as the *language of business*.

Each chapter was dedicated to introducing and demonstrating concepts and activities involved in each of the systematic steps in the accounting process:

1. In chapter 1 we introduced the two most important concepts in accounting: (1) the accounting equation and (2) the double-entry concept of accounting, upon which all modern accounting systems are based.
2. In chapter 2 we defined business transactions and introduced the chart of accounts (COA) and general journal (JL) and special journals and demonstrated how they are used to record business transactions of an organization.
3. The general ledger (GL) and trial balance (TB) and the mechanics of "T" accounts

were discussed in chapter 3.

4. In chapter 4 we discussed the general ledger accounts—elements that make up the balance sheet of an organization and defined major classification found in the balance sheets: assets, liabilities, and equity. These provide details of the summarized relationships of the accounting equation. The difference between an expense and expenditure was also explained in the chapter.

5. We described the elements—general ledger accounts found in the income statement along with the two main classifications, revenue and expenses, in chapter 5.

6. In chapter 6 we looked at end-of-period accounting activities including adjusting entries, closing entries, and the income summary account and introduced the concept of net income.

7. The information in chapter 7 was devoted to financial reporting statements including: the income statement, balance sheet, statement of retained earnings, and changes in the owner's equity account.

8. Simple payroll techniques and activities and payroll expenses were introduced in chapter 8 and provided some examples of IRS Federal income tax withholding tables and other IRS payroll resources found on the IRS.gov website.

9. In chapter 9 we explored the direct and indirect methods of preparing cash flows statements as well as how to prepare a bank reconciliation statement.

10. An introduction to financial ratios and trend analysis was provided in chapter 10 and noted that financial ratios and trend analyses are done at more advanced stages in accounting by experienced accountants.

You have now been introduced to accounting and bookkeeping and should now see that the subject can be learned with minimum knowledge of mathematics. I encourage you to search the Web, public libraries, or your favorite online bookstores to further explore the self-help, introductory, or other accounting resources that are readily available.

I wish you success in your academic and professional careers.

Denver G. Pettigrew, CPA, PhD, MBA

Appendixes

Appendix A: Combined Chart of Accounts and Trial Balance

A Simple Combined Chart of Accounts and Trial Balance

CHART OF ACCOUNTS Account #, Classification, and General Ledger Descriptions	TRIAL BALANCE	
	Debit $$	Credit $$
Balance Sheet		
Assets: 1000		
• 1010 Cash	XXXX.XX	
• 1020 Accounts Receivable	XXXX.XX	
• 1021 Allowance for Bad Debts		XXXX.XX
• 1030 Merchandise Inventory	XXXX.XX	
• 1040 Prepaid Accounts	XXXX.XX	
• 1050 Fixed Assets	XXXX.XX	
• 1051 Accumulated Depreciation		XXXX.XX
Liabilities: 2000		
• 2010 Accounts Payable		XXXX.XX
• 2020 Salaries & Wages Payable		XXXX.XX
• 2030 Long-term Payable		XXXX.XX
• 2040 Unearned Revenue		XXXX.XX
Equity: 3000		
• 3010 Owner's Capital/Equity		XXXX.XX
• 3020 Drawing	XXXX.XX	
• 3030 Retained Earnings		XXXX.XX
Income Statement		
Revenue: 4000		
• 4010 Sales Revenue		XXXX.XX
• 4020 Other Revenue		XXXX.XX
• 4030 Cost of Goods Sold (COGS)	XXXX.XX	
Expenses: 5000		
• 5010 Rent Expense	XXXX.XX	
• 5020 Salaries & Wages	XXXX.XX	
• 5030 Office Expenses & Supplies	XXXX.XX	
• 5040 Utilities Expense	XXXX.XX	
• 5050 Insurance Expense	XXXX.XX	
• 5060 Advertising & Promotion Expense	XXXX.XX	
• 5070 Depreciation Expense	XXXX.XX	
• 5080 Vehicle, Travelling & Entertainment Expense	XXXX.XX	
• 5090 Bad Debt Expense	XXXX.XX	
TOTAL	XXXX.XX	XXXX.XX

Appendix B: Typical Check Register

ITEM NO. OR TRANS. CODE (a)	DATE (b)	TRANSACTION DESCRIPTION (c)	ADDITIONS: AMT OF DEPOSITS OR INTEREST (+) (d)	✓ T	FEE IF ANY (-) (e)	SUBTRACTIONS: AMT OF PAYMENTS OR WITHDRAWALS (-) (f)	BALANCE (g)

PLEASE MAKE SURE TO DEDUCT CHARGES THAT AFFECT YOUR ACCOUNT

Appendixes
Appendix C: General Journal

General Journal				Page No.____
Date 2____	Description	GL Ref.	Debit Amount	Credit Amount

Appendix D: General Ledger

General Ledger						
Account Name: **No.:** _____					**Account**	
Date 20__	Trans. Description	JL Ref.	Post JL here		Updated Balance	
			Debit	Credit	Debit	Credit

Appendixes

Appendix E: Combined Income Statement & Retained Earnings

Combined Income Statement & Retained Earnings For Period Ended _____, 20___		
Sales Revenue	$	$
Sales:		
Less Cost of Goods Sold:		
Gross Profit		
Expenses	$	$
Rent Expense		
Salaries & Wages		
Office Expenses & Supplies		
Utilities Expense		
Insurance Expense		
Advertising & Promotion Expense		
Depreciation Expense		
Vehicle, Trav. & Ent. Expenses		
Bad Debt Expenses		
Total Expenses		
Net Income		
Add Previous Retained Earnings Balance		
Less Drawings by Owner for Period		
Current Y/E Retained Earnings Balance		

Appendix F: Balance Sheet

Balance Sheet as at Period Ending _____, 20____		
	$$	$$
Assets		
Cash		
Accounts Receivable		
Less Allowance for Bad Debts		
Net Accounts Receivable		
Merchandise Inventory		
Current Assets		
Fixed Assets		
Less Accumulated Depreciation		
Net Fixed Assets		
Total Assets (A)		
Liabilities		
Accounts Payable		
Salaries & Wages Payable		
Current Liabilities		
Long-term Payable		
Unearned Revenue		
Long-term Liabilities		
Total Liabilities (L)		
Owners' Equity		
Owners' Capital/Equity		
Drawing		
Retained Earnings		
Total Equity (E)		
Total Liabilities + Equity (L+E) = (A)		

Appendixes
Appendix G: IRS Percentage Method Tables for Income Tax Withholding

Percentage Method Tables for Income Tax Withholding

(For Wages Paid in 2018)

TABLE 1—WEEKLY Payroll Period

(a) SINGLE person (including head of household)—

If the amount of wages (after subtracting withholding allowances) is: Not over $71 . . . . The amount of income tax to withhold is: $0

Over—	But not over—		of excess over—
$71	—$254	$0.00 plus 10%	—$71
$254	—$815	$18.30 plus 12%	—$254
$815	—$1,658	$85.62 plus 22%	—$815
$1,658	—$3,100	$271.08 plus 24%	—$1,658
$3,100	—$3,917	$617.16 plus 32%	—$3,100
$3,917	—$9,687	$878.60 plus 35%	—$3,917
$9,687		$2,898.10 plus 37%	—$9,687

(b) MARRIED person—

If the amount of wages (after subtracting withholding allowances) is: Not over $222 . . . . The amount of income tax to withhold is: $0

Over—	But not over—		of excess over—
$222	—$588	$0.00 plus 10%	—$222
$588	—$1,711	$36.60 plus 12%	—$588
$1,711	—$3,395	$171.36 plus 22%	—$1,711
$3,395	—$6,280	$541.84 plus 24%	—$3,395
$6,280	—$7,914	$1,234.24 plus 32%	—$6,280
$7,914	—$11,761	$1,757.12 plus 35%	—$7,914
$11,761		$3,103.57 plus 37%	—$11,761

TABLE 2—BIWEEKLY Payroll Period

(a) SINGLE person (including head of household)—

If the amount of wages (after subtracting withholding allowances) is: Not over $142 . . . . The amount of income tax to withhold is: $0

Over—	But not over—		of excess over—
$142	—$509	$0.00 plus 10%	—$142
$509	—$1,631	$36.70 plus 12%	—$509
$1,631	—$3,315	$171.34 plus 22%	—$1,631
$3,315	—$6,200	$541.82 plus 24%	—$3,315
$6,200	—$7,835	$1,234.22 plus 32%	—$6,200
$7,835	—$19,373	$1,757.42 plus 35%	—$7,835
$19,373		$5,795.72 plus 37%	—$19,373

(b) MARRIED person—

If the amount of wages (after subtracting withholding allowances) is: Not over $444 . . . . The amount of income tax to withhold is: $0

Over—	But not over—		of excess over—
$444	—$1,177	$0.00 plus 10%	—$444
$1,177	—$3,421	$73.30 plus 12%	—$1,177
$3,421	—$6,790	$342.58 plus 22%	—$3,421
$6,790	—$12,560	$1,083.76 plus 24%	—$6,790
$12,560	—$15,829	$2,468.56 plus 32%	—$12,560
$15,829	—$23,521	$3,514.64 plus 35%	—$15,829
$23,521		$6,206.84 plus 37%	—$23,521

TABLE 3—SEMIMONTHLY Payroll Period

(a) SINGLE person (including head of household)—

If the amount of wages (after subtracting withholding allowances) is: Not over $154 . . . . The amount of income tax to withhold is: $0

Over—	But not over—		of excess over—
$154	—$551	$0.00 plus 10%	—$154
$551	—$1,767	$39.70 plus 12%	—$551
$1,767	—$3,592	$185.62 plus 22%	—$1,767
$3,592	—$6,717	$587.12 plus 24%	—$3,592
$6,717	—$8,488	$1,337.12 plus 32%	—$6,717
$8,488	—$20,988	$1,903.84 plus 35%	—$8,488
$20,988		$6,278.84 plus 37%	—$20,988

(b) MARRIED person—

If the amount of wages (after subtracting withholding allowances) is: Not over $481 . . . . The amount of income tax to withhold is: $0

Over—	But not over—		of excess over—
$481	—$1,275	$0.00 plus 10%	—$481
$1,275	—$3,706	$79.40 plus 12%	—$1,275
$3,706	—$7,356	$371.12 plus 22%	—$3,706
$7,356	—$13,606	$1,174.12 plus 24%	—$7,356
$13,606	—$17,148	$2,674.12 plus 32%	—$13,606
$17,148	—$25,481	$3,807.56 plus 35%	—$17,148
$25,481		$6,724.11 plus 37%	—$25,481

TABLE 4—MONTHLY Payroll Period

(a) SINGLE person (including head of household)—

If the amount of wages (after subtracting withholding allowances) is: Not over $308 . . . . The amount of income tax to withhold is: $0

Over—	But not over—		of excess over—
$308	—$1,102	$0.00 plus 10%	—$308
$1,102	—$3,533	$79.40 plus 12%	—$1,102
$3,533	—$7,183	$371.12 plus 22%	—$3,533
$7,183	—$13,433	$1,174.12 plus 24%	—$7,183
$13,433	—$16,975	$2,674.12 plus 32%	—$13,433
$16,975	—$41,975	$3,807.56 plus 35%	—$16,975
$41,975		$12,557.56 plus 37%	—$41,975

(b) MARRIED person—

If the amount of wages (after subtracting withholding allowances) is: Not over $963 . . . . The amount of income tax to withhold is: $0

Over—	But not over—		of excess over—
$963	—$2,550	$0.00 plus 10%	—$963
$2,550	—$7,413	$158.70 plus 12%	—$2,550
$7,413	—$14,713	$742.26 plus 22%	—$7,413
$14,713	—$27,213	$2,348.26 plus 24%	—$14,713
$27,213	—$34,296	$5,348.26 plus 32%	—$27,213
$34,296	—$50,963	$7,614.82 plus 35%	—$34,296
$50,963		$13,448.27 plus 37%	—$50,963

Images copied from Circular E, Pub. 15, IRS Employer Tax Guide 2018 published on the IRS website WWW.IRS.gov

Accounting 101: Easy Accounting and Bookkeeping for Beginners

Percentage Method Tables for Income Tax Withholding (continued)

(For Wages Paid in 2018)

TABLE 5—QUARTERLY Payroll Period

(a) SINGLE person (including head of household)—
If the amount of wages (after subtracting withholding allowances) is:
Not over $925 . . . . $0

Over—	But not over—	The amount of income tax to withhold is:	of excess over—
$925	—$3,306	$0.00 plus 10%	—$925
$3,306	—$10,600	$238.10 plus 12%	—$3,306
$10,600	—$21,550	$1,113.38 plus 22%	—$10,600
$21,550	—$40,300	$3,522.38 plus 24%	—$21,550
$40,300	—$50,925	$8,022.38 plus 32%	—$40,300
$50,925	—$125,925	$11,422.38 plus 35%	—$50,925
$125,925		$37,672.38 plus 37%	—$125,925

(b) MARRIED person—
If the amount of wages (after subtracting withholding allowances) is:
Not over $2,888 . . . . $0

Over—	But not over—	The amount of income tax to withhold is:	of excess over—
$2,888	—$7,650	$0.00 plus 10%	—$2,888
$7,650	—$22,238	$476.20 plus 12%	—$7,650
$22,238	—$44,138	$2,226.76 plus 22%	—$22,238
$44,138	—$81,638	$7,044.76 plus 24%	—$44,138
$81,638	—$102,888	$16,044.76 plus 32%	—$81,638
$102,888	—$152,888	$22,844.76 plus 35%	—$102,888
$152,888		$40,344.76 plus 37%	—$152,888

TABLE 6—SEMIANNUAL Payroll Period

(a) SINGLE person (including head of household)—
If the amount of wages (after subtracting withholding allowances) is:
Not over $1,850 . . . . $0

Over—	But not over—	The amount of income tax to withhold is:	of excess over—
$1,850	—$6,613	$0.00 plus 10%	—$1,850
$6,613	—$21,200	$476.30 plus 12%	—$6,613
$21,200	—$43,100	$2,226.74 plus 22%	—$21,200
$43,100	—$80,600	$7,044.74 plus 24%	—$43,100
$80,600	—$101,850	$16,044.74 plus 32%	—$80,600
$101,850	—$251,850	$22,844.74 plus 35%	—$101,850
$251,850		$75,344.74 plus 37%	—$251,850

(b) MARRIED person—
If the amount of wages (after subtracting withholding allowances) is:
Not over $5,775 . . . . $0

Over—	But not over—	The amount of income tax to withhold is:	of excess over—
$5,775	—$15,300	$0.00 plus 10%	—$5,775
$15,300	—$44,475	$952.50 plus 12%	—$15,300
$44,475	—$88,275	$4,453.50 plus 22%	—$44,475
$88,275	—$163,275	$14,089.50 plus 24%	—$88,275
$163,275	—$205,775	$32,089.50 plus 32%	—$163,275
$205,775	—$305,775	$45,689.50 plus 35%	—$205,775
$305,775		$80,689.50 plus 37%	—$305,775

TABLE 7—ANNUAL Payroll Period

(a) SINGLE person (including head of household)—
If the amount of wages (after subtracting withholding allowances) is:
Not over $3,700 . . . . $0

Over—	But not over—	The amount of income tax to withhold is:	of excess over—
$3,700	—$13,225	$0.00 plus 10%	—$3,700
$13,225	—$42,400	$952.50 plus 12%	—$13,225
$42,400	—$86,200	$4,453.50 plus 22%	—$42,400
$86,200	—$161,200	$14,089.50 plus 24%	—$86,200
$161,200	—$203,700	$32,089.50 plus 32%	—$161,200
$203,700	—$503,700	$45,689.50 plus 35%	—$203,700
$503,700		$150,689.50 plus 37%	—$503,700

(b) MARRIED person—
If the amount of wages (after subtracting withholding allowances) is:
Not over $11,550 . . . . $0

Over—	But not over—	The amount of income tax to withhold is:	of excess over—
$11,550	—$30,600	$0.00 plus 10%	—$11,550
$30,600	—$88,950	$1,905.00 plus 12%	—$30,600
$88,950	—$176,550	$8,907.00 plus 22%	—$88,950
$176,550	—$326,550	$28,179.00 plus 24%	—$176,550
$326,550	—$411,550	$64,179.00 plus 32%	—$326,550
$411,550	—$611,550	$91,379.00 plus 35%	—$411,550
$611,550		$161,379.00 plus 37%	—$611,550

TABLE 8—DAILY or MISCELLANEOUS Payroll Period

(a) SINGLE person (including head of household)—
If the amount of wages (after subtracting withholding allowances) divided by the number of days in the payroll period is:
Not over $14.20 . . . . $0

Over—	But not over—	The amount of income tax to withhold per day is:	of excess over—
$14.20	—$50.90	$0.00 plus 10%	—$14.20
$50.90	—$163.10	$3.67 plus 12%	—$50.90
$163.10	—$331.50	$17.13 plus 22%	—$163.10
$331.50	—$620.00	$54.18 plus 24%	—$331.50
$620.00	—$783.50	$123.42 plus 32%	—$620.00
$783.50	—$1,937.30	$175.74 plus 35%	—$783.50
$1,937.30		$579.57 plus 37%	—$1,937.30

(b) MARRIED person—
If the amount of wages (after subtracting withholding allowances) divided by the number of days in the payroll period is:
Not over $44.40 . . . . $0

Over—	But not over—	The amount of income tax to withhold per day is:	of excess over—
$44.40	—$117.70	$0.00 plus 10%	—$44.40
$117.70	—$342.10	$7.33 plus 12%	—$117.70
$342.10	—$679.00	$34.26 plus 22%	—$342.10
$679.00	—$1,256.00	$108.38 plus 24%	—$679.00
$1,256.00	—$1,582.90	$246.86 plus 32%	—$1,256.00
$1,582.90	—$2,352.10	$351.47 plus 35%	—$1,582.90
$2,352.10		$620.69 plus 37%	—$2,352.10

Images copied from Circular E, Pub. 15, IRS Employer Tax Guide 2018 published on the IRS website WWW.IRS.gov

Appendixes

Appendix H: IRS Wage Bracket Tables for Income Tax Withholding 2018

Wage Bracket Method Tables for Income Tax Withholding

SINGLE Persons—WEEKLY Payroll Period

(For Wages Paid through December 31, 2018)

And the wages are—		And the number of withholding allowances claimed is—										
At least	But less than	0	1	2	3	4	5	6	7	8	9	10
		The amount of income tax to be withheld is—										
$0	$75	$0	$0	$0	$0	$0	$0	$0	$0	$0	$0	$0
75	80	1	0	0	0	0	0	0	0	0	0	0
80	85	1	0	0	0	0	0	0	0	0	0	0
85	90	2	0	0	0	0	0	0	0	0	0	0
90	95	2	0	0	0	0	0	0	0	0	0	0
95	100	3	0	0	0	0	0	0	0	0	0	0
100	105	3	0	0	0	0	0	0	0	0	0	0
105	110	4	0	0	0	0	0	0	0	0	0	0
110	115	4	0	0	0	0	0	0	0	0	0	0
115	120	5	0	0	0	0	0	0	0	0	0	0
120	125	5	0	0	0	0	0	0	0	0	0	0
125	130	6	0	0	0	0	0	0	0	0	0	0
130	135	6	0	0	0	0	0	0	0	0	0	0
135	140	7	0	0	0	0	0	0	0	0	0	0
140	145	7	0	0	0	0	0	0	0	0	0	0
145	150	8	0	0	0	0	0	0	0	0	0	0
150	155	8	0	0	0	0	0	0	0	0	0	0
155	160	9	1	0	0	0	0	0	0	0	0	0
160	165	9	1	0	0	0	0	0	0	0	0	0
165	170	10	2	0	0	0	0	0	0	0	0	0
170	175	10	2	0	0	0	0	0	0	0	0	0
175	180	11	3	0	0	0	0	0	0	0	0	0
180	185	11	3	0	0	0	0	0	0	0	0	0
185	190	12	4	0	0	0	0	0	0	0	0	0
190	195	12	4	0	0	0	0	0	0	0	0	0
195	200	13	5	0	0	0	0	0	0	0	0	0
200	210	13	5	0	0	0	0	0	0	0	0	0
210	220	14	6	0	0	0	0	0	0	0	0	0
220	230	15	7	0	0	0	0	0	0	0	0	0
230	240	16	8	0	0	0	0	0	0	0	0	0
240	250	17	9	1	0	0	0	0	0	0	0	0
250	260	18	10	2	0	0	0	0	0	0	0	0
260	270	20	11	3	0	0	0	0	0	0	0	0
270	280	21	12	4	0	0	0	0	0	0	0	0
280	290	22	13	5	0	0	0	0	0	0	0	0
290	300	23	14	6	0	0	0	0	0	0	0	0
300	310	24	15	7	0	0	0	0	0	0	0	0
310	320	26	16	8	0	0	0	0	0	0	0	0
320	330	27	17	9	1	0	0	0	0	0	0	0
330	340	28	18	10	2	0	0	0	0	0	0	0
340	350	29	20	11	3	0	0	0	0	0	0	0
350	360	30	21	12	4	0	0	0	0	0	0	0
360	370	32	22	13	5	0	0	0	0	0	0	0
370	380	33	23	14	6	0	0	0	0	0	0	0
380	390	34	24	15	7	0	0	0	0	0	0	0
390	400	35	26	16	8	0	0	0	0	0	0	0
400	410	36	27	17	9	1	0	0	0	0	0	0
410	420	38	28	18	10	2	0	0	0	0	0	0
420	430	39	29	20	11	3	0	0	0	0	0	0
430	440	40	30	21	12	4	0	0	0	0	0	0
440	450	41	32	22	13	5	0	0	0	0	0	0
450	460	42	33	23	14	6	0	0	0	0	0	0
460	470	44	34	24	15	7	0	0	0	0	0	0
470	480	45	35	26	16	8	0	0	0	0	0	0
480	490	46	36	27	17	9	1	0	0	0	0	0
490	500	47	38	28	18	10	2	0	0	0	0	0
500	510	48	39	29	20	11	3	0	0	0	0	0
510	520	50	40	30	21	12	4	0	0	0	0	0
520	530	51	41	32	22	13	5	0	0	0	0	0
530	540	52	42	33	23	14	6	0	0	0	0	0
540	550	53	44	34	24	15	7	0	0	0	0	0
550	560	54	45	35	26	16	8	1	0	0	0	0
560	570	56	46	36	27	17	9	2	0	0	0	0
570	580	57	47	38	28	18	10	3	0	0	0	0
580	590	58	48	39	29	20	11	4	0	0	0	0
590	600	59	50	40	30	21	12	5	0	0	0	0
600	610	60	51	41	32	22	13	6	0	0	0	0
610	620	62	52	42	33	23	14	7	0	0	0	0
620	630	63	53	44	34	24	15	8	0	0	0	0
630	640	64	54	45	35	26	16	9	1	0	0	0

Images copied from Circular E, Pub. 15, IRS Employer Tax Guide 2018 published on the IRS website WWW.IRS.gov

Wage Bracket Method Tables for Income Tax Withholding

SINGLE Persons—WEEKLY Payroll Period

(For Wages Paid through December 31, 2018)

And the wages are—		And the number of withholding allowances claimed is—										
At least	But less than	0	1	2	3	4	5	6	7	8	9	10
		The amount of income tax to be withheld is—										
$640	$650	$65	$56	$46	$36	$27	$17	$10	$2	$0	$0	$0
650	660	66	57	47	38	28	19	11	3	0	0	0
660	670	68	58	48	39	29	20	12	4	0	0	0
670	680	69	59	50	40	30	21	13	5	0	0	0
680	690	70	60	51	41	32	22	14	6	0	0	0
690	700	71	62	52	42	33	23	15	7	0	0	0
700	710	72	63	53	44	34	25	16	8	0	0	0
710	720	74	64	54	45	35	26	17	9	1	0	0
720	730	75	65	56	46	36	27	18	10	2	0	0
730	740	76	66	57	47	38	28	19	11	3	0	0
740	750	77	68	58	48	39	29	20	12	4	0	0
750	760	78	69	59	50	40	31	21	13	5	0	0
760	770	80	70	60	51	41	32	22	14	6	0	0
770	780	81	71	62	52	42	33	23	15	7	0	0
780	790	82	72	63	53	44	34	25	16	8	0	0
790	800	83	74	64	54	45	35	26	17	9	1	0
800	810	84	75	65	56	46	37	27	18	10	2	0
810	820	86	76	66	57	47	38	28	19	11	3	0
820	830	88	77	68	58	48	39	29	20	12	4	0
830	840	90	78	69	59	50	40	31	21	13	5	0
840	850	92	80	70	60	51	41	32	22	14	6	0
850	860	94	81	71	62	52	43	33	23	15	7	0
860	870	97	82	72	63	53	44	34	25	16	8	0
870	880	99	83	74	64	54	45	35	26	17	9	1
880	890	101	84	75	65	56	46	37	27	18	10	2
890	900	103	86	76	66	57	47	38	28	19	11	3
900	910	105	88	77	68	58	49	39	29	20	12	4
910	920	108	90	78	69	59	50	40	31	21	13	5
920	930	110	92	80	70	60	51	41	32	22	14	6
930	940	112	94	81	71	62	52	43	33	23	15	7
940	950	114	97	82	72	63	53	44	34	25	16	8
950	960	116	99	83	74	64	55	45	35	26	17	9
960	970	119	101	84	75	65	56	46	37	27	18	10
970	980	121	103	86	76	66	57	47	38	28	19	11
980	990	123	105	88	77	68	58	49	39	29	20	12
990	1,000	125	108	90	78	69	59	50	40	31	21	13
1,000	1,010	127	110	92	80	70	61	51	41	32	22	14
1,010	1,020	130	112	94	81	71	62	52	43	33	23	15
1,020	1,030	132	114	97	82	72	63	53	44	34	25	16
1,030	1,040	134	116	99	83	74	64	55	45	35	26	17
1,040	1,050	136	119	101	84	75	65	56	46	37	27	18
1,050	1,060	138	121	103	86	76	67	57	47	38	28	19
1,060	1,070	141	123	105	88	77	68	58	49	39	29	20
1,070	1,080	143	125	108	90	78	69	59	50	40	31	21
1,080	1,090	145	127	110	92	80	70	61	51	41	32	22
1,090	1,100	147	130	112	94	81	71	62	52	43	33	23
1,100	1,110	149	132	114	97	82	73	63	53	44	34	25
1,110	1,120	152	134	116	99	83	74	64	55	45	35	26
1,120	1,130	154	136	119	101	84	75	65	56	46	37	27
1,130	1,140	156	138	121	103	86	76	67	57	47	38	28
1,140	1,150	158	141	123	105	88	77	68	58	49	39	29
1,150	1,160	160	143	125	108	90	79	69	59	50	40	31
1,160	1,170	163	145	127	110	92	80	70	61	51	41	32
1,170	1,180	165	147	130	112	95	81	71	62	52	43	33
1,180	1,190	167	149	132	114	97	82	73	63	53	44	34
1,190	1,200	169	152	134	116	99	83	74	64	55	45	35
1,200	1,210	171	154	136	119	101	85	75	65	56	46	37
1,210	1,220	174	156	138	121	103	86	76	67	57	47	38
1,220	1,230	176	158	141	123	106	88	77	68	58	49	39
1,230	1,240	178	160	143	125	108	90	79	69	59	50	40
1,240	1,250	180	163	145	127	110	92	80	70	61	51	41
1,250	1,260	182	165	147	130	112	95	81	71	62	52	43
1,260	1,270	185	167	149	132	114	97	82	73	63	53	44
1,270	1,280	187	169	152	134	117	99	83	74	64	55	45
1,280	1,290	189	171	154	136	119	101	85	75	65	56	46

$1,290 and over — Use Table 1(a) for a SINGLE person on page 46. Also see the instructions on page 44.

Images copied from Circular E, Pub. 15, IRS Employer Tax Guide 2018 published on the IRS website WWW.IRS.gov

Appendixes

Wage Bracket Method Tables for Income Tax Withholding

MARRIED Persons—WEEKLY Payroll Period

(For Wages Paid through December 31, 2018)

And the wages are—		And the number of withholding allowances claimed is—										
At least	But less than	0	1	2	3	4	5	6	7	8	9	10
		The amount of income tax to be withheld is—										
$0	$225	$0	$0	$0	$0	$0	$0	$0	$0	$0	$0	$0
225	235	1	0	0	0	0	0	0	0	0	0	0
235	245	2	0	0	0	0	0	0	0	0	0	0
245	255	3	0	0	0	0	0	0	0	0	0	0
255	265	4	0	0	0	0	0	0	0	0	0	0
265	275	5	0	0	0	0	0	0	0	0	0	0
275	285	6	0	0	0	0	0	0	0	0	0	0
285	295	7	0	0	0	0	0	0	0	0	0	0
295	305	8	0	0	0	0	0	0	0	0	0	0
305	315	9	1	0	0	0	0	0	0	0	0	0
315	325	10	2	0	0	0	0	0	0	0	0	0
325	335	11	3	0	0	0	0	0	0	0	0	0
335	345	12	4	0	0	0	0	0	0	0	0	0
345	355	13	5	0	0	0	0	0	0	0	0	0
355	365	14	6	0	0	0	0	0	0	0	0	0
365	375	15	7	0	0	0	0	0	0	0	0	0
375	385	16	8	0	0	0	0	0	0	0	0	0
385	395	17	9	1	0	0	0	0	0	0	0	0
395	405	18	10	2	0	0	0	0	0	0	0	0
405	415	19	11	3	0	0	0	0	0	0	0	0
415	425	20	12	4	0	0	0	0	0	0	0	0
425	435	21	13	5	0	0	0	0	0	0	0	0
435	445	22	14	6	0	0	0	0	0	0	0	0
445	455	23	15	7	0	0	0	0	0	0	0	0
455	465	24	16	8	0	0	0	0	0	0	0	0
465	475	25	17	9	1	0	0	0	0	0	0	0
475	485	26	18	10	2	0	0	0	0	0	0	0
485	495	27	19	11	3	0	0	0	0	0	0	0
495	505	28	20	12	4	0	0	0	0	0	0	0
505	515	29	21	13	5	0	0	0	0	0	0	0
515	525	30	22	14	6	0	0	0	0	0	0	0
525	535	31	23	15	7	0	0	0	0	0	0	0
535	545	32	24	16	8	0	0	0	0	0	0	0
545	555	33	25	17	9	1	0	0	0	0	0	0
555	565	34	26	18	10	2	0	0	0	0	0	0
565	575	35	27	19	11	3	0	0	0	0	0	0
575	585	36	28	20	12	4	0	0	0	0	0	0
585	595	37	29	21	13	5	0	0	0	0	0	0
595	605	38	30	22	14	6	0	0	0	0	0	0
605	615	39	31	23	15	7	0	0	0	0	0	0
615	625	40	32	24	16	8	0	0	0	0	0	0
625	635	42	33	25	17	9	1	0	0	0	0	0
635	645	43	34	26	18	10	2	0	0	0	0	0
645	655	44	35	27	19	11	3	0	0	0	0	0
655	665	45	36	28	20	12	4	0	0	0	0	0
665	675	46	37	29	21	13	5	0	0	0	0	0
675	685	48	38	30	22	14	6	0	0	0	0	0
685	695	49	39	31	23	15	7	0	0	0	0	0
695	705	50	40	32	24	16	8	0	0	0	0	0
705	715	51	42	33	25	17	9	1	0	0	0	0
715	725	52	43	34	26	18	10	2	0	0	0	0
725	735	54	44	35	27	19	11	3	0	0	0	0
735	745	55	45	36	28	20	12	4	0	0	0	0
745	755	56	46	37	29	21	13	5	0	0	0	0
755	765	57	48	38	30	22	14	6	0	0	0	0
765	775	58	49	39	31	23	15	7	0	0	0	0
775	785	60	50	40	32	24	16	8	0	0	0	0
785	795	61	51	42	33	25	17	9	1	0	0	0
795	805	62	52	43	34	26	18	10	2	0	0	0
805	815	63	54	44	35	27	19	11	3	0	0	0
815	825	64	55	45	36	28	20	12	4	0	0	0
825	835	66	56	46	37	29	21	13	5	0	0	0
835	845	67	57	48	38	30	22	14	6	0	0	0
845	855	68	58	49	39	31	23	15	7	0	0	0
855	865	69	60	50	40	32	24	16	8	0	0	0
865	875	70	61	51	42	33	25	17	9	1	0	0
875	885	72	62	52	43	34	26	18	10	2	0	0
885	895	73	63	54	44	35	27	19	11	3	0	0
895	905	74	64	55	45	36	28	20	12	4	0	0
905	915	75	66	56	46	37	29	21	13	5	0	0

Images copied from Circular E, Pub. 15, IRS Employer Tax Guide 2018 published on the IRS website WWW.IRS.gov

Wage Bracket Method Tables for Income Tax Withholding

MARRIED Persons—WEEKLY Payroll Period

(For Wages Paid through December 31, 2018)

And the wages are—		And the number of withholding allowances claimed is—										
At least	But less than	0	1	2	3	4	5	6	7	8	9	10
		The amount of income tax to be withheld is—										
$915	$925	$76	$67	$57	$48	$38	$30	$22	$14	$6	$0	$0
925	935	78	68	58	49	39	31	23	15	7	0	0
935	945	79	69	60	50	41	32	24	16	8	0	0
945	955	80	70	61	51	42	33	25	17	9	1	0
955	965	81	72	62	52	43	34	26	18	10	2	0
965	975	82	73	63	54	44	35	27	19	11	3	0
975	985	84	74	64	55	45	36	28	20	12	4	0
985	995	85	75	66	56	47	37	29	21	13	5	0
995	1,005	86	76	67	57	48	38	30	22	14	6	0
1,005	1,015	87	78	68	58	49	39	31	23	15	7	0
1,015	1,025	88	79	69	60	50	41	32	24	16	8	0
1,025	1,035	90	80	70	61	51	42	33	25	17	9	1
1,035	1,045	91	81	72	62	53	43	34	26	18	10	2
1,045	1,055	92	82	73	63	54	44	35	27	19	11	3
1,055	1,065	93	84	74	64	55	45	36	28	20	12	4
1,065	1,075	94	85	75	66	56	47	37	29	21	13	5
1,075	1,085	96	86	76	67	57	48	38	30	22	14	6
1,085	1,095	97	87	78	68	59	49	39	31	23	15	7
1,095	1,105	98	88	79	69	60	50	41	32	24	16	8
1,105	1,115	99	90	80	70	61	51	42	33	25	17	9
1,115	1,125	100	91	81	72	62	53	43	34	26	18	10
1,125	1,135	102	92	82	73	63	54	44	35	27	19	11
1,135	1,145	103	93	84	74	65	55	45	36	28	20	12
1,145	1,155	104	94	85	75	66	56	47	37	29	21	13
1,155	1,165	105	96	86	76	67	57	48	38	30	22	14
1,165	1,175	106	97	87	78	68	59	49	39	31	23	15
1,175	1,185	108	98	88	79	69	60	50	41	32	24	16
1,185	1,195	109	99	90	80	71	61	51	42	33	25	17
1,195	1,205	110	100	91	81	72	62	53	43	34	26	18
1,205	1,215	111	102	92	82	73	63	54	44	35	27	19
1,215	1,225	112	103	93	84	74	65	55	45	36	28	20
1,225	1,235	114	104	94	85	75	66	56	47	37	29	21
1,235	1,245	115	105	96	86	77	67	57	48	38	30	22
1,245	1,255	116	106	97	87	78	68	59	49	39	31	23
1,255	1,265	117	108	98	88	79	69	60	50	41	32	24
1,265	1,275	118	109	99	90	80	71	61	51	42	33	25
1,275	1,285	120	110	100	91	81	72	62	53	43	34	26
1,285	1,295	121	111	102	92	83	73	63	54	44	35	27
1,295	1,305	122	112	103	93	84	74	65	55	45	36	28
1,305	1,315	123	114	104	94	85	75	66	56	47	37	29
1,315	1,325	124	115	105	96	86	77	67	57	48	38	30
1,325	1,335	126	116	106	97	87	78	68	59	49	39	31
1,335	1,345	127	117	108	98	89	79	69	60	50	41	32
1,345	1,355	128	118	109	99	90	80	71	61	51	42	33
1,355	1,365	129	120	110	100	91	81	72	62	53	43	34
1,365	1,375	130	121	111	102	92	83	73	63	54	44	35
1,375	1,385	132	122	112	103	93	84	74	65	55	45	36
1,385	1,395	133	123	114	104	95	85	75	66	56	47	37
1,395	1,405	134	124	115	105	96	86	77	67	57	48	38
1,405	1,415	135	126	116	106	97	87	78	68	59	49	39
1,415	1,425	136	127	117	108	98	89	79	69	60	50	41
1,425	1,435	138	128	118	109	99	90	80	71	61	51	42
1,435	1,445	139	129	120	110	101	91	81	72	62	53	43
1,445	1,455	140	130	121	111	102	92	83	73	63	54	44
1,455	1,465	141	132	122	112	103	93	84	74	65	55	45
1,465	1,475	142	133	123	114	104	95	85	75	66	56	47
1,475	1,485	144	134	124	115	105	96	86	77	67	57	48
1,485	1,495	145	135	126	116	107	97	87	78	68	59	49
1,495	1,505	146	136	127	117	108	98	89	79	69	60	50
1,505	1,515	147	138	128	118	109	99	90	80	71	61	51
1,515	1,525	148	139	129	120	110	101	91	81	72	62	53
1,525	1,535	150	140	130	121	111	102	92	83	73	63	54
1,535	1,545	151	141	132	122	113	103	93	84	74	65	55
1,545	1,555	152	142	133	123	114	104	95	85	75	66	56
1,555	1,565	153	144	134	124	115	105	96	86	77	67	57
1,565	1,575	154	145	135	126	116	107	97	87	78	68	59

$1,575 and over   Use Table 1(b) for a MARRIED person on page 46. Also see the instructions on page 44.

Images copied from Circular E, Pub. 15, IRS Employer Tax Guide 2018 published on the IRS website WWW.IRS.gov

Appendixes

Wage Bracket Method Tables for Income Tax Withholding
SINGLE Persons—BIWEEKLY Payroll Period
(For Wages Paid through December 31, 2018)

And the wages are—		And the number of withholding allowances claimed is—										
At least	But less than	0	1	2	3	4	5	6	7	8	9	10
		The amount of income tax to be withheld is—										
$0	$145	$0	$0	$0	$0	$0	$0	$0	$0	$0	$0	$0
145	150	1	0	0	0	0	0	0	0	0	0	0
150	155	1	0	0	0	0	0	0	0	0	0	0
155	160	2	0	0	0	0	0	0	0	0	0	0
160	165	2	0	0	0	0	0	0	0	0	0	0
165	170	3	0	0	0	0	0	0	0	0	0	0
170	175	3	0	0	0	0	0	0	0	0	0	0
175	180	4	0	0	0	0	0	0	0	0	0	0
180	185	4	0	0	0	0	0	0	0	0	0	0
185	190	5	0	0	0	0	0	0	0	0	0	0
190	195	5	0	0	0	0	0	0	0	0	0	0
195	200	6	0	0	0	0	0	0	0	0	0	0
200	205	6	0	0	0	0	0	0	0	0	0	0
205	210	7	0	0	0	0	0	0	0	0	0	0
210	215	7	0	0	0	0	0	0	0	0	0	0
215	220	8	0	0	0	0	0	0	0	0	0	0
220	225	8	0	0	0	0	0	0	0	0	0	0
225	230	9	0	0	0	0	0	0	0	0	0	0
230	235	9	0	0	0	0	0	0	0	0	0	0
235	240	10	0	0	0	0	0	0	0	0	0	0
240	245	10	0	0	0	0	0	0	0	0	0	0
245	250	11	0	0	0	0	0	0	0	0	0	0
250	260	11	0	0	0	0	0	0	0	0	0	0
260	270	12	0	0	0	0	0	0	0	0	0	0
270	280	13	0	0	0	0	0	0	0	0	0	0
280	290	14	0	0	0	0	0	0	0	0	0	0
290	300	15	0	0	0	0	0	0	0	0	0	0
300	310	16	0	0	0	0	0	0	0	0	0	0
310	320	17	1	0	0	0	0	0	0	0	0	0
320	330	18	2	0	0	0	0	0	0	0	0	0
330	340	19	3	0	0	0	0	0	0	0	0	0
340	350	20	4	0	0	0	0	0	0	0	0	0
350	360	21	5	0	0	0	0	0	0	0	0	0
360	370	22	6	0	0	0	0	0	0	0	0	0
370	380	23	7	0	0	0	0	0	0	0	0	0
380	390	24	8	0	0	0	0	0	0	0	0	0
390	400	25	9	0	0	0	0	0	0	0	0	0
400	410	26	10	0	0	0	0	0	0	0	0	0
410	420	27	11	0	0	0	0	0	0	0	0	0
420	430	28	12	0	0	0	0	0	0	0	0	0
430	440	29	13	0	0	0	0	0	0	0	0	0
440	450	30	14	0	0	0	0	0	0	0	0	0
450	460	31	15	0	0	0	0	0	0	0	0	0
460	470	32	16	0	0	0	0	0	0	0	0	0
470	480	33	17	1	0	0	0	0	0	0	0	0
480	490	34	18	2	0	0	0	0	0	0	0	0
490	500	35	19	3	0	0	0	0	0	0	0	0
500	520	37	21	5	0	0	0	0	0	0	0	0
520	540	39	23	7	0	0	0	0	0	0	0	0
540	560	42	25	9	0	0	0	0	0	0	0	0
560	580	44	27	11	0	0	0	0	0	0	0	0
580	600	46	29	13	0	0	0	0	0	0	0	0
600	620	49	31	15	0	0	0	0	0	0	0	0
620	640	51	33	17	1	0	0	0	0	0	0	0
640	660	54	35	19	3	0	0	0	0	0	0	0
660	680	56	37	21	5	0	0	0	0	0	0	0
680	700	58	39	23	7	0	0	0	0	0	0	0
700	720	61	42	25	9	0	0	0	0	0	0	0
720	740	63	44	27	11	0	0	0	0	0	0	0
740	760	66	46	29	13	0	0	0	0	0	0	0
760	780	68	49	31	15	0	0	0	0	0	0	0
780	800	70	51	33	17	1	0	0	0	0	0	0
800	820	73	54	35	19	3	0	0	0	0	0	0
820	840	75	56	37	21	5	0	0	0	0	0	0
840	860	78	58	39	23	7	0	0	0	0	0	0
860	880	80	61	42	25	9	0	0	0	0	0	0
880	900	82	63	44	27	11	0	0	0	0	0	0
900	920	85	66	46	29	13	0	0	0	0	0	0
920	940	87	68	49	31	15	0	0	0	0	0	0
940	960	90	70	51	33	17	1	0	0	0	0	0

Images copied from Circular E, Pub. 15, IRS Employer Tax Guide 2018 published on the IRS website WWW.IRS.gov

Wage Bracket Method Tables for Income Tax Withholding

SINGLE Persons—BIWEEKLY Payroll Period
(For Wages Paid through December 31, 2018)

And the wages are—		And the number of withholding allowances claimed is—										
At least	But less than	0	1	2	3	4	5	6	7	8	9	10
		The amount of income tax to be withheld is—										
$960	$980	$92	$73	$54	$35	$19	$3	$0	$0	$0	$0	$0
980	1,000	94	75	56	37	21	5	0	0	0	0	0
1,000	1,020	97	78	58	39	23	7	0	0	0	0	0
1,020	1,040	99	80	61	42	25	9	0	0	0	0	0
1,040	1,060	102	82	63	44	27	11	0	0	0	0	0
1,060	1,080	104	85	66	47	29	13	0	0	0	0	0
1,080	1,100	106	87	68	49	31	15	0	0	0	0	0
1,100	1,120	109	90	70	51	33	17	1	0	0	0	0
1,120	1,140	111	92	73	54	35	19	3	0	0	0	0
1,140	1,160	114	94	75	56	37	21	5	0	0	0	0
1,160	1,180	116	97	78	59	39	23	7	0	0	0	0
1,180	1,200	118	99	80	61	42	25	9	0	0	0	0
1,200	1,220	121	102	82	63	44	27	11	0	0	0	0
1,220	1,240	123	104	85	66	47	29	13	0	0	0	0
1,240	1,260	126	106	87	68	49	31	15	0	0	0	0
1,260	1,280	128	109	90	71	51	33	17	1	0	0	0
1,280	1,300	130	111	92	73	54	35	19	3	0	0	0
1,300	1,320	133	114	94	75	56	37	21	5	0	0	0
1,320	1,340	135	116	97	78	59	39	23	7	0	0	0
1,340	1,360	138	118	99	80	61	42	25	9	0	0	0
1,360	1,380	140	121	102	83	63	44	27	11	0	0	0
1,380	1,400	142	123	104	85	66	47	29	13	0	0	0
1,400	1,420	145	126	106	87	68	49	31	15	0	0	0
1,420	1,440	147	128	109	90	71	51	33	17	1	0	0
1,440	1,460	150	130	111	92	73	54	35	19	3	0	0
1,460	1,480	152	133	114	95	75	56	37	21	5	0	0
1,480	1,500	154	135	116	97	78	59	39	23	7	0	0
1,500	1,520	157	138	118	99	80	61	42	25	9	0	0
1,520	1,540	159	140	121	102	83	63	44	27	11	0	0
1,540	1,560	162	142	123	104	85	66	47	29	13	0	0
1,560	1,580	164	145	126	107	87	68	49	31	15	0	0
1,580	1,600	166	147	128	109	90	71	51	33	17	1	0
1,600	1,620	169	150	130	111	92	73	54	35	19	3	0
1,620	1,640	171	152	133	114	95	75	56	37	21	5	0
1,640	1,660	176	154	135	116	97	78	59	40	23	7	0
1,660	1,680	180	157	138	119	99	80	61	42	25	9	0
1,680	1,700	184	159	140	121	102	83	63	44	27	11	0
1,700	1,720	189	162	142	123	104	85	66	47	29	13	0
1,720	1,740	193	164	145	126	107	87	68	49	31	15	0
1,740	1,760	198	166	147	128	109	90	71	52	33	17	1
1,760	1,780	202	169	150	131	111	92	73	54	35	19	3
1,780	1,800	206	171	152	133	114	95	75	56	37	21	5
1,800	1,820	211	176	154	135	116	97	78	59	40	23	7
1,820	1,840	215	180	157	138	119	99	80	61	42	25	9
1,840	1,860	220	184	159	140	121	102	83	64	44	27	11
1,860	1,880	224	189	162	143	123	104	85	66	47	29	13
1,880	1,900	228	193	164	145	126	107	87	68	49	31	15
1,900	1,920	233	198	166	147	128	109	90	71	52	33	17
1,920	1,940	237	202	169	150	131	111	92	73	54	35	19
1,940	1,960	242	206	171	152	133	114	95	76	56	37	21
1,960	1,980	246	211	176	155	135	116	97	78	59	40	23
1,980	2,000	250	215	180	157	138	119	99	80	61	42	25
2,000	2,020	255	220	184	159	140	121	102	83	64	44	27
2,020	2,040	259	224	189	162	143	123	104	85	66	47	29
2,040	2,060	264	228	193	164	145	126	107	88	68	49	31
2,060	2,080	268	233	198	167	147	128	109	90	71	52	33
2,080	2,100	272	237	202	169	150	131	111	92	73	54	35
2,100	2,120	277	242	206	171	152	133	114	95	76	56	37
2,120	2,140	281	246	211	176	155	135	116	97	78	59	40
2,140	2,160	286	250	215	180	157	138	119	100	80	61	42
2,160	2,180	290	255	220	185	159	140	121	102	83	64	44
2,180	2,200	294	259	224	189	162	143	123	104	85	66	47
2,200	2,220	299	264	228	193	164	145	126	107	88	68	49
2,220	2,240	303	268	233	198	167	147	128	109	90	71	52
2,240	2,260	308	272	237	202	169	150	131	112	92	73	54

$2,260 and over   Use Table 2(a) for a SINGLE person on page 46. Also see the instructions on page 44.

Images copied from Circular E, Pub. 15, IRS Employer Tax Guide 2018 published on the IRS website WWW.IRS.gov

Appendixes

Wage Bracket Method Tables for Income Tax Withholding

MARRIED Persons—BIWEEKLY Payroll Period

(For Wages Paid through December 31, 2018)

And the wages are—		And the number of withholding allowances claimed is—										
At least	But less than	0	1	2	3	4	5	6	7	8	9	10
		The amount of income tax to be withheld is—										
$0	$445	$0	$0	$0	$0	$0	$0	$0	$0	$0	$0	$0
445	455	1	0	0	0	0	0	0	0	0	0	0
455	465	2	0	0	0	0	0	0	0	0	0	0
465	475	3	0	0	0	0	0	0	0	0	0	0
475	485	4	0	0	0	0	0	0	0	0	0	0
485	495	5	0	0	0	0	0	0	0	0	0	0
495	505	6	0	0	0	0	0	0	0	0	0	0
505	525	7	0	0	0	0	0	0	0	0	0	0
525	545	9	0	0	0	0	0	0	0	0	0	0
545	565	11	0	0	0	0	0	0	0	0	0	0
565	585	13	0	0	0	0	0	0	0	0	0	0
585	605	15	0	0	0	0	0	0	0	0	0	0
605	625	17	1	0	0	0	0	0	0	0	0	0
625	645	19	3	0	0	0	0	0	0	0	0	0
645	665	21	5	0	0	0	0	0	0	0	0	0
665	685	23	7	0	0	0	0	0	0	0	0	0
685	705	25	9	0	0	0	0	0	0	0	0	0
705	725	27	11	0	0	0	0	0	0	0	0	0
725	745	29	13	0	0	0	0	0	0	0	0	0
745	765	31	15	0	0	0	0	0	0	0	0	0
765	785	33	17	1	0	0	0	0	0	0	0	0
785	805	35	19	3	0	0	0	0	0	0	0	0
805	825	37	21	5	0	0	0	0	0	0	0	0
825	845	39	23	7	0	0	0	0	0	0	0	0
845	865	41	25	9	0	0	0	0	0	0	0	0
865	885	43	27	11	0	0	0	0	0	0	0	0
885	905	45	29	13	0	0	0	0	0	0	0	0
905	925	47	31	15	0	0	0	0	0	0	0	0
925	945	49	33	17	1	0	0	0	0	0	0	0
945	965	51	35	19	3	0	0	0	0	0	0	0
965	985	53	37	21	5	0	0	0	0	0	0	0
985	1,005	55	39	23	7	0	0	0	0	0	0	0
1,005	1,025	57	41	25	9	0	0	0	0	0	0	0
1,025	1,045	59	43	27	11	0	0	0	0	0	0	0
1,045	1,065	61	45	29	13	0	0	0	0	0	0	0
1,065	1,085	63	47	31	15	0	0	0	0	0	0	0
1,085	1,105	65	49	33	17	1	0	0	0	0	0	0
1,105	1,125	67	51	35	19	3	0	0	0	0	0	0
1,125	1,145	69	53	37	21	5	0	0	0	0	0	0
1,145	1,165	71	55	39	23	7	0	0	0	0	0	0
1,165	1,185	73	57	41	25	9	0	0	0	0	0	0
1,185	1,205	75	59	43	27	11	0	0	0	0	0	0
1,205	1,225	78	61	45	29	13	0	0	0	0	0	0
1,225	1,245	80	63	47	31	15	0	0	0	0	0	0
1,245	1,265	83	65	49	33	17	1	0	0	0	0	0
1,265	1,285	85	67	51	35	19	3	0	0	0	0	0
1,285	1,305	87	69	53	37	21	5	0	0	0	0	0
1,305	1,325	90	71	55	39	23	7	0	0	0	0	0
1,325	1,345	92	73	57	41	25	9	0	0	0	0	0
1,345	1,365	95	75	59	43	27	11	0	0	0	0	0
1,365	1,385	97	78	61	45	29	13	0	0	0	0	0
1,385	1,405	99	80	63	47	31	15	0	0	0	0	0
1,405	1,425	102	83	65	49	33	17	1	0	0	0	0
1,425	1,445	104	85	67	51	35	19	3	0	0	0	0
1,445	1,465	107	87	69	53	37	21	5	0	0	0	0
1,465	1,485	109	90	71	55	39	23	7	0	0	0	0
1,485	1,505	111	92	73	57	41	25	9	0	0	0	0
1,505	1,525	114	95	76	59	43	27	11	0	0	0	0
1,525	1,545	116	97	78	61	45	29	13	0	0	0	0
1,545	1,565	119	99	80	63	47	31	15	0	0	0	0
1,565	1,585	121	102	83	65	49	33	17	1	0	0	0
1,585	1,605	123	104	85	67	51	35	19	3	0	0	0
1,605	1,625	126	107	88	69	53	37	21	5	0	0	0
1,625	1,645	128	109	90	71	55	39	23	7	0	0	0
1,645	1,665	131	111	92	73	57	41	25	9	0	0	0
1,665	1,685	133	114	95	76	59	43	27	11	0	0	0
1,685	1,705	135	116	97	78	61	45	29	13	0	0	0
1,705	1,725	138	119	100	80	63	47	31	15	0	0	0
1,725	1,745	140	121	102	83	65	49	33	17	1	0	0
1,745	1,765	143	123	104	85	67	51	35	19	3	0	0

Images copied from Circular E, Pub. 15, IRS Employer Tax Guide 2018 published on the IRS website WWW.IRS.gov

Wage Bracket Method Tables for Income Tax Withholding

MARRIED Persons—BIWEEKLY Payroll Period

(For Wages Paid through December 31, 2018)

And the wages are—		And the number of withholding allowances claimed is—										
At least	But less than	0	1	2	3	4	5	6	7	8	9	10
		The amount of income tax to be withheld is—										
$1,765	$1,785	$145	$126	$107	$88	$69	$53	$37	$21	$5	$0	$0
1,785	1,805	147	128	109	90	71	55	39	23	7	0	0
1,805	1,825	150	131	112	92	73	57	41	25	9	0	0
1,825	1,845	152	133	114	95	76	59	43	27	11	0	0
1,845	1,865	155	135	116	97	78	61	45	29	13	0	0
1,865	1,885	157	138	119	100	80	63	47	31	15	0	0
1,885	1,905	159	140	121	102	83	65	49	33	17	1	0
1,905	1,925	162	143	124	104	85	67	51	35	19	3	0
1,925	1,945	164	145	126	107	88	69	53	37	21	5	0
1,945	1,965	167	147	128	109	90	71	55	39	23	7	0
1,965	1,985	169	150	131	112	92	73	57	41	25	9	0
1,985	2,005	171	152	133	114	95	76	59	43	27	11	0
2,005	2,025	174	155	136	116	97	78	61	45	29	13	0
2,025	2,045	176	157	138	119	100	80	63	47	31	15	0
2,045	2,065	179	159	140	121	102	83	65	49	33	17	1
2,065	2,085	181	162	143	124	104	85	67	51	35	19	3
2,085	2,105	183	164	145	126	107	88	69	53	37	21	5
2,105	2,125	186	167	148	128	109	90	71	55	39	23	7
2,125	2,145	188	169	150	131	112	92	73	57	41	25	9
2,145	2,165	191	171	152	133	114	95	76	59	43	27	11
2,165	2,185	193	174	155	136	116	97	78	61	45	29	13
2,185	2,205	195	176	157	138	119	100	81	63	47	31	15
2,205	2,225	198	179	160	140	121	102	83	65	49	33	17
2,225	2,245	200	181	162	143	124	104	85	67	51	35	19
2,245	2,265	203	183	164	145	126	107	88	69	53	37	21
2,265	2,285	205	186	167	148	128	109	90	71	55	39	23
2,285	2,305	207	188	169	150	131	112	93	73	57	41	25
2,305	2,325	210	191	172	152	133	114	95	76	59	43	27
2,325	2,345	212	193	174	155	136	116	97	78	61	45	29
2,345	2,365	215	195	176	157	138	119	100	81	63	47	31
2,365	2,385	217	198	179	160	140	121	102	83	65	49	33
2,385	2,405	219	200	181	162	143	124	105	85	67	51	35
2,405	2,425	222	203	184	164	145	126	107	88	69	53	37
2,425	2,445	224	205	186	167	148	128	109	90	71	55	39
2,445	2,465	227	207	188	169	150	131	112	93	73	57	41
2,465	2,485	229	210	191	172	152	133	114	95	76	59	43
2,485	2,505	231	212	193	174	155	136	117	97	78	61	45
2,505	2,525	234	215	196	176	157	138	119	100	81	63	47
2,525	2,545	236	217	198	179	160	140	121	102	83	65	49
2,545	2,565	239	219	200	181	162	143	124	105	85	67	51
2,565	2,585	241	222	203	184	164	145	126	107	88	69	53
2,585	2,605	243	224	205	186	167	148	129	109	90	71	55
2,605	2,625	246	227	208	188	169	150	131	112	93	73	57
2,625	2,645	248	229	210	191	172	152	133	114	95	76	59
2,645	2,665	251	231	212	193	174	155	136	117	97	78	61
2,665	2,685	253	234	215	196	176	157	138	119	100	81	63
2,685	2,705	255	236	217	198	179	160	141	121	102	83	65
2,705	2,725	258	239	220	200	181	162	143	124	105	85	67
2,725	2,745	260	241	222	203	184	164	145	126	107	88	69
2,745	2,765	263	243	224	205	186	167	148	129	109	90	71
2,765	2,785	265	246	227	208	188	169	150	131	112	93	74
2,785	2,805	267	248	229	210	191	172	153	133	114	95	76
2,805	2,825	270	251	232	212	193	174	155	136	117	97	78
2,825	2,845	272	253	234	215	196	176	157	138	119	100	81
2,845	2,865	275	255	236	217	198	179	160	141	121	102	83
2,865	2,885	277	258	239	220	200	181	162	143	124	105	86
2,885	2,905	279	260	241	222	203	184	165	145	126	107	88
2,905	2,925	282	263	244	224	205	186	167	148	129	109	90
2,925	2,945	284	265	246	227	208	188	169	150	131	112	93
2,945	2,965	287	267	248	229	210	191	172	153	133	114	95
2,965	2,985	289	270	251	232	212	193	174	155	136	117	98
2,985	3,005	291	272	253	234	215	196	177	157	138	119	100
3,005	3,025	294	275	256	236	217	198	179	160	141	121	102
3,025	3,045	296	277	258	239	220	200	181	162	143	124	105
3,045	3,065	299	279	260	241	222	203	184	165	145	126	107
3,065	3,085	301	282	263	244	224	205	186	167	148	129	110

$3,085 and over   Use Table 2(b) for a MARRIED person on page 46. Also see the instructions on page 44.

Images copied from Circular E, Pub. 15, IRS Employer Tax Guide 2018 published on the IRS website WWW.IRS.gov

Appendixes

Wage Bracket Method Tables for Income Tax Withholding

SINGLE Persons—SEMIMONTHLY Payroll Period
(For Wages Paid through December 31, 2018)

And the wages are—		And the number of withholding allowances claimed is—										
At least	But less than	0	1	2	3	4	5	6	7	8	9	10
		The amount of income tax to be withheld is—										
$0	$160	$0	$0	$0	$0	$0	$0	$0	$0	$0	$0	$0
160	165	1	0	0	0	0	0	0	0	0	0	0
165	170	1	0	0	0	0	0	0	0	0	0	0
170	175	2	0	0	0	0	0	0	0	0	0	0
175	180	2	0	0	0	0	0	0	0	0	0	0
180	185	3	0	0	0	0	0	0	0	0	0	0
185	190	3	0	0	0	0	0	0	0	0	0	0
190	195	4	0	0	0	0	0	0	0	0	0	0
195	200	4	0	0	0	0	0	0	0	0	0	0
200	205	5	0	0	0	0	0	0	0	0	0	0
205	210	5	0	0	0	0	0	0	0	0	0	0
210	215	6	0	0	0	0	0	0	0	0	0	0
215	220	6	0	0	0	0	0	0	0	0	0	0
220	225	7	0	0	0	0	0	0	0	0	0	0
225	230	7	0	0	0	0	0	0	0	0	0	0
230	235	8	0	0	0	0	0	0	0	0	0	0
235	240	8	0	0	0	0	0	0	0	0	0	0
240	245	9	0	0	0	0	0	0	0	0	0	0
245	250	9	0	0	0	0	0	0	0	0	0	0
250	260	10	0	0	0	0	0	0	0	0	0	0
260	270	11	0	0	0	0	0	0	0	0	0	0
270	280	12	0	0	0	0	0	0	0	0	0	0
280	290	13	0	0	0	0	0	0	0	0	0	0
290	300	14	0	0	0	0	0	0	0	0	0	0
300	310	15	0	0	0	0	0	0	0	0	0	0
310	320	16	0	0	0	0	0	0	0	0	0	0
320	330	17	0	0	0	0	0	0	0	0	0	0
330	340	18	1	0	0	0	0	0	0	0	0	0
340	350	19	2	0	0	0	0	0	0	0	0	0
350	360	20	3	0	0	0	0	0	0	0	0	0
360	370	21	4	0	0	0	0	0	0	0	0	0
370	380	22	5	0	0	0	0	0	0	0	0	0
380	390	23	6	0	0	0	0	0	0	0	0	0
390	400	24	7	0	0	0	0	0	0	0	0	0
400	410	25	8	0	0	0	0	0	0	0	0	0
410	420	26	9	0	0	0	0	0	0	0	0	0
420	430	27	10	0	0	0	0	0	0	0	0	0
430	440	28	11	0	0	0	0	0	0	0	0	0
440	450	29	12	0	0	0	0	0	0	0	0	0
450	460	30	13	0	0	0	0	0	0	0	0	0
460	470	31	14	0	0	0	0	0	0	0	0	0
470	480	32	15	0	0	0	0	0	0	0	0	0
480	490	33	16	0	0	0	0	0	0	0	0	0
490	500	34	17	0	0	0	0	0	0	0	0	0
500	520	36	18	1	0	0	0	0	0	0	0	0
520	540	38	20	3	0	0	0	0	0	0	0	0
540	560	40	22	5	0	0	0	0	0	0	0	0
560	580	42	24	7	0	0	0	0	0	0	0	0
580	600	44	26	9	0	0	0	0	0	0	0	0
600	620	47	28	11	0	0	0	0	0	0	0	0
620	640	49	30	13	0	0	0	0	0	0	0	0
640	660	52	32	15	0	0	0	0	0	0	0	0
660	680	54	34	17	0	0	0	0	0	0	0	0
680	700	56	36	19	2	0	0	0	0	0	0	0
700	720	59	38	21	4	0	0	0	0	0	0	0
720	740	61	40	23	6	0	0	0	0	0	0	0
740	760	64	43	25	8	0	0	0	0	0	0	0
760	780	66	45	27	10	0	0	0	0	0	0	0
780	800	68	48	29	12	0	0	0	0	0	0	0
800	820	71	50	31	14	0	0	0	0	0	0	0
820	840	73	52	33	16	0	0	0	0	0	0	0
840	860	76	55	35	18	0	0	0	0	0	0	0
860	880	78	57	37	20	2	0	0	0	0	0	0
880	900	80	60	39	22	4	0	0	0	0	0	0
900	920	83	62	41	24	6	0	0	0	0	0	0
920	940	85	64	44	26	8	0	0	0	0	0	0
940	960	88	67	46	28	10	0	0	0	0	0	0
960	980	90	69	48	30	12	0	0	0	0	0	0
980	1,000	92	72	51	32	14	0	0	0	0	0	0
1,000	1,020	95	74	53	34	16	0	0	0	0	0	0

Images copied from Circular E, Pub. 15, IRS Employer Tax Guide 2018 published on the IRS website WWW.IRS.gov

Wage Bracket Method Tables for Income Tax Withholding

SINGLE Persons—SEMIMONTHLY Payroll Period

(For Wages Paid through December 31, 2018)

And the wages are—		And the number of withholding allowances claimed is—										
At least	But less than	0	1	2	3	4	5	6	7	8	9	10
		The amount of income tax to be withheld is—										
$1,020	$1,040	$97	$76	$56	$36	$18	$1	$0	$0	$0	$0	$0
1,040	1,060	100	79	58	38	20	3	0	0	0	0	0
1,060	1,080	102	81	60	40	22	5	0	0	0	0	0
1,080	1,100	104	84	63	42	24	7	0	0	0	0	0
1,100	1,120	107	86	65	45	26	9	0	0	0	0	0
1,120	1,140	109	88	68	47	28	11	0	0	0	0	0
1,140	1,160	112	91	70	49	30	13	0	0	0	0	0
1,160	1,180	114	93	72	52	32	15	0	0	0	0	0
1,180	1,200	116	96	75	54	34	17	0	0	0	0	0
1,200	1,220	119	98	77	57	36	19	2	0	0	0	0
1,220	1,240	121	100	80	59	38	21	4	0	0	0	0
1,240	1,260	124	103	82	61	41	23	6	0	0	0	0
1,260	1,280	126	105	84	64	43	25	8	0	0	0	0
1,280	1,300	128	108	87	66	45	27	10	0	0	0	0
1,300	1,320	131	110	89	69	48	29	12	0	0	0	0
1,320	1,340	133	112	92	71	50	31	14	0	0	0	0
1,340	1,360	136	115	94	73	53	33	16	0	0	0	0
1,360	1,380	138	117	96	76	55	35	18	1	0	0	0
1,380	1,400	140	120	99	78	57	37	20	3	0	0	0
1,400	1,420	143	122	101	81	60	39	22	5	0	0	0
1,420	1,440	145	124	104	83	62	41	24	7	0	0	0
1,440	1,460	148	127	106	85	65	44	26	9	0	0	0
1,460	1,480	150	129	108	88	67	46	28	11	0	0	0
1,480	1,500	152	132	111	90	69	49	30	13	0	0	0
1,500	1,520	155	134	113	93	72	51	32	15	0	0	0
1,520	1,540	157	136	116	95	74	53	34	17	0	0	0
1,540	1,560	160	139	118	97	77	56	36	19	1	0	0
1,560	1,580	162	141	120	100	79	58	38	21	3	0	0
1,580	1,600	164	144	123	102	81	61	40	23	5	0	0
1,600	1,620	167	146	125	105	84	63	42	25	7	0	0
1,620	1,640	169	148	128	107	86	65	45	27	9	0	0
1,640	1,660	172	151	130	109	89	68	47	29	11	0	0
1,660	1,680	174	153	132	112	91	70	49	31	13	0	0
1,680	1,700	176	156	135	114	93	73	52	33	15	0	0
1,700	1,720	179	158	137	117	96	75	54	35	17	0	0
1,720	1,740	181	160	140	119	98	77	57	37	19	2	0
1,740	1,760	184	163	142	121	101	80	59	39	21	4	0
1,760	1,780	186	165	144	124	103	82	61	41	23	6	0
1,780	1,800	191	168	147	126	105	85	64	43	25	8	0
1,800	1,820	195	170	149	129	108	87	66	46	27	10	0
1,820	1,840	199	172	152	131	110	89	69	48	29	12	0
1,840	1,860	204	175	154	133	113	92	71	50	31	14	0
1,860	1,880	208	177	156	136	115	94	73	53	33	16	0
1,880	1,900	213	180	159	138	117	97	76	55	35	18	1
1,900	1,920	217	182	161	141	120	99	78	58	37	20	3
1,920	1,940	221	184	164	143	122	101	81	60	39	22	5
1,940	1,960	226	188	166	145	125	104	83	62	42	24	7
1,960	1,980	230	192	168	148	127	106	85	65	44	26	9
1,980	2,000	235	197	171	150	129	109	88	67	46	28	11
2,000	2,020	239	201	173	153	132	111	90	70	49	30	13
2,020	2,040	243	205	176	155	134	113	93	72	51	32	15
2,040	2,060	248	210	178	157	137	116	95	74	54	34	17
2,060	2,080	252	214	180	160	139	118	97	77	56	36	19
2,080	2,100	257	219	183	162	141	121	100	79	58	38	21
2,100	2,120	261	223	185	165	144	123	102	82	61	40	23
2,120	2,140	265	227	189	167	146	125	105	84	63	42	25
2,140	2,160	270	232	194	169	149	128	107	86	66	45	27
2,160	2,180	274	236	198	172	151	130	109	89	68	47	29
2,180	2,200	279	241	203	174	153	133	112	91	70	50	31
2,200	2,220	283	245	207	177	156	135	114	94	73	52	33
2,220	2,240	287	249	211	179	158	137	117	96	75	54	35
2,240	2,260	292	254	216	181	161	140	119	98	78	57	37
2,260	2,280	296	258	220	184	163	142	121	101	80	59	39
2,280	2,300	301	263	225	187	165	145	124	103	82	62	41
2,300	2,320	305	267	229	191	168	147	126	106	85	64	43

$2,320 and over   Use Table 3(a) for a SINGLE person on page 46. Also see the instructions on page 44.

Images copied from Circular E, Pub. 15, IRS Employer Tax Guide 2018 published on the IRS website WWW.IRS.gov

Appendixes

Wage Bracket Method Tables for Income Tax Withholding

MARRIED Persons—SEMIMONTHLY Payroll Period

(For Wages Paid through December 31, 2018)

And the wages are—		And the number of withholding allowances claimed is—										
At least	But less than	0	1	2	3	4	5	6	7	8	9	10
		The amount of income tax to be withheld is—										
$0	$485	$0	$0	$0	$0	$0	$0	$0	$0	$0	$0	$0
485	495	1	0	0	0	0	0	0	0	0	0	0
495	505	2	0	0	0	0	0	0	0	0	0	0
505	525	3	0	0	0	0	0	0	0	0	0	0
525	545	5	0	0	0	0	0	0	0	0	0	0
545	565	7	0	0	0	0	0	0	0	0	0	0
565	585	9	0	0	0	0	0	0	0	0	0	0
585	605	11	0	0	0	0	0	0	0	0	0	0
605	625	13	0	0	0	0	0	0	0	0	0	0
625	645	15	0	0	0	0	0	0	0	0	0	0
645	665	17	0	0	0	0	0	0	0	0	0	0
665	685	19	2	0	0	0	0	0	0	0	0	0
685	705	21	4	0	0	0	0	0	0	0	0	0
705	725	23	6	0	0	0	0	0	0	0	0	0
725	745	25	8	0	0	0	0	0	0	0	0	0
745	765	27	10	0	0	0	0	0	0	0	0	0
765	785	29	12	0	0	0	0	0	0	0	0	0
785	805	31	14	0	0	0	0	0	0	0	0	0
805	825	33	16	0	0	0	0	0	0	0	0	0
825	845	35	18	1	0	0	0	0	0	0	0	0
845	865	37	20	3	0	0	0	0	0	0	0	0
865	885	39	22	5	0	0	0	0	0	0	0	0
885	905	41	24	7	0	0	0	0	0	0	0	0
905	925	43	26	9	0	0	0	0	0	0	0	0
925	945	45	28	11	0	0	0	0	0	0	0	0
945	965	47	30	13	0	0	0	0	0	0	0	0
965	985	49	32	15	0	0	0	0	0	0	0	0
985	1,005	51	34	17	0	0	0	0	0	0	0	0
1,005	1,025	53	36	19	2	0	0	0	0	0	0	0
1,025	1,045	55	38	21	4	0	0	0	0	0	0	0
1,045	1,065	57	40	23	6	0	0	0	0	0	0	0
1,065	1,085	59	42	25	8	0	0	0	0	0	0	0
1,085	1,105	61	44	27	10	0	0	0	0	0	0	0
1,105	1,125	63	46	29	12	0	0	0	0	0	0	0
1,125	1,145	65	48	31	14	0	0	0	0	0	0	0
1,145	1,165	67	50	33	16	0	0	0	0	0	0	0
1,165	1,185	69	52	35	18	0	0	0	0	0	0	0
1,185	1,205	71	54	37	20	2	0	0	0	0	0	0
1,205	1,225	73	56	39	22	4	0	0	0	0	0	0
1,225	1,245	75	58	41	24	6	0	0	0	0	0	0
1,245	1,265	77	60	43	26	8	0	0	0	0	0	0
1,265	1,285	79	62	45	28	10	0	0	0	0	0	0
1,285	1,305	82	64	47	30	12	0	0	0	0	0	0
1,305	1,325	84	66	49	32	14	0	0	0	0	0	0
1,325	1,345	87	68	51	34	16	0	0	0	0	0	0
1,345	1,365	89	70	53	36	18	1	0	0	0	0	0
1,365	1,385	91	72	55	38	20	3	0	0	0	0	0
1,385	1,405	94	74	57	40	22	5	0	0	0	0	0
1,405	1,425	96	76	59	42	24	7	0	0	0	0	0
1,425	1,445	99	78	61	44	26	9	0	0	0	0	0
1,445	1,465	101	80	63	46	28	11	0	0	0	0	0
1,465	1,485	103	83	65	48	30	13	0	0	0	0	0
1,485	1,505	106	85	67	50	32	15	0	0	0	0	0
1,505	1,525	108	87	69	52	34	17	0	0	0	0	0
1,525	1,545	111	90	71	54	36	19	2	0	0	0	0
1,545	1,565	113	92	73	56	38	21	4	0	0	0	0
1,565	1,585	115	95	75	58	40	23	6	0	0	0	0
1,585	1,605	118	97	77	60	42	25	8	0	0	0	0
1,605	1,625	120	99	79	62	44	27	10	0	0	0	0
1,625	1,645	123	102	81	64	46	29	12	0	0	0	0
1,645	1,665	125	104	83	66	48	31	14	0	0	0	0
1,665	1,685	127	107	86	68	50	33	16	0	0	0	0
1,685	1,705	130	109	88	70	52	35	18	0	0	0	0
1,705	1,725	132	111	91	72	54	37	20	2	0	0	0
1,725	1,745	135	114	93	74	56	39	22	4	0	0	0
1,745	1,765	137	116	95	76	58	41	24	6	0	0	0
1,765	1,785	139	119	98	78	60	43	26	8	0	0	0
1,785	1,805	142	121	100	80	62	45	28	10	0	0	0
1,805	1,825	144	123	103	82	64	47	30	12	0	0	0
1,825	1,845	147	126	105	84	66	49	32	14	0	0	0

Images copied from Circular E, Pub. 15, IRS Employer Tax Guide 2018 published on the IRS website WWW.IRS.gov

Wage Bracket Method Tables for Income Tax Withholding
MARRIED Persons—SEMIMONTHLY Payroll Period
(For Wages Paid through December 31, 2018)

And the wages are—		And the number of withholding allowances claimed is—										
At least	But less than	0	1	2	3	4	5	6	7	8	9	10
		The amount of income tax to be withheld is—										
$1,845	$1,865	$149	$128	$107	$87	$68	$51	$34	$16	$0	$0	$0
1,865	1,885	151	131	110	89	70	53	36	18	1	0	0
1,885	1,905	154	133	112	92	72	55	38	20	3	0	0
1,905	1,925	156	135	115	94	74	57	40	22	5	0	0
1,925	1,945	159	138	117	96	76	59	42	24	7	0	0
1,945	1,965	161	140	119	99	78	61	44	26	9	0	0
1,965	1,985	163	143	122	101	80	63	46	28	11	0	0
1,985	2,005	166	145	124	104	83	65	48	30	13	0	0
2,005	2,025	168	147	127	106	85	67	50	32	15	0	0
2,025	2,045	171	150	129	108	88	69	52	34	17	0	0
2,045	2,065	173	152	131	111	90	71	54	36	19	2	0
2,065	2,085	175	155	134	113	92	73	56	38	21	4	0
2,085	2,105	178	157	136	116	95	75	58	40	23	6	0
2,105	2,125	180	159	139	118	97	77	60	42	25	8	0
2,125	2,145	183	162	141	120	100	79	62	44	27	10	0
2,145	2,165	185	164	143	123	102	81	64	46	29	12	0
2,165	2,185	187	167	146	125	104	84	66	48	31	14	0
2,185	2,205	190	169	148	128	107	86	68	50	33	16	0
2,205	2,225	192	171	151	130	109	88	70	52	35	18	0
2,225	2,245	195	174	153	132	112	91	72	54	37	20	2
2,245	2,265	197	176	155	135	114	93	74	56	39	22	4
2,265	2,285	199	179	158	137	116	96	76	58	41	24	6
2,285	2,305	202	181	160	140	119	98	78	60	43	26	8
2,305	2,325	204	183	163	142	121	100	80	62	45	28	10
2,325	2,345	207	186	165	144	124	103	82	64	47	30	12
2,345	2,365	209	188	167	147	126	105	84	66	49	32	14
2,365	2,385	211	191	170	149	128	108	87	68	51	34	16
2,385	2,405	214	193	172	152	131	110	89	70	53	36	18
2,405	2,425	216	195	175	154	133	112	92	72	55	38	20
2,425	2,445	219	198	177	156	136	115	94	74	57	40	22
2,445	2,465	221	200	179	159	138	117	96	76	59	42	24
2,465	2,485	223	203	182	161	140	120	99	78	61	44	26
2,485	2,505	226	205	184	164	143	122	101	81	63	46	28
2,505	2,525	228	207	187	166	145	124	104	83	65	48	30
2,525	2,545	231	210	189	168	148	127	106	85	67	50	32
2,545	2,565	233	212	191	171	150	129	108	88	69	52	34
2,565	2,585	235	215	194	173	152	132	111	90	71	54	36
2,585	2,605	238	217	196	176	155	134	113	93	73	56	38
2,605	2,625	240	219	199	178	157	136	116	95	75	58	40
2,625	2,645	243	222	201	180	160	139	118	97	77	60	42
2,645	2,665	245	224	203	183	162	141	120	100	79	62	44
2,665	2,685	247	227	206	185	164	144	123	102	81	64	46
2,685	2,705	250	229	208	188	167	146	125	105	84	66	48
2,705	2,725	252	231	211	190	169	148	128	107	86	68	50
2,725	2,745	255	234	213	192	172	151	130	109	89	70	52
2,745	2,765	257	236	215	195	174	153	132	112	91	72	54
2,765	2,785	259	239	218	197	176	156	135	114	93	74	56
2,785	2,805	262	241	220	200	179	158	137	117	96	76	58
2,805	2,825	264	243	223	202	181	160	140	119	98	78	60
2,825	2,845	267	246	225	204	184	163	142	121	101	80	62
2,845	2,865	269	248	227	207	186	165	144	124	103	82	64
2,865	2,885	271	251	230	209	188	168	147	126	105	85	66
2,885	2,905	274	253	232	212	191	170	149	129	108	87	68
2,905	2,925	276	255	235	214	193	172	152	131	110	89	70
2,925	2,945	279	258	237	216	196	175	154	133	113	92	72
2,945	2,965	281	260	239	219	198	177	156	136	115	94	74
2,965	2,985	283	263	242	221	200	180	159	138	117	97	76
2,985	3,005	286	265	244	224	203	182	161	141	120	99	78
3,005	3,025	288	267	247	226	205	184	164	143	122	101	81
3,025	3,045	291	270	249	228	208	187	166	145	125	104	83
3,045	3,065	293	272	251	231	210	189	168	148	127	106	85
3,065	3,085	295	275	254	233	212	192	171	150	129	109	88
3,085	3,105	298	277	256	236	215	194	173	153	132	111	90
3,105	3,125	300	279	259	238	217	196	176	155	134	113	93
3,125	3,145	303	282	261	240	220	199	178	157	137	116	95
3,145	3,165	305	284	263	243	222	201	180	160	139	118	97

$3,165 and over   Use Table 3(b) for a MARRIED person on page 46. Also see the instructions on page 44.

Images copied from Circular E, Pub. 15, IRS Employer Tax Guide 2018 published on the IRS website WWW.IRS.gov

Appendixes

Wage Bracket Method Tables for Income Tax Withholding
SINGLE Persons—MONTHLY Payroll Period
(For Wages Paid through December 31, 2018)

And the wages are—		And the number of withholding allowances claimed is—										
At least	But less than	0	1	2	3	4	5	6	7	8	9	10
		The amount of income tax to be withheld is—										
$0	$305	$0	$0	$0	$0	$0	$0	$0	$0	$0	$0	$0
305	325	1	0	0	0	0	0	0	0	0	0	0
325	345	3	0	0	0	0	0	0	0	0	0	0
345	365	5	0	0	0	0	0	0	0	0	0	0
365	385	7	0	0	0	0	0	0	0	0	0	0
385	405	9	0	0	0	0	0	0	0	0	0	0
405	425	11	0	0	0	0	0	0	0	0	0	0
425	445	13	0	0	0	0	0	0	0	0	0	0
445	465	15	0	0	0	0	0	0	0	0	0	0
465	485	17	0	0	0	0	0	0	0	0	0	0
485	505	19	0	0	0	0	0	0	0	0	0	0
505	525	21	0	0	0	0	0	0	0	0	0	0
525	545	23	0	0	0	0	0	0	0	0	0	0
545	565	25	0	0	0	0	0	0	0	0	0	0
565	585	27	0	0	0	0	0	0	0	0	0	0
585	605	29	0	0	0	0	0	0	0	0	0	0
605	645	32	0	0	0	0	0	0	0	0	0	0
645	685	36	1	0	0	0	0	0	0	0	0	0
685	725	40	5	0	0	0	0	0	0	0	0	0
725	765	44	9	0	0	0	0	0	0	0	0	0
765	805	48	13	0	0	0	0	0	0	0	0	0
805	845	52	17	0	0	0	0	0	0	0	0	0
845	885	56	21	0	0	0	0	0	0	0	0	0
885	925	60	25	0	0	0	0	0	0	0	0	0
925	965	64	29	0	0	0	0	0	0	0	0	0
965	1,005	68	33	0	0	0	0	0	0	0	0	0
1,005	1,045	72	37	3	0	0	0	0	0	0	0	0
1,045	1,085	76	41	7	0	0	0	0	0	0	0	0
1,085	1,125	80	45	11	0	0	0	0	0	0	0	0
1,125	1,165	85	49	15	0	0	0	0	0	0	0	0
1,165	1,205	89	53	19	0	0	0	0	0	0	0	0
1,205	1,245	94	57	23	0	0	0	0	0	0	0	0
1,245	1,285	99	61	27	0	0	0	0	0	0	0	0
1,285	1,325	104	65	31	0	0	0	0	0	0	0	0
1,325	1,365	109	69	35	0	0	0	0	0	0	0	0
1,365	1,405	113	73	39	4	0	0	0	0	0	0	0
1,405	1,445	118	77	43	8	0	0	0	0	0	0	0
1,445	1,485	123	81	47	12	0	0	0	0	0	0	0
1,485	1,525	128	86	51	16	0	0	0	0	0	0	0
1,525	1,565	133	91	55	20	0	0	0	0	0	0	0
1,565	1,605	137	96	59	24	0	0	0	0	0	0	0
1,605	1,645	142	101	63	28	0	0	0	0	0	0	0
1,645	1,685	147	105	67	32	0	0	0	0	0	0	0
1,685	1,725	152	110	71	36	1	0	0	0	0	0	0
1,725	1,765	157	115	75	40	5	0	0	0	0	0	0
1,765	1,805	161	120	79	44	9	0	0	0	0	0	0
1,805	1,845	166	125	83	48	13	0	0	0	0	0	0
1,845	1,885	171	129	88	52	17	0	0	0	0	0	0
1,885	1,925	176	134	93	56	21	0	0	0	0	0	0
1,925	1,965	181	139	98	60	25	0	0	0	0	0	0
1,965	2,005	185	144	102	64	29	0	0	0	0	0	0
2,005	2,045	190	149	107	68	33	0	0	0	0	0	0
2,045	2,085	195	153	112	72	37	3	0	0	0	0	0
2,085	2,125	200	158	117	76	41	7	0	0	0	0	0
2,125	2,165	205	163	122	80	45	11	0	0	0	0	0
2,165	2,205	209	168	126	85	49	15	0	0	0	0	0
2,205	2,245	214	173	131	90	53	19	0	0	0	0	0
2,245	2,285	219	177	136	94	57	23	0	0	0	0	0
2,285	2,325	224	182	141	99	61	27	0	0	0	0	0
2,325	2,365	229	187	146	104	65	31	0	0	0	0	0
2,365	2,405	233	192	150	109	69	35	0	0	0	0	0
2,405	2,445	238	197	155	114	73	39	4	0	0	0	0
2,445	2,485	243	201	160	118	77	43	8	0	0	0	0
2,485	2,525	248	206	165	123	82	47	12	0	0	0	0
2,525	2,565	253	211	170	128	87	51	16	0	0	0	0
2,565	2,605	257	216	174	133	91	55	20	0	0	0	0
2,605	2,645	262	221	179	138	96	59	24	0	0	0	0
2,645	2,685	267	225	184	142	101	63	28	0	0	0	0
2,685	2,725	272	230	189	147	106	67	32	0	0	0	0
2,725	2,765	277	235	194	152	111	71	36	2	0	0	0

Images copied from Circular E, Pub. 15, IRS Employer Tax Guide 2018 published on the IRS website WWW.IRS.gov

Wage Bracket Method Tables for Income Tax Withholding

SINGLE Persons—MONTHLY Payroll Period

(For Wages Paid through December 31, 2018)

And the wages are—		And the number of withholding allowances claimed is—										
At least	But less than	0	1	2	3	4	5	6	7	8	9	10
		The amount of income tax to be withheld is—										
$2,765	$2,805	$281	$240	$198	$157	$115	$75	$40	$6	$0	$0	$0
2,805	2,845	286	245	203	162	120	79	44	10	0	0	0
2,845	2,885	291	249	208	166	125	83	48	14	0	0	0
2,885	2,925	296	254	213	171	130	88	52	18	0	0	0
2,925	2,965	301	259	218	176	135	93	56	22	0	0	0
2,965	3,005	305	264	222	181	139	98	60	26	0	0	0
3,005	3,045	310	269	227	186	144	103	64	30	0	0	0
3,045	3,085	315	273	232	190	149	107	68	34	0	0	0
3,085	3,125	320	278	237	195	154	112	72	38	3	0	0
3,125	3,165	325	283	242	200	159	117	76	42	7	0	0
3,165	3,205	329	288	246	205	163	122	80	46	11	0	0
3,205	3,245	334	293	251	210	168	127	85	50	15	0	0
3,245	3,285	339	297	256	214	173	131	90	54	19	0	0
3,285	3,325	344	302	261	219	178	136	95	58	23	0	0
3,325	3,365	349	307	266	224	183	141	100	62	27	0	0
3,365	3,405	353	312	270	229	187	146	104	66	31	0	0
3,405	3,445	358	317	275	234	192	151	109	70	35	0	0
3,445	3,485	363	321	280	238	197	155	114	74	39	4	0
3,485	3,525	368	326	285	243	202	160	119	78	43	8	0
3,525	3,565	374	331	290	248	207	165	124	82	47	12	0
3,565	3,605	382	336	294	253	211	170	128	87	51	16	0
3,605	3,645	391	341	299	258	216	175	133	92	55	20	0
3,645	3,685	400	345	304	262	221	179	138	96	59	24	0
3,685	3,725	409	350	309	267	226	184	143	101	63	28	0
3,725	3,765	418	355	314	272	231	189	148	106	67	32	0
3,765	3,805	426	360	318	277	235	194	152	111	71	36	2
3,805	3,845	435	365	323	282	240	199	157	116	75	40	6
3,845	3,885	444	369	328	286	245	203	162	120	79	44	10
3,885	3,925	453	377	333	291	250	208	167	125	84	48	14
3,925	3,965	462	386	338	296	255	213	172	130	89	52	18
3,965	4,005	470	394	342	301	259	218	176	135	93	56	22
4,005	4,045	479	403	347	306	264	223	181	140	98	60	26
4,045	4,085	488	412	352	310	269	227	186	144	103	64	30
4,085	4,125	497	421	357	315	274	232	191	149	108	68	34
4,125	4,165	506	430	362	320	279	237	196	154	113	72	38
4,165	4,205	514	438	366	325	283	242	200	159	117	76	42
4,205	4,245	523	447	371	330	288	247	205	164	122	81	46
4,245	4,285	532	456	380	334	293	251	210	168	127	85	50
4,285	4,325	541	465	389	339	298	256	215	173	132	90	54
4,325	4,365	550	474	398	344	303	261	220	178	137	95	58
4,365	4,405	558	482	406	349	307	266	224	183	141	100	62
4,405	4,445	567	491	415	354	312	271	229	188	146	105	66
4,445	4,485	576	500	424	358	317	275	234	192	151	109	70
4,485	4,525	585	509	433	363	322	280	239	197	156	114	74
4,525	4,565	594	518	442	368	327	285	244	202	161	119	78
4,565	4,605	602	526	450	374	331	290	248	207	165	124	82
4,605	4,645	611	535	459	383	336	295	253	212	170	129	87
4,645	4,685	620	544	468	392	341	299	258	216	175	133	92
4,685	4,725	629	553	477	401	346	304	263	221	180	138	97
4,725	4,765	638	562	486	409	351	309	268	226	185	143	102
4,765	4,805	646	570	494	418	355	314	272	231	189	148	106
4,805	4,845	655	579	503	427	360	319	277	236	194	153	111
4,845	4,885	664	588	512	436	365	323	282	240	199	157	116
4,885	4,925	673	597	521	445	370	328	287	245	204	162	121
4,925	4,965	682	606	530	453	377	333	292	250	209	167	126
4,965	5,005	690	614	538	462	386	338	296	255	213	172	130
5,005	5,045	699	623	547	471	395	343	301	260	218	177	135
5,045	5,085	708	632	556	480	404	347	306	264	223	181	140
5,085	5,125	717	641	565	489	413	352	311	269	228	186	145
5,125	5,165	726	650	574	497	421	357	316	274	233	191	150
5,165	5,205	734	658	582	506	430	362	320	279	237	196	154
5,205	5,245	743	667	591	515	439	367	325	284	242	201	159
5,245	5,285	752	676	600	524	448	372	330	288	247	205	164
5,285	5,325	761	685	609	533	457	380	335	293	252	210	169
5,325	5,365	770	694	618	541	465	389	340	298	257	215	174
5,365	5,405	778	702	626	550	474	398	344	303	261	220	178

$5,405 and over   Use Table 4(a) for a SINGLE person on page 46. Also see the instructions on page 44.

Images copied from Circular E, Pub. 15, IRS Employer Tax Guide 2018 published on the IRS website WWW.IRS.gov

Appendixes

Wage Bracket Method Tables for Income Tax Withholding
MARRIED Persons—MONTHLY Payroll Period
(For Wages Paid through December 31, 2018)

And the wages are—		And the number of withholding allowances claimed is—										
At least	But less than	0	1	2	3	4	5	6	7	8	9	10
		The amount of income tax to be withheld is—										
$0	$950	$0	$0	$0	$0	$0	$0	$0	$0	$0	$0	$0
950	990	1	0	0	0	0	0	0	0	0	0	0
990	1,030	5	0	0	0	0	0	0	0	0	0	0
1,030	1,070	9	0	0	0	0	0	0	0	0	0	0
1,070	1,110	13	0	0	0	0	0	0	0	0	0	0
1,110	1,150	17	0	0	0	0	0	0	0	0	0	0
1,150	1,190	21	0	0	0	0	0	0	0	0	0	0
1,190	1,230	25	0	0	0	0	0	0	0	0	0	0
1,230	1,270	29	0	0	0	0	0	0	0	0	0	0
1,270	1,310	33	0	0	0	0	0	0	0	0	0	0
1,310	1,350	37	2	0	0	0	0	0	0	0	0	0
1,350	1,390	41	6	0	0	0	0	0	0	0	0	0
1,390	1,430	45	10	0	0	0	0	0	0	0	0	0
1,430	1,470	49	14	0	0	0	0	0	0	0	0	0
1,470	1,510	53	18	0	0	0	0	0	0	0	0	0
1,510	1,550	57	22	0	0	0	0	0	0	0	0	0
1,550	1,590	61	26	0	0	0	0	0	0	0	0	0
1,590	1,630	65	30	0	0	0	0	0	0	0	0	0
1,630	1,670	69	34	0	0	0	0	0	0	0	0	0
1,670	1,710	73	38	4	0	0	0	0	0	0	0	0
1,710	1,750	77	42	8	0	0	0	0	0	0	0	0
1,750	1,790	81	46	12	0	0	0	0	0	0	0	0
1,790	1,830	85	50	16	0	0	0	0	0	0	0	0
1,830	1,870	89	54	20	0	0	0	0	0	0	0	0
1,870	1,910	93	58	24	0	0	0	0	0	0	0	0
1,910	1,950	97	62	28	0	0	0	0	0	0	0	0
1,950	1,990	101	66	32	0	0	0	0	0	0	0	0
1,990	2,030	105	70	36	1	0	0	0	0	0	0	0
2,030	2,070	109	74	40	5	0	0	0	0	0	0	0
2,070	2,110	113	78	44	9	0	0	0	0	0	0	0
2,110	2,150	117	82	48	13	0	0	0	0	0	0	0
2,150	2,190	121	86	52	17	0	0	0	0	0	0	0
2,190	2,230	125	90	56	21	0	0	0	0	0	0	0
2,230	2,270	129	94	60	25	0	0	0	0	0	0	0
2,270	2,310	133	98	64	29	0	0	0	0	0	0	0
2,310	2,350	137	102	68	33	0	0	0	0	0	0	0
2,350	2,390	141	106	72	37	2	0	0	0	0	0	0
2,390	2,430	145	110	76	41	6	0	0	0	0	0	0
2,430	2,470	149	114	80	45	10	0	0	0	0	0	0
2,470	2,510	153	118	84	49	14	0	0	0	0	0	0
2,510	2,550	157	122	88	53	18	0	0	0	0	0	0
2,550	2,590	161	126	92	57	22	0	0	0	0	0	0
2,590	2,630	166	130	96	61	26	0	0	0	0	0	0
2,630	2,670	171	134	100	65	30	0	0	0	0	0	0
2,670	2,710	176	138	104	69	34	0	0	0	0	0	0
2,710	2,750	180	142	108	73	38	4	0	0	0	0	0
2,750	2,790	185	146	112	77	42	8	0	0	0	0	0
2,790	2,830	190	150	116	81	46	12	0	0	0	0	0
2,830	2,870	195	154	120	85	50	16	0	0	0	0	0
2,870	2,910	200	158	124	89	54	20	0	0	0	0	0
2,910	2,950	204	163	128	93	58	24	0	0	0	0	0
2,950	2,990	209	168	132	97	62	28	0	0	0	0	0
2,990	3,030	214	172	136	101	66	32	0	0	0	0	0
3,030	3,070	219	177	140	105	70	36	1	0	0	0	0
3,070	3,110	224	182	144	109	74	40	5	0	0	0	0
3,110	3,150	228	187	148	113	78	44	9	0	0	0	0
3,150	3,190	233	192	152	117	82	48	13	0	0	0	0
3,190	3,230	238	196	156	121	86	52	17	0	0	0	0
3,230	3,270	243	201	160	125	90	56	21	0	0	0	0
3,270	3,310	248	206	165	129	94	60	25	0	0	0	0
3,310	3,350	252	211	169	133	98	64	29	0	0	0	0
3,350	3,390	257	216	174	137	102	68	33	0	0	0	0
3,390	3,430	262	220	179	141	106	72	37	3	0	0	0
3,430	3,470	267	225	184	145	110	76	41	7	0	0	0
3,470	3,510	272	230	189	149	114	80	45	11	0	0	0
3,510	3,550	276	235	193	153	118	84	49	15	0	0	0
3,550	3,590	281	240	198	157	122	88	53	19	0	0	0
3,590	3,630	286	244	203	161	126	92	57	23	0	0	0
3,630	3,670	291	249	208	166	130	96	61	27	0	0	0
3,670	3,710	296	254	213	171	134	100	65	31	0	0	0

Images copied from Circular E, Pub. 15, IRS Employer Tax Guide 2018 published on the IRS website WWW.IRS.gov

Wage Bracket Method Tables for Income Tax Withholding

MARRIED Persons—MONTHLY Payroll Period

(For Wages Paid through December 31, 2018)

And the wages are—		And the number of withholding allowances claimed is—										
At least	But less than	0	1	2	3	4	5	6	7	8	9	10
		The amount of income tax to be withheld is—										
$3,710	$3,750	$300	$259	$217	$176	$138	$104	$69	$35	$0	$0	$0
3,750	3,790	305	264	222	181	142	108	73	39	4	0	0
3,790	3,830	310	268	227	185	146	112	77	43	8	0	0
3,830	3,870	315	273	232	190	150	116	81	47	12	0	0
3,870	3,910	320	278	237	195	154	120	85	51	16	0	0
3,910	3,950	324	283	241	200	158	124	89	55	20	0	0
3,950	3,990	329	288	246	205	163	128	93	59	24	0	0
3,990	4,030	334	292	251	209	168	132	97	63	28	0	0
4,030	4,070	339	297	256	214	173	136	101	67	32	0	0
4,070	4,110	344	302	261	219	178	140	105	71	36	2	0
4,110	4,150	348	307	265	224	182	144	109	75	40	6	0
4,150	4,190	353	312	270	229	187	148	113	79	44	10	0
4,190	4,230	358	316	275	233	192	152	117	83	48	14	0
4,230	4,270	363	321	280	238	197	156	121	87	52	18	0
4,270	4,310	368	326	285	243	202	160	125	91	56	22	0
4,310	4,350	372	331	289	248	206	165	129	95	60	26	0
4,350	4,390	377	336	294	253	211	170	133	99	64	30	0
4,390	4,430	382	340	299	257	216	174	137	103	68	34	0
4,430	4,470	387	345	304	262	221	179	141	107	72	38	3
4,470	4,510	392	350	309	267	226	184	145	111	76	42	7
4,510	4,550	396	355	313	272	230	189	149	115	80	46	11
4,550	4,590	401	360	318	277	235	194	153	119	84	50	15
4,590	4,630	406	364	323	281	240	198	157	123	88	54	19
4,630	4,670	411	369	328	286	245	203	162	127	92	58	23
4,670	4,710	416	374	333	291	250	208	167	131	96	62	27
4,710	4,750	420	379	337	296	254	213	171	135	100	66	31
4,750	4,790	425	384	342	301	259	218	176	139	104	70	35
4,790	4,830	430	388	347	305	264	222	181	143	108	74	39
4,830	4,870	435	393	352	310	269	227	186	147	112	78	43
4,870	4,910	440	398	357	315	274	232	191	151	116	82	47
4,910	4,950	444	403	361	320	278	237	195	155	120	86	51
4,950	4,990	449	408	366	325	283	242	200	159	124	90	55
4,990	5,030	454	412	371	329	288	246	205	163	128	94	59
5,030	5,070	459	417	376	334	293	251	210	168	132	98	63
5,070	5,110	464	422	381	339	298	256	215	173	136	102	67
5,110	5,150	468	427	385	344	302	261	219	178	140	106	71
5,150	5,190	473	432	390	349	307	266	224	183	144	110	75
5,190	5,230	478	436	395	353	312	270	229	187	148	114	79
5,230	5,270	483	441	400	358	317	275	234	192	152	118	83
5,270	5,310	488	446	405	363	322	280	239	197	156	122	87
5,310	5,350	492	451	409	368	326	285	243	202	160	126	91
5,350	5,390	497	456	414	373	331	290	248	207	165	130	95
5,390	5,430	502	460	419	377	336	294	253	211	170	134	99
5,430	5,470	507	465	424	382	341	299	258	216	175	138	103
5,470	5,510	512	470	429	387	346	304	263	221	180	142	107
5,510	5,550	516	475	433	392	350	309	267	226	184	146	111
5,550	5,590	521	480	438	397	355	314	272	231	189	150	115
5,590	5,630	526	484	443	401	360	318	277	235	194	154	119
5,630	5,670	531	489	448	406	365	323	282	240	199	158	123
5,670	5,710	536	494	453	411	370	328	287	245	204	162	127
5,710	5,750	540	499	457	416	374	333	291	250	208	167	131
5,750	5,790	545	504	462	421	379	338	296	255	213	172	135
5,790	5,830	550	508	467	425	384	342	301	259	218	176	139
5,830	5,870	555	513	472	430	389	347	306	264	223	181	143
5,870	5,910	560	518	477	435	394	352	311	269	228	186	147
5,910	5,950	564	523	481	440	398	357	315	274	232	191	151
5,950	5,990	569	528	486	445	403	362	320	279	237	196	155
5,990	6,030	574	532	491	449	408	366	325	283	242	200	159
6,030	6,070	579	537	496	454	413	371	330	288	247	205	164
6,070	6,110	584	542	501	459	418	376	335	293	252	210	169
6,110	6,150	588	547	505	464	422	381	339	298	256	215	173
6,150	6,190	593	552	510	469	427	386	344	303	261	220	178
6,190	6,230	598	556	515	473	432	390	349	307	266	224	183
6,230	6,270	603	561	520	478	437	395	354	312	271	229	188
6,270	6,310	608	566	525	483	442	400	359	317	276	234	193
6,310	6,350	612	571	529	488	446	405	363	322	280	239	197

$6,350 and over   Use Table 4(b) for a MARRIED person on page 46. Also see the instructions on page 44.

Images copied from Circular E, Pub. 15, IRS Employer Tax Guide 2018 published on the IRS website WWW.IRS.gov

Appendixes

Wage Bracket Method Tables for Income Tax Withholding
SINGLE Persons—DAILY Payroll Period
(For Wages Paid through December 31, 2018)

And the wages are—		And the number of withholding allowances claimed is—										
At least	But less than	0	1	2	3	4	5	6	7	8	9	10
		The amount of income tax to be withheld is—										
$0	$18	$0	$0	$0	$0	$0	$0	$0	$0	$0	$0	$0
18	21	1	0	0	0	0	0	0	0	0	0	0
21	24	1	0	0	0	0	0	0	0	0	0	0
24	27	1	0	0	0	0	0	0	0	0	0	0
27	30	1	0	0	0	0	0	0	0	0	0	0
30	33	2	0	0	0	0	0	0	0	0	0	0
33	36	2	0	0	0	0	0	0	0	0	0	0
36	39	2	1	0	0	0	0	0	0	0	0	0
39	42	3	1	0	0	0	0	0	0	0	0	0
42	45	3	1	0	0	0	0	0	0	0	0	0
45	48	3	2	0	0	0	0	0	0	0	0	0
48	51	4	2	0	0	0	0	0	0	0	0	0
51	54	4	2	1	0	0	0	0	0	0	0	0
54	57	4	3	1	0	0	0	0	0	0	0	0
57	60	5	3	1	0	0	0	0	0	0	0	0
60	63	5	3	2	0	0	0	0	0	0	0	0
63	66	5	3	2	0	0	0	0	0	0	0	0
66	69	6	4	2	1	0	0	0	0	0	0	0
69	72	6	4	2	1	0	0	0	0	0	0	0
72	75	6	4	3	1	0	0	0	0	0	0	0
75	78	7	5	3	1	0	0	0	0	0	0	0
78	81	7	5	3	2	0	0	0	0	0	0	0
81	84	7	6	4	2	0	0	0	0	0	0	0
84	87	8	6	4	2	1	0	0	0	0	0	0
87	90	8	6	4	3	1	0	0	0	0	0	0
90	93	9	7	5	3	1	0	0	0	0	0	0
93	96	9	7	5	3	2	0	0	0	0	0	0
96	99	9	7	5	4	2	0	0	0	0	0	0
99	102	10	8	6	4	2	1	0	0	0	0	0
102	105	10	8	6	4	3	1	0	0	0	0	0
105	108	10	8	7	5	3	1	0	0	0	0	0
108	111	11	9	7	5	3	2	0	0	0	0	0
111	114	11	9	7	5	3	2	0	0	0	0	0
114	117	11	10	8	6	4	2	1	0	0	0	0
117	120	12	10	8	6	4	2	1	0	0	0	0
120	123	12	10	8	6	4	3	1	0	0	0	0
123	126	12	11	9	7	5	3	1	0	0	0	0
126	129	13	11	9	7	5	3	2	0	0	0	0
129	132	13	11	9	7	6	4	2	0	0	0	0
132	135	14	12	10	8	6	4	2	1	0	0	0
135	138	14	12	10	8	6	4	3	1	0	0	0
138	141	14	12	10	9	7	5	3	1	0	0	0
141	144	15	13	11	9	7	5	3	2	0	0	0
144	147	15	13	11	9	7	5	4	2	0	0	0
147	150	15	13	12	10	8	6	4	2	1	0	0
150	153	16	14	12	10	8	6	4	3	1	0	0
153	156	16	14	12	10	8	7	5	3	1	0	0
156	159	16	15	13	11	9	7	5	3	2	0	0
159	162	17	15	13	11	9	7	5	3	2	0	0
162	165	17	15	13	11	10	8	6	4	2	1	0
165	168	18	16	14	12	10	8	6	4	2	1	0
168	171	19	16	14	12	10	8	6	4	3	1	0
171	174	19	16	14	13	11	9	7	5	3	1	0
174	177	20	17	15	13	11	9	7	5	3	2	0
177	180	21	17	15	13	11	9	7	6	4	2	0
180	183	21	18	16	14	12	10	8	6	4	2	1
183	186	22	18	16	14	12	10	8	6	4	3	1
186	189	23	19	16	14	12	10	9	7	5	3	1
189	192	23	20	17	15	13	11	9	7	5	3	2
192	195	24	20	17	15	13	11	9	7	5	4	2
195	198	24	21	17	15	13	12	10	8	6	4	2
198	201	25	22	18	16	14	12	10	8	6	4	3
201	204	26	22	19	16	14	12	10	8	7	5	3
204	207	26	23	19	16	15	13	11	9	7	5	3
207	210	27	24	20	17	15	13	11	9	7	5	3
210	213	28	24	21	17	15	13	11	10	8	6	4
213	216	28	25	21	18	16	14	12	10	8	6	4
216	219	29	26	22	19	16	14	12	10	8	6	5
219	222	30	26	23	19	16	14	13	11	9	7	5
222	225	30	27	23	20	17	15	13	11	9	7	5

Images copied from Circular E, Pub. 15, IRS Employer Tax Guide 2018 published on the IRS website WWW.IRS.gov

Wage Bracket Method Tables for Income Tax Withholding

SINGLE Persons—DAILY Payroll Period
(For Wages Paid through December 31, 2018)

And the wages are—		And the number of withholding allowances claimed is—										
At least	But less than	0	1	2	3	4	5	6	7	8	9	10
		The amount of income tax to be withheld is—										
$225	$228	$31	$28	$24	$21	$17	$15	$13	$11	$9	$8	$6
228	231	32	28	25	21	18	16	14	12	10	8	6
231	234	32	29	25	22	18	16	14	12	10	8	6
234	237	33	30	26	23	19	16	14	12	10	9	7
237	240	34	30	27	23	20	17	15	13	11	9	7
240	243	34	31	27	24	20	17	15	13	11	9	7
243	246	35	32	28	25	21	17	15	13	12	10	8
246	249	36	32	29	25	22	18	16	14	12	10	8
249	252	36	33	29	26	22	19	16	14	12	10	8
252	255	37	34	30	26	23	19	16	15	13	11	9
255	258	38	34	31	27	24	20	17	15	13	11	9
258	261	38	35	31	28	24	21	17	15	13	11	10
261	264	39	35	32	28	25	21	18	16	14	12	10
264	267	40	36	33	29	26	22	19	16	14	12	10
267	270	40	37	33	30	26	23	19	16	14	13	11
270	273	41	37	34	30	27	23	20	17	15	13	11
273	276	42	38	35	31	28	24	21	17	15	13	11
276	279	42	39	35	32	28	25	21	18	16	14	12
279	282	43	39	36	32	29	25	22	18	16	14	12
282	285	44	40	37	33	30	26	23	19	16	14	12
285	288	44	41	37	34	30	27	23	20	17	15	13
288	291	45	41	38	34	31	27	24	20	17	15	13
291	294	46	42	39	35	32	28	25	21	18	15	14
294	297	46	43	39	36	32	29	25	22	18	16	14
297	300	47	43	40	36	33	29	26	22	19	16	14
300	303	48	44	41	37	34	30	27	23	19	17	15
303	306	48	45	41	38	34	31	27	24	20	17	15
306	309	49	45	42	38	35	31	28	24	21	17	15
309	312	50	46	43	39	36	32	28	25	21	18	16
312	315	50	47	43	40	36	33	29	26	22	19	16
315	318	51	47	44	40	37	33	30	26	23	19	16
318	321	52	48	45	41	37	34	30	27	23	20	17
321	324	52	49	45	42	38	35	31	28	24	21	17
324	327	53	49	46	42	39	35	32	28	25	21	18
327	330	54	50	46	43	39	36	32	29	25	22	18
330	333	54	51	47	44	40	37	33	30	26	23	19
333	336	55	51	48	44	41	37	34	30	27	23	20
336	339	56	52	48	45	41	38	34	31	27	24	20
339	341	56	53	49	46	42	38	35	31	28	24	21
341	343	57	53	49	46	42	39	35	32	28	25	21
343	345	57	53	50	46	43	39	36	32	29	25	22
345	347	58	54	50	47	43	40	36	33	29	26	22
347	349	58	54	51	47	44	40	37	33	30	26	23
349	351	59	55	51	48	44	41	37	34	30	27	23
351	353	59	55	52	48	45	41	38	34	31	27	24
353	355	60	56	52	49	45	42	38	35	31	28	24
355	357	60	56	53	49	46	42	39	35	31	28	24
357	359	61	57	53	49	46	42	39	35	32	28	25
359	361	61	57	53	50	46	43	39	36	32	29	25
361	363	62	58	54	50	47	43	40	36	33	29	26
363	365	62	58	54	51	47	44	40	37	33	30	26
365	367	62	59	55	51	48	44	41	37	34	30	27
367	369	63	59	55	52	48	45	41	38	34	31	27
369	371	63	60	56	52	49	45	42	38	35	31	28
371	373	64	60	56	53	49	46	42	39	35	31	28
373	375	64	61	57	53	49	46	42	39	35	32	28
375	377	65	61	57	53	50	46	43	39	36	32	29
377	379	65	62	58	54	50	47	43	40	36	33	29
379	381	66	62	58	54	51	47	44	40	37	33	30
381	383	66	62	59	55	51	48	44	41	37	34	30
383	385	67	63	59	55	52	48	45	41	38	34	31
385	387	67	63	60	56	52	49	45	42	38	35	31
387	389	68	64	60	56	53	49	46	42	39	35	31
389	391	68	64	61	57	53	49	46	42	39	35	32
391	393	69	65	61	57	53	50	46	43	39	36	32
393	395	69	65	62	58	54	50	47	43	40	36	33

$395 and over   Use Table 8(a) for a SINGLE person on page 47. Also see the instructions on page 44.

Images copied from Circular E, Pub. 15, IRS Employer Tax Guide 2018 published on the IRS website WWW.IRS.gov

Appendixes

Wage Bracket Method Tables for Income Tax Withholding
MARRIED Persons—DAILY Payroll Period
(For Wages Paid through December 31, 2018)

And the wages are—		And the number of withholding allowances claimed is—										
At least	But less than	0	1	2	3	4	5	6	7	8	9	10
		The amount of income tax to be withheld is—										
$0	$50	$0	$0	$0	$0	$0	$0	$0	$0	$0	$0	$0
50	53	1	0	0	0	0	0	0	0	0	0	0
53	56	1	0	0	0	0	0	0	0	0	0	0
56	59	1	0	0	0	0	0	0	0	0	0	0
59	62	2	0	0	0	0	0	0	0	0	0	0
62	65	2	0	0	0	0	0	0	0	0	0	0
65	68	2	1	0	0	0	0	0	0	0	0	0
68	71	3	1	0	0	0	0	0	0	0	0	0
71	74	3	1	0	0	0	0	0	0	0	0	0
74	77	3	2	0	0	0	0	0	0	0	0	0
77	80	3	2	0	0	0	0	0	0	0	0	0
80	83	4	2	1	0	0	0	0	0	0	0	0
83	86	4	2	1	0	0	0	0	0	0	0	0
86	89	4	3	1	0	0	0	0	0	0	0	0
89	92	5	3	1	0	0	0	0	0	0	0	0
92	95	5	3	2	0	0	0	0	0	0	0	0
95	98	5	4	2	0	0	0	0	0	0	0	0
98	101	6	4	2	1	0	0	0	0	0	0	0
101	104	6	4	3	1	0	0	0	0	0	0	0
104	107	6	5	3	1	0	0	0	0	0	0	0
107	110	6	5	3	2	0	0	0	0	0	0	0
110	113	7	5	4	2	0	0	0	0	0	0	0
113	116	7	5	4	2	1	0	0	0	0	0	0
116	119	7	6	4	3	1	0	0	0	0	0	0
119	122	8	6	4	3	1	0	0	0	0	0	0
122	125	8	6	5	3	2	0	0	0	0	0	0
125	128	8	7	5	3	2	0	0	0	0	0	0
128	131	9	7	5	4	2	1	0	0	0	0	0
131	134	9	7	6	4	2	1	0	0	0	0	0
134	137	9	8	6	4	3	1	0	0	0	0	0
137	140	10	8	6	5	3	1	0	0	0	0	0
140	143	10	8	7	5	3	2	0	0	0	0	0
143	146	11	9	7	5	4	2	0	0	0	0	0
146	149	11	9	7	6	4	2	1	0	0	0	0
149	152	11	9	7	6	4	3	1	0	0	0	0
152	155	12	10	8	6	5	3	1	0	0	0	0
155	158	12	10	8	6	5	3	2	0	0	0	0
158	161	12	10	9	7	5	4	2	0	0	0	0
161	164	13	11	9	7	5	4	2	1	0	0	0
164	167	13	11	9	7	6	4	3	1	0	0	0
167	170	13	12	10	8	6	4	3	1	0	0	0
170	173	14	12	10	8	6	5	3	2	0	0	0
173	176	14	12	10	8	7	5	3	2	0	0	0
176	179	15	13	11	9	7	5	4	2	1	0	0
179	182	15	13	11	9	7	6	4	2	1	0	0
182	185	15	13	11	9	8	6	4	3	1	0	0
185	188	16	14	12	10	8	6	5	3	1	0	0
188	191	16	14	12	10	8	7	5	3	2	0	0
191	194	16	14	12	11	9	7	5	4	2	0	0
194	197	17	15	13	11	9	7	6	4	2	1	0
197	200	17	15	13	11	9	7	6	4	3	1	0
200	203	17	15	14	12	10	8	6	5	3	1	0
203	206	18	16	14	12	10	8	6	5	3	2	0
206	209	18	16	14	12	10	9	7	5	4	2	0
209	212	18	17	15	13	11	9	7	5	4	2	1
212	215	19	17	15	13	11	9	7	6	4	3	1
215	218	19	17	15	13	12	10	8	6	4	3	1
218	221	20	18	16	14	12	10	8	6	5	3	2
221	224	20	18	16	14	12	10	8	7	5	3	2
224	227	20	18	16	15	13	11	9	7	5	4	2
227	230	21	19	17	15	13	11	9	7	6	4	2
230	233	21	19	17	15	13	11	9	8	6	4	3
233	236	21	19	18	16	14	12	10	8	6	5	3
236	239	22	20	18	16	14	12	10	8	7	5	3
239	242	22	20	18	16	14	12	11	9	7	5	4
242	245	22	21	19	17	15	13	11	9	7	6	4
245	248	23	21	19	17	15	13	11	9	7	6	4
248	251	23	21	19	17	15	14	12	10	8	6	5
251	254	24	22	20	18	16	14	12	10	8	6	5
254	257	24	22	20	18	16	14	12	10	9	7	5

Images copied from Circular E, Pub. 15, IRS Employer Tax Guide 2018 published on the IRS website WWW.IRS.gov

Wage Bracket Method Tables for Income Tax Withholding

MARRIED Persons—DAILY Payroll Period

(For Wages Paid through December 31, 2018)

And the wages are—		And the number of withholding allowances claimed is—										
At least	But less than	0	1	2	3	4	5	6	7	8	9	10
		The amount of income tax to be withheld is—										
$257	$260	$24	$22	$20	$18	$17	$15	$13	$11	$9	$7	$5
260	263	25	23	21	19	17	15	13	11	9	7	6
263	266	25	23	21	19	17	15	13	12	10	8	6
266	269	25	23	21	20	18	16	14	12	10	8	6
269	272	26	24	22	20	18	16	14	12	10	8	7
272	275	26	24	22	20	18	16	15	13	11	9	7
275	278	26	24	23	21	19	17	15	13	11	9	7
278	281	27	25	23	21	19	17	15	13	11	10	8
281	284	27	25	23	21	19	18	16	14	12	10	8
284	287	27	26	24	22	20	18	16	14	12	10	8
287	290	28	26	24	22	20	18	16	14	13	11	9
290	293	28	26	24	22	21	19	17	15	13	11	9
293	296	29	27	25	23	21	19	17	15	13	11	9
296	299	29	27	25	23	21	19	17	15	14	12	10
299	302	29	27	25	24	22	20	18	16	14	12	10
302	305	30	28	26	24	22	20	18	16	14	12	10
305	308	30	28	26	24	22	20	19	17	15	13	11
308	311	30	28	27	25	23	21	19	17	15	13	11
311	314	31	29	27	25	23	21	19	17	15	13	12
314	317	31	29	27	25	23	21	20	18	16	14	12
317	320	31	30	28	26	24	22	20	18	16	14	12
320	323	32	30	28	26	24	22	20	18	16	15	13
323	326	32	30	28	26	24	23	21	19	17	15	13
326	329	33	31	29	27	25	23	21	19	17	15	13
329	332	33	31	29	27	25	23	21	19	18	16	14
332	335	33	31	29	27	26	24	22	20	18	16	14
335	338	34	32	30	28	26	24	22	20	18	16	14
338	341	34	32	30	28	26	24	22	21	19	17	15
341	343	34	32	30	28	27	25	23	21	19	17	15
343	345	35	33	31	29	27	25	23	21	19	17	15
345	347	35	33	31	29	27	25	23	21	19	17	16
347	349	36	33	31	29	27	25	23	22	20	18	16
349	351	36	33	31	29	28	26	24	22	20	18	16
351	353	36	34	32	30	28	26	24	22	20	18	16
353	355	37	34	32	30	28	26	24	22	20	18	17
355	357	37	34	32	30	28	26	24	23	21	19	17
357	359	38	34	32	30	29	27	25	23	21	19	17
359	361	38	35	33	31	29	27	25	23	21	19	17
361	363	39	35	33	31	29	27	25	23	21	19	17
363	365	39	36	33	31	29	27	25	23	22	20	18
365	367	40	36	33	31	29	28	26	24	22	20	18
367	369	40	36	34	32	30	28	26	24	22	20	18
369	371	40	37	34	32	30	28	26	24	22	20	18
371	373	41	37	34	32	30	28	26	24	23	21	19
373	375	41	38	34	32	30	29	27	25	23	21	19
375	377	42	38	35	33	31	29	27	25	23	21	19
377	379	42	39	35	33	31	29	27	25	23	21	19
379	381	43	39	36	33	31	29	27	25	23	22	20
381	383	43	40	36	33	31	29	28	26	24	22	20
383	385	43	40	36	34	32	30	28	26	24	22	20
385	387	44	40	37	34	32	30	28	26	24	22	20
387	389	44	41	37	34	32	30	28	26	24	23	21
389	391	45	41	38	34	32	30	29	27	25	23	21
391	393	45	42	38	35	33	31	29	27	25	23	21
393	395	46	42	39	35	33	31	29	27	25	23	21
395	397	46	43	39	36	33	31	29	27	25	23	22
397	399	47	43	40	36	33	31	29	28	26	24	22
399	401	47	43	40	36	34	32	30	28	26	24	22
401	403	47	44	40	37	34	32	30	28	26	24	22
403	405	48	44	41	37	34	32	30	28	26	24	23
405	407	48	45	41	38	34	32	30	29	27	25	23
407	409	49	45	42	38	35	33	31	29	27	25	23
409	411	49	46	42	39	35	33	31	29	27	25	23
411	413	50	46	43	39	36	33	31	29	27	25	23
413	415	50	47	43	40	36	33	31	29	28	26	24
415	417	51	47	43	40	36	34	32	30	28	26	24

$417 and over — Use Table 8(b) for a MARRIED person on page 47. Also see the instructions on page 44.

Images copied from Circular E, Pub. 15, IRS Employer Tax Guide 2018 published on the IRS website WWW.IRS.gov

www.ingramcontent.com/pod-product-compliance
Lightning Source LLC
Chambersburg PA
CBHW062321220526
45469CB00008B/2587